Harmony versus Conflict in Asian Business

Palgrave Macmillan Asian Business Series Centre for the Study of Emerging Markets Series

Series Editor: **Harukiyo Hasegawa** is Professor at Doshisha Business School, Kyoto, Japan, and Honourable Research Fellow at the University of Sheffield's School of East Asian Studies, where he was formerly Director of the Centre for Japanese Studies.

The Palgrave Macmillan Asian Business Series seeks to publish theoretical and empirical studies that contribute forward-looking social perspectives on the study of management issues not just in Asia, but by implication elsewhere. The series specifically aims at the development of new frontiers in the scope, themes and methods of business and management studies in Asia, a region which is seen as key to studies of modern management, organization, strategies, human resources and technologies.

The series invites practitioners, policy-makers and academic researchers to join us at the cutting edge of constructive perspectives on Asian management, seeking to contribute towards the development of civil societies in Asia and further afield.

Titles include:

Glenn D. Hook and Harukiyo Hasegawa (*editors*)
JAPANESE RESPONSES TO GLOBALIZATION IN THE 21ST CENTURY
Politics, Security, Economics and Business

Diane Rosemary Sharpe and Harukiyo Hasegawa (*editors*)
NEW HORIZONS IN ASIAN MANAGEMENT
Emerging Issues and Critical Perspectives

Sten Söderman (*editor*)
EMERGING MULTIPLICITY
Integration and Responsiveness in Asian Business Development

Oliver H.M. Yau and Raymond P.M. Chow (*editors*)
HARMONY VERSUS CONFLICT IN ASIAN BUSINESS
Managing in a Turbulent Era

Palgrave Macmillan Asian Business Series
Series Standing Order ISBN 1–4039–9841–8

You can receive future titles in this series as they are published by placing a standing order. Please contact your bookseller or, in case of difficulty, write to us at the address below with your name and address, the title of the series and one of the ISBNs quoted above.

Customer Services Department, Macmillan Distribution Ltd, Houndmills, Basingstoke, Hampshire RG21 6XS, England

Harmony versus Conflict in Asian Business

Managing in a Turbulent Era

Edited by

Oliver H.M. Yau and Raymond P.M. Chow

First published 2007 by
PALGRAVE MACMILLAN
Houndmills, Basingstoke, Hampshire RG21 6XS and
175 Fifth Avenue, New York, N.Y. 10010
Companies and representatives throughout the world

PALGRAVE MACMILLAN is the global academic imprint of the Palgrave
Macmillan division of St. Martin's Press, LLC and of Palgrave Macmillan
Ltd. Macmillan® is a registered trademark in the United States, United
Kingdom and other countries. Palgrave is a registered trademark in the
European Union and other countries.

ISBN-13: 978-0-230-54292-1   hardback
ISBN-10: 0-230-54292-1   hardback

This book is printed on paper suitable for recycling and made from fully
managed and sustained forest sources. Logging, pulping and manufacturing processes are expected to conform to the environmental regulations
of the country of origin.

A catalogue record for this book is available from the British Library.

A catalog record for this book is available from the Library of Congress.

10 9 8 7 6 5 4 3 2 1
16 15 14 13 12 11 10 09 08 07

Printed and bound in Great Britain by
Antony Rowe Ltd, Chippenham and Eastbourne

Contents

List of Figures

List of Tables

Contributors

Simone C.L. Cheng is a PhD candidate in the Department of Marketing at the City University of Hong Kong.

Fanny S.L. Cheung is Assistant Professor in the Department of Marketing at the City University of Hong Kong.

Wah Leung Cheung is Associate Professor in the Department of Marketing at the Hong Kong Baptist University, Hong Kong.

Cheris W.C. Chow is a PhD candidate in the Department of Marketing at the City University of Hong Kong.

Raymond P.M. Chow is Assistant Professor in the School of Business and Administration at the Open University of Hong Kong.

Lena Croft is at the Department of Management, Chinese University of Hong Kong.

Wolfgang Dorow is at European University Viadrina, Frankfurt (Oder), Germany.

Martin Hemmert is Assistant Professor at Korea University Business School, Seoul, Korea.

John Kidd is with the Operations and Information Management Group, Aston Business School, Birmingham.

K.F. Lau is at The Hong Kong Polytechnic University, Hong Kong.

Leo Leung is at Lingnan University, Hong Kong.

W.F. Leung is Director (Higher Education) at Hong Kong College of Technology, Hong Kong.

Xue Li is on a Doctoral Programme, at Aston Business School, Bermingham.

Shige Makino is Professor in the Department of Management, Chinese University of Hong Kong.

Sharon Moore is Professor of International Business and Strategic Management, Sydney Graduate School, Australia.

Gerard Prendergast is Associate Professor in the Department of Marketing at the Hong Kong Baptist University, Hong Kong.

Che-Jen Su is with the Department of Restaurant, Hotel & Institutional Management, Fu-Jen Catholic University, Taiwan.

Cheng-Chien Wang is with the Department of Restaurant, Hotel & Institutional Management, Fu-Jen Catholic University, Taiwan.

Julie Jie Wen is Lecturer in the University of Western Sydney, Australia.

Oliver H.M. Yau is Chair Professor at the Department of Marketing at the City University of Hong Kong.

Pamela Yeow is at Kent Business School, University of Kent, Canterbury, UK.

Preface

In his book, *A Tale of Two Cities*, Charles Dickens says, '… it was the worst of times, … it was the age of foolishness, … it was the epoch of incredulity, … it was the season of Darkness, …'[1] We are now living in a world that is no better than Charles Dickens' world, a world that is full of anger, abhorrence, antipathy, hypocrisy and hostility, especially when we see that both regional and international terrorisms have emerged and been fighting against each other on selfish grounds. The rise of an almost hegemony has already shaken the harmony of this planet. The business arena is exception. Therefore, it is high time that we needed to contemplate harmonious relationships among nations, partners, and even among our enemies. The Chinese always say, 'Being harmonious is a noble act'. This book provides a good source on how a harmonious business environment can be created, by and for, managers and firms, so as to enhance performance in terms of both financial and human indicators. We firmly believe that the ideas in this book can foster the development of new and creative approaches to managing harmony in international business.

Harmony is a central concept in the Asian spiritual and social thought. Although similar concepts and ideas can be found in the West, they do not play as decisive a role as in the Asian context. In Asian culture, the problem of harmony and conflict can be perceived as the problem of explaining and justifying the creation or pursuit of harmony, or the problem of providing a resolution of conflict in the interests of harmony. As such, the basic purpose of this book is to provide a timely evaluation of how a harmonious business environment can be created and managed successfully in an increasingly turbulent business environment.

In fact, this book is mostly a result of the Euro-Asia Management Studies Association (EAMSA) annual conference in 2004, which is a unique forum in which academicians and professionals with a concern about management and development of international business came together face-to-face to forge ties. From 37 papers in the conference, we selected 10 and incorporated them in this book as chapters. We also include a paper that has already been published (Chapter 2) because of its consistency with the central theme of this book. All of these chapters illustrate the diversity of perspectives and disciplines in Asian business.

[1] Dickens, Charles (1895), *A Tale of Two Cities* (London: Pan Books), p. 29.

In terms of the organization of this book, Chapter 1 is a summary of the whole book. All the other 11 chapters pivot on the themes of harmony and conflict. From the harmony perspective, Part I consists of seven chapters while from the conflict perspective, Part II contains four chapters.

This book can be used for students and researchers in Asian and international studies at both undergraduate and graduate levels. General readers with an interest in globalization and Asian politics and business may also find this book stimulating.

This is one of a few books with a theme in harmony. It is a must for major university libraries in Asia, North America, and Europe, especially for libraries of business schools.

Finally, we take this opportunity to thank Professor Yoshiaki Takahashi, Chuo University, Japan, Chairman of EAMSA, and Professor Harukiyo Hasegawa, the General Editor of the Palgrave Macmillan Asian Business and Management Series for his couragement. Also we thank the Unit for Chinese Management Development, Department of Marketing, City University of Hong Kong who assisted in the preparation of the manuscript of this book. This indicates the Unit's sheer endeavour in the expansion of the scope of knowledge in the new economy. Special thanks are due to my assistants, Miss Christy Chui and Miss Yen Au, for their unceasing attention in the preparation of the manuscript. We are also grateful to the reviewers for their kind support and assistance, and who would like to remain anonymous.

Oliver H.M. Yau,
Raymond P.M. Chow

1
Introduction

Oliver H.M. Yau and Raymond P.M. Chow

Harmony is a central concept in the Asian spiritual and social thought. Although similar concepts and ideals can be found in the West, they do not play as decisive a role as in the Asian context. In the context of the Asian culture, the problem of harmony and conflict can be perceived as the problem of explaining and justifying the creation or pursuit of harmony, or the problem of providing a resolution of conflict in the interests of harmony. It is the basic purpose of this book to provide a timely evaluation of how a harmonious business environment can be created and managed successfully in an increasingly turbulent business environment.

This introduction has two objectives: first, to provide readers with a road map for this book, detailing its structure and, second, to serve as a guideline for recent developments in harmony and conflict management. This chapter thus provides a perspective for the book as a whole, underlining its novelty and innovative aspects of problems and challenges emerging as a result of recent economic reforms and development in Asia.

This book contains 12 chapters and is divided into two parts – the Harmony Perspective (Part I) and the Conflict Perspective (Part II). A brief account of each is given below.

Part I: The Harmony Perspective

Part I includes seven chapters that examine various issues on how Asian firms endeavour to harmonize the business environment. First, we deal with the long existing concept of harmony and its impact on joint venture performance. Second, we look into how the economic reform in China shapes the gender situation into a more equitable situation. Third, we explain that the benefit from harmonious interactions between Chinese and German firms on environment behaviour would accrue to both nations. This is followed by three chapters going deeper into the concept of trust at large. First, we examine the role of trust in knowledge generation and dissemination. As the Asian business environment is changing rapidly, the issue of trust is further explored by tracking how trust is likely to shift over time in international joint alliances in southwest China. We then investigate how harmonizing processes such as trust building, communication, leadership, shared goals and commitment differ within the context of the cultural framework of global companies. The final chapter in this part deals with an empirical study on trust, commitment, relationship quality, and behavioural consequences for international tourist hotels in Taiwan. These chapters provide a sound foundation for readers who do not have a good knowledge of how harmony and conflicts are dealt with in Asian business.

In Chapter 2, Raymond Chow and Oliver Yau report on the development and validation of a set of multi-item scales for the measurement of harmony using established procedures from the measurement development literature. A brief review of previous related studies on the roles of harmony in joint venture performance is provided, followed by the hypothesized dimensions of harmony and then a description of the procedures to construct the subscales and assess their psychometric properties.

The results presented in this chapter are relevant both to business academicians and to practitioners. From the theoretical perspective, the harmony orientation (HO) scale developed not only helps to enrich the content and meaning of the construct, but it also helps to enhance our understanding of the importance of harmony in business ventures in general and in the Chinese business environment in particular. From the managerial perspective, this chapter provides empirical support for the importance of harmony in conducting business in China, and has significant implications for international marketers. When formulating new venture strategies in the greater China market, the scale developed can help to gauge the degree of HO held by international joint venture (IJV) partners.

In Chapter 3, Sharon Moore and Julie Jie Wen look into how economic reform in China has been shaping the gender situation in business areas. They identify that the economic and social status of women in China can be viewed in three historical stages. The first stage reflects over two millennia of Confucian culture and patriarchy, when the gap between two genders was seen as infinite. The second stage (1949–78), represents the Chinese Communist party goal to promote equity and eliminate social differences between men and women. The third stage, from 1978, is the current era of economic reforms.

They analyse the historical and political factors affecting the economic and social status of women in terms of these three historical periods, concluding that although the economic and social status of women continues to rise in China, the gap in career opportunities available for men and women shows little sign of narrowing. In a society where men are traditionally regarded as superior, the economic reforms actually undercut women's status by withdrawing state assistance and increasing gender-based inequality. Both primary and secondary data sources are utilized to describe the current position of women in management roles, a privileged class compared to other women in the workforce.

A sample of 316 Chinese male and female business managers was surveyed. Along the same lines, another group of 85 women managers were also focus group interviewed in Guangzhou, China during 2003–04. They applied gender history and theory to the current working day reality of middle to senior level women managers in China. Although focusing on women's opinions and experience in the interview and focus group study, they also uncovered the experience and organizational issues of male managers to minimize any potential bias, and maximize validity and reliability. Strategies that developed through interview and focus group data to advance women's employment in China are explored.

In Chapter 4, Lena Croft and Shige Makino present a conceptual framework depicting the relation between corporate environmental values and corporate environmental behaviour (CEB) to explain why firms proactively go beyond profit maximization to combat environmental problems. Interaction between a German firm, which puts environment pollution as a primacy, and firms from China where 'no regret' policy in promoting the economic growth is in practice, is discussed. The result demonstrates that placing emphasis on CEB can transform a conflicting issue to achieve a harmonious result.

The proposing construct advances existing knowledge by further deriving categorization, dynamic patterns of categorization and taxonomy of CEB suggesting future direction of study within the area of organization and the natural environment. Through the exploration of the new construct, this chapter intends to generate new debates that lead to enrichment of theoretical development to a relatively new area in the pressing natural environment, and practitioners are still adopting a 'learning-by-doing' attitude to tackle this complicated issue.

In Chapter 5, Leo Leung and K.F. Lau examine the role of trust in knowledge generation and dissemination. Distinction is made between perceived trust at interpersonal level and inter-organizational level (or group level). Two strands of research streams are employed to understand the role of trust in knowledge management process at these two levels. First, social exchange theory is used to explore the interactions among individuals in developing trust at interpersonal level. Then, transaction cost analysis is adopted to investigate the role of trust as a coordinating mechanism in organizing functional activities within and between organizations in addition to the use of either market or hierarchy. Both theories provide a conceptual foundation to understand the development of trust in facilitating knowledge creation and transfer.

Different forms of trust may emerge throughout different stages of the knowledge management process. Developing unconditional trust requires time, costs and commitment of resources. Some empirical research studies have demonstrated a positive relationship between trust and knowledge generation/dissemination. An appropriate organizational setting such as team orientation, market-oriented culture and open-communication climate is important to trust-building. Various strategies for building trust are discussed at the end of this chapter.

In Chapter 6, John Kidd and Xue Li review several aspects of trust, distrust and its dynamics in international joint ventures. Further, they indicate how 'trust' is likely to shift over time, and then links these suggestions to findings from fieldwork conducted in southwest China.

There is a considerable body of research upon international joint alliances, their mode of entry and their sociometrics, but there is little research on the shift in attitudes about their inter-organizational trust as time progresses. That is, from 'early' to 'late', as the alliance moves towards maturity. The overall research, partially reported in this chapter, is to look at the concept of trust in joint alliance relationships in China and how this construct may change over time as both parties get to know each other better. The data collection supporting the research is based upon a questionnaire and on data culled from semi-structured interviews.

Their analyses indicate that there is a drift in trust between the partners (on both sides of the alliance) that indicate the preference of outsider firms is to move from a joint operation to one that is wholly owned. They also suggest that all IJV staff must become aware of 'the needs of the other party' and to be attentive to subtle changes in both their (and the others') attitudes and expectancy as the alliance matures. Such attention might obviate the need to break up the alliance prematurely; or conversely, it may allow the dissolution of the alliance without recrimination through the recognition of the needs of the other party.

In Chapter 7, Pamela Yeow and Wolfgang Dorow present preliminary empirical evidence of a German organization and look at the problems and solutions of integrating subsidiaries into the global parent company. They look specifically at intercultural aspects of shared goals, trust and communication and discuss the implications of the findings within the context of globalization and integration of corporate culture at top management levels. The premise is that the effective management of different cultures is a key factor for corporate survival in this turbulent world.

Their chapter reveals that 'trust' was seen as a particularly critical cultural variable in the interaction relationships between local and foreign executives. Within the 'trust' dimension, it was found that in general, the Japanese significantly did not feel that they could rely on their foreign subordinates or superiors. They report that the Japanese preferred to have a more formalized procedure within the organization, significantly more so than the Germans or the Americans. Shared basic values (e.g., employee and quality focus, long-term thinking) have facilitated the evolution of a culture of trust between European (specifically German) and Japanese executives. However, this trust relationship is at risk from stereotypes that have developed over the past two decades, partially based on short-term deployment practices. The heavily criticized increase in explicit, formal monitoring, which is interpreted as a policy of suspicion, should be reviewed by the parent companies with a view to building trust. Language barriers exacerbate the problem of intercultural trust building by obscuring the authenticity of the communication partner. Trust building is a long-term management task; its advantage lies in reduced monitoring expenses.

In Chapter 8, Che-Jen Su and Cheng-Chien Wang integrate marketing literature and offer a model and hypotheses that demonstrate the mediating role of relationship quality among trust, commitment, and behavioural intention in the international tourist hotel industry. Data were collected from a field survey of 182 qualified consumers in Taiwan, and structural equation modelling (SEM) was utilized to examine structural linkages and to analyse their relative impacts. Results reported in this chapter indicate that relationship quality appears to have a remarkably positive impact on all behavioural consequences, namely, relationship continuity, word-of-mouth, and share of purchases. Specifically, hotel commitment positively shapes relationship quality more strongly than do other antecedents. Overall, hotel commitment was confirmed to be the dominating construct in the framework. The implications of these findings for tourist practice and future research are discussed.

This chapter expands the knowledge of relationship quality's mediating role in the process of improving behavioural consequences of relational customers in the international tourist hotel industry. A remarkable finding is that commitment to the hotel explains more variance than the other antecedents of relationship quality and behavioural consequences. This chapter provides greater support for past findings in a more comprehensive framework.

Part II: The Conflict Perspective

This part focuses on the conflict aspects in Asian business and consists of four chapters. First, we deal with the moderating effects of situation factors on the relationship between Chinese cultural values and consumers' complaint behaviour. Second, we look into the profile and perceptions of buyers of pirated products, a serious problem confronted by many multinational companies doing business in Asia. This is followed by a chapter in which we explore a new framework to analyse the competitive potential of business groups in Asia, a subject that have attracted much interest and attention from researchers and practitioners. In the final chapter, we attempt to address the different impacts of economic crises and health crises on marketing activities, which are critical for a firm's business development and even a firm's survival in an increasingly turbulent business environment.

The effects of Chinese cultural values on consumers' complaint behaviour in the restaurant setting are the subject of Chapter 9. In this chapter, Simone Cheng and Oliver Yau describe some distinctive Chinese values, including the desire for harmony and conflict avoidance, the Doctrine of the Mean, face, and their effects on consumers' complaint intentions, which are seldom discussed in studies conducted in the West. Further, some situation factors do moderate the relationship between Chinese cultural values and consumers' complaint behaviour. These situation factors include in-group versus out-group, seniority versus people in the same generation, and the impression management.

This chapter proposes that distinctive Chinese cultural values influence the complaint behaviour of Chinese consumers. It also examines the relationship between Chinese cultural values, situation factors, and the complaint behaviour of Chinese consumers. The study presented in this chapter makes several contributions. First, it is the first attempt to explain Chinese' consumer complaint behaviour based on traditional Chinese values other than collectivism. This chapter advances the current knowledge on the complaint behaviour of Chinese. Second, despite a general conception that Chinese consumers are reluctant to complain even when they are dissatisfied with products and services, no previous study on consumer behaviour proposed the importance of situation factors in moderating the relationship between cultural values and complaint behaviour in the Chinese setting. This chapter asserts that the complaint intention of Chinese consumers is largely moderated by situations. Although the complaint intention of Chinese consumers is low in many situations, they may complain to facilitate impression management. As such, this chapter takes a step further by including the moderating effect of situation factors in Chinese complaint behaviour.

In Chapter 10, in contrast to previous studies, Wah-leung Cheung and Gerard Prendergast profile heavy and light buyers of pirated VCDs/DVDs, their demographics, buying behaviour, and perceptions of pirated VCDs/DVDs vis-à-vis their original equivalents.

Product piracy in many parts of Asia is a serious problem for multinationals wishing to do business there. Different from previous studies on product piracy, the study presented in this chapter surveys actual buyers of pirated products in Hong Kong. In particular, the focus is on heavy and light buyers of pirated VCDs/DVDs. Personal interviews with more than 350 pirated product buyers revealed that pirated VCDs/DVDs, which are most often purchased for the buyers and/or their families, are identified mainly by their price and buying location. Purchasing appears to be prominent among males. Pirated VCDs/DVDs were perceived as being in adequate supply and having adequate variety, and to be up to date. Comparing consumer perceptions of pirated VCDs/DVDs with their expectations from original equivalents, pirated VCDs/DVDs were felt to underperform in all respects, but most notably in the areas of variety, quality, their ethical and legal aspects, and after sales service. Based on the findings, recommendations are made for reducing pirated product buying.

Diversified business groups from Asian countries have attracted much attention from researchers and practitioners, with their competitive potential being one main point of interest. In Chapter 11, Martin Hemmert proposes a new framework to analyse the competitive potential of business groups by assessing (1) their market-based competitive potential; (2) their resource-based competitive potential; and (3) the extent to which managerial control can be exerted over them.

This framework is applied to Japanese and Korean business groups (*kigyo shudan* and *chaebol*). It is shown that both Japanese and Korean business groups have only a limited market-based competitive potential, but a high resource-based competitive potential. Whereas Japanese business groups are loose network-type organizations with no managerial control, however, Korean business groups are hierarchically structured and centrally managed. They have utilized their high competitive potential during recent decades to create competitive advantage through internal resource sharing.

At the same time, their centralized management has also resulted in often unsound diversification strategies which forced many of them into bankruptcy or reorganization after the Asian financial crisis of 1997.

During the outbreak of severe acute respiratory syndrome (SARS), the analysts generally predicted a recession to follow the crisis. However, the results showed a surprising strong economic growth. In Chapter 12, Oliver Yau and his associates attempt to address the different impacts of economic crises (or financial crises) and health crises on marketing activities, which are critical for a firm's business development and even a firm's survival.

A life-cycle model is applied to show the different effects under an economic crisis and a health crisis. A health crisis, such as SARS, brings higher current consumption rather than lower consumption under an economic crisis. An economic crisis lowers the expected income and thus the current consumption is lower in order to maintain savings for future consumption. A health crisis lowers expectancy life but the current consumption is raised as savings are cut for smaller future consumption is expected. For marketers, correct marketing strategies under a crisis will provide competitive advantages over the rival firms. Thus, marketing implications are provided for practitioners in developing marketing strategies during a crisis. Precision judgement is critical to the success of the marketing strategy.

Concluding remarks

This book tries to provide the readers with tools for understanding, researching and managing Asian business. All contributions are grouped into one of the two parts – the harmony aspect or the conflict aspect. In each chapter, we also focus on a particular area of interest in managing businesses in the Asian perspective. In particular, the harmony-oriented approaches to problem solving and conflict resolution are dealt with in great length. In addition to the contribution in providing insights into recent developments, problems that were encountered and challenges that are being faced by Asian and foreign executives are discussed. We are confident that in understanding these problems and challenges, it will help prepare strategies for enhanced performance in Asia in this turbulent era.

Part I
The Harmony Perspective

2
In Search of Harmony

Raymond P.M. Chow and Oliver H.M. Yau[1]

Introduction

Since 1978, China has embarked on one of the most unprecedented economic reforms in modern history. Among all of the contemporary changes in China, the most important is the transformation of its centrally planned economy into a market-oriented economy. Since China launched its open door policy in the late 1970s and actively pursued the development of a market-driven economy, numerous foreign companies have entered the market through the establishment of joint ventures. By the end of 2002, a total of 278,811 Chinese-foreign joint ventures had been approved (Hu, 2003). While there is a huge market in China, unfamiliarity with local cultural values, systems and practices has presented the foreign partners with challenges as well as opportunities.

Prior research on international joint venture (IJV) performance has regarded harmony as an important element in maintaining the partnership relationship, thus as significantly affecting the effectiveness of IJVs (Anderson, 1990; Antoniou and Whitman, 1998; Sulej, 1998). However, these studies have generally been vague regarding specific measurements of harmony. Besides, there has been minimal primary research conducted on the relationships between harmony and the performance related measures of IJVs.

To fill this gap in the literature, this chapter reports the development and validation of a set of multi-item scales for the measurement of harmony using established procedures from the measurement development literature. A brief review of past related studies on the roles of harmony in IJV performance is first provided. The hypothesized dimensions of harmony are then set out, and this is followed with a description of the procedure to construct the subscales and assess their psychometric properties.

A discussion of the implications of the research findings and directions for future research conclude the chapter.

Previous research on harmony and its impact on IJV performance

Asians regard harmony and personal relationships as the foundations on which society can be organized (Selmer, 1996). In the case of the Chinese, under the influence of the Confucianism that has become an integral part of the Chinese social, economic and cultural inheritance, working to achieve harmony is considered an imperative to which all other goals are subordinate (Chen and Pan, 1993; Cragg, 1995).

Chinese culture, often viewed as a high-context culture, regards harmony as more important than competition, and thus developing interpersonal relationships and mutual understanding is a prerequisite for business success (Hall and Hall, 1987). In contrast to the low context cultural norm of the pursuit of individualism and the promotion of egoism, Chinese culture advocates collectivism and likes to seek harmony in the family, in organizations, and in society (Helms, 1992). The importance of harmony in social and business dealings has frequently been emphasized in studies on China and Chinese culture (Bond, 1993; Kelly and Shenkar, 1993; Redding, 1993; Chen, 1995). Among the basic tenets of Confucian philosophy, harmony is particularly relevant to interpersonal behaviour. In the Chinese business context, the concept of harmony reflects an aspiration toward a conflict-free, group-based system of social relations (Antoniou and Whitman, 1998), and harmony thus should be maintained in the work environment and in the decision-making process (Chen, 1995).

Joint venture management involves complex partnership relationships. When corporate parents bicker and executives take sides with one parent company against the other, a joint venture may lose its focus, causing more harm than harmony (Sparks, 1999). A review of the joint venture management literature suggests that harmony is an important element in the effective and successful operations of IJVs. Despite the significance of this important constituent of IJV partner relations, there has been minimal primary research directed toward operationalizing this concept more rigorously, and empirically examining the impact of harmony on IJV performance. Several studies did, however, lay some groundwork for this important issue. Major findings of these studies are outlined below.

Using primary data from China, Antoniou and Whitman (1998) conducted a study to examine the personal value systems of professionals and managers. Results of their study indicated that the Chinese have a high regard for harmony and form as elements that constitute essential components of a meaningful life.

Sulej (1998) examined the pattern of activity in joint venture formation in technological industries focusing on equity joint ventures formed between 1945 and 1989. He commented on the need to focus on soft elements of the joint venture relationship rather than hard issues when examining the context and performance outcomes of international strategic alliances and equity joint ventures.

In a paper focused on succeeding in China in the 21st century, Wong (1995) identified 10 most common problems foreign investors encounter in China. He noted that, among the different aspects of Chinese culture, harmony is the key objective that the Chinese seek to achieve through a network of relationships.

In a study exploring the nature and roots of selected conflicts experienced by Chinese and westerners when attempting to work together in a joint venture, O'Keefe and O'Keefe (1997) suggested that the Confucian principle of seeking harmony rather than conflict may help both parties to work more effectively together.

Taking an integrative approach to studying the determinants of conflict management styles in Chinese joint ventures, Ding (1995) commented that the impact of Chinese culture on conflict-management behaviour is characterized by, among other determinants, an emphasis on harmony. In business dealings, the Chinese attempt to seek harmony with other parties with whom they are dealing instead of engaging in head-on competition or confrontation (Wang, 1994).

The findings from these studies confirm that collectivism and group harmony are emphasized in the Chinese social and business environment. In fact, it is the underlying belief among the Chinese that harmony, along with other values advocated in Confucianism, is the proper base for all business relationships (DeMonte, 1989).

A close examination of the constructs of the value measurement instruments that can be found in the business research literature reveals that harmony is often included as one of the dimensions or components. In Rokeach's (1973) study, which consists of two sets of values, inner harmony is listed as one of the terminal values. In Schwartz's (1992) study, which contains seven motivational domains, harmony is listed as the opposite domain to mastery. In the Chinese value survey (Chinese Cultural Connection, 1987), harmony with others is treated as an attribute of integration, one of the four dimensions of the scale. In Yau's (1994) Chinese cultural value scale, both harmony with the universe and harmony with people are listed. Although harmony is not listed as an integral component in Hofstede's (1980) cultural value dimensions, group harmony is considered as the core value of collectivism in the scale. It is interesting to note that in all the value scales, perhaps with the exception of Yau's scale, harmony is treated as a single dimension or as a component of a multi-dimensional scale. Given the importance and complexity of this particular value dimension, it would seem necessary to explore further the root, notions and dimensionality of the concept of harmony.

The dimensions of harmony orientation in a Chinese context

Based on a review of the literature, and as a result of a series of in-depth interviews with senior managers in over 30 Chinese-foreign joint ventures in six major cities in China, a proposition was formulated to the effect that harmony orientation in the context of Chinese culture resembles closely the notion of accompaniment in Chinese opera.

Musical harmony

Music and its social and cosmological implications have been understood throughout the ages and across different cultures. In Chinese tradition, the Confucian notions of music have significant implications for self-mastery and social harmony. Music, by its nature, is concerned with harmony and proper resonance. Hence in imperial China, political theorists regarded music as an essential component of the emperor's harmonizing function.

In Confucianism, music as an expression of human emotion is regarded as essential to human life, and music serves as 'the inner bond of harmony' to form or transform human character (Legge, 1967) and to achieve societal harmony. Confucians ordered society according to hierarchical distinctions and simultaneously attempted to harmonize differentiated classes through music.

According to Yueji, music gives expression to unchanging feelings (Legge, 1967), as all tones emerge from the human heart. The relation among the elements of music, as Yueji understands them, parallels the proper relation among the elements of society (Saussy, 2002), as 'music is that which penetrates the principles of social relation' and 'music and government are directly connected with one another' (Lin, 1994). Music is built on the foundation of harmony and harmony is the essence of music. This suggests that harmony is the principle component of music in Chinese thought.

Accompaniment in Chinese opera

Musical harmony can be broadly defined as the sound of two or more notes heard simultaneously. It is the succession of harmonies that gives a piece of music its distinctive personality. In music, an accompaniment is a part, usually instrumental, performed together with the main part for richer effect. It attempts to balance all the constituent parts to produce a pleasing harmony of various elements in a musical composition. It creates a harmonic background to the melody and enhances the rhythmic quality of the music. In Chinese opera, traditional Chinese string and percussion instruments provide a strong rhythmic accompaniment to the acting, which was done mainly based on illusionary tactics, with frequent hand gestures mixed throughout.

Beijing and Cantonese operas are two of the various different regional opera styles commonly performed in China today. While Beijing opera is nationwide and Cantonese opera is more prevalent in the Pearl River delta area, each has its own unique quality. Beijing opera is the most popular and widespread, and so becomes the standard to which others are compared. Cantonese opera represents the vivacious and elegant spirit of the people of southern China. The regional characteristics are fully reflected in the vocal and dramatic styles of the plays, while the orchestral accompaniment adds an enriching touch to the highly entertaining performances.

Accompaniment in Cantonese opera is known as *pai-he*. The word *pai* implies 'to join up', 'to attach to' or 'to accompany', and *he* means 'to harmonize'. Literally it means 'to accompany' and it implies 'mutual enhancement'. While it might not embody the same harmonic concepts found in Western musical theory, it does carry the spirit of harmony. It aims at creating a harmonious relationship between the vocal part and the instrumental accompaniment (Loo and Lai, 1999). It is an indispensable component of Cantonese opera performance, although it appears to assume a role subordinate to the vocal part. Fundamentally, musical accompaniment is a performing art aimed at enriching the vocal part of the opera so as to enhance the rhythmic quality of the performance.

In general, the most essential aesthetic objective of *pai-he* is to embellish and intensify the vocal part. It enriches the melodic line. In practice, different melodic types require specific *pai-he* approaches (Loo and Lai, 1999). While there are various *pai-he* concepts, the encapsulation put forward by Loo and Lai would seem to be comprehensive enough for the purposes of this study. Their five different types of *pai-he* can be summarized as:

(1) Enrichment (*bu*): accompaniment used to enrich the rests between vocal lines;

(2) Introduction (*yin*): an improvised introductory passage which will lead into the proper vocal part;
(3) Bridge (*da*): a transitional section used to link different musical phrases, themes or vocal lines;
(4) Unison (*qi*): simultaneous playing of the same note or tune;
(5) Off-beat Imitation (*sui*): a melodic idea is presented in one voice (part) and restated in another while the first voice continues with new material.

Accompaniment is an inclusive form of the performing arts, characterized by its unlimited variations of a monophonic melody. The different accompaniment techniques described above reflect the close harmonious relationship between the vocal part and its accompaniment.

The five components of a harmony orientation scale

Departing from the above proposition, a harmony-orientation (HO) scale can be visualized as a multi-dimensional construct consisting of five components: Enrichment, Leading, Bridging, Synchronizing and Imitation (see Figure 2.1).

Enrichment

In joint ventures, strategic advantage is generated from the combined resources of the partners, which enable the IJV to benefit from economies of scale, expanded market access, spread of investment and complementary skill sets. However, it is necessary to effectively integrate all such resources to continuously enrich the product/service offerings in the light of local conditions, and satisfy the needs of different interests. This would

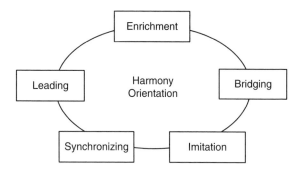

Figure 2.1:   The five dimensions of harmony orientation (HO)

require that partners in IJVs assist each other in order that their combined strengths can be effectively deployed to fill in for the shortcomings or weaknesses of either party. In a case where one partner cannot solve a problem alone, the other would need to give a helping hand or might even need to settle the problem on behalf of the other. This is often the case when a foreign partner may not be familiar with or even unaware of local customs and practices, making it difficult if not impossible to effectively handle specific local situations. Mutual effort by IJV partners can help to promote, extend and enhance their combined strengths, and are capable of boosting IJV performance.

Leading

Success in any IJV requires the concerted and mutually supportive efforts of the partners. Under certain circumstances, it may require a specific partner to take a leading role in areas where that partner may be in a better or more advantageous position to accomplish a particular goal. This is very important, especially in the startup phase, when either partner may not be familiar with the environment and systems of the other. The foreign investing partner would require the local partner to take the lead in establishing needed local government, industrial and business connections. Likewise, the local hosting partner would look to the foreign partner to take the initiative in instituting a network of organizations and markets external to the hosting location. Such concerted efforts would surely enhance the ongoing success of the IJV.

Bridging

Strongly linked bridge ties are valuable in IJVs, as they provide a more robust basis for inter-partner cooperation. To a great extent, an IJV is an inter-organizational collaboration involving distinct management groups representing the interests of the partnering firms. To be effective, members of the IJV management team must bridge the needs of all the partners. Like other forms of collaboration, bridging between IJV partners relies on collaborative efforts and commitment to the success of the operation. A high degree of organizational interpenetration and coordination can build a strongly linked bridge between the partners and enhance the performance of the venture.

Synchronizing

Different partners in an IJV may have different incentives and interests. Should they all strive to optimize their individual objectives independently, the resulting performance of the joint venture could be compromised.

The best efforts of one partner could be wasted if the other partners are not synchronizing their efforts. Building a successful and very active joint venture requires strong alignment between partners playing in unison. To accomplish synchrony, partners need to help each other wholeheartedly so that the partners and the joint venture progress together. Joint decision making focusing on the common interest and aiming at the overall benefits of the joint venture is likely to be important to success.

Imitation

In any alliance, a party with superior expertise in certain strategic essentials would naturally take the lead in that area, with other members of the team trying to follow and imitate, aiming to learn and acquire the skills of the leader. In a joint venture setting with members working in close relationships, there would naturally be leaders and followers in specific business practices. While one partner may be leading the way, members of the other partner would follow the directions set. To a certain extent, the following members would even adjust their own structures, expectations, and ways of conducting business to harmonize and synchronize with what is being orchestrated by the leading partner, thus achieving enrichment and embellishment effects. Mutual respect and support can be enhanced, and superior performance can be achieved.

Methodology

Sampling

A total of 500 respondents were sampled in the study, covering joint venture companies in the Chinese cities of Beijing, Tianjin, and Shanghai, and other IJVs from the Chinese provinces of Jiangsu, Guangdong and Fujian. The target sample was defined as senior executives who had at least three years of managerial experience in one or more international joint venture companies. Stratified sampling with proportional allocation according to quotas was adopted, taking into consideration the large population size and diversity of industries, locations, company sizes, and origins of the foreign-partnered firms. Respondents were selected randomly and each stratum contributed proportionately to the number of successful cases.

The data were collected by Marketing Decision Research (Pacific) Ltd, a professional full-service research agency covering all major cities in China. Specific procedures were taken to minimize the non-response rate, including making appointments with the respondents before conducting interviews and repeated calls and visits. The response rate was 8.4 percent.

The proportional quota combined with the stated selection criteria added to the complication and difficulties in achieving a higher success rate.

An interviewer visited the selected respondents for an in-depth interview. The respondents were requested to fill out a structured questionnaire, written in Chinese, which was divided into three major sections: a harmony-orientation scale, statements on performance and questions soliciting demographic data.

The final data set constituted a representative sample of IJVs in the selected cities and provinces including (1) at the company level – joint ventures in different locations, in various industries, of various company sizes, and with a variety of number of years since their establishment; and (2) at the respondent level – age, position and years of service in the company. The respondents in this survey tended to be middle-aged, holding a senior managerial position, with an average of 6.4 years of service in the joint venture companies. An analysis of the respondents indicates a fairly representative cross-section of ages, positions and JV experience.

Construct measurement

In this study, harmony orientation (HO) is defined as the common values preferred and held by Chinese in the pursuit of harmony that is driven by a value placed on harmony rather any other goals that are facilitated by harmonious relationships.

Based on a review of the literature and in-depth interviews with IJV managers, 38 statements were first generated to capture the various dimensions of harmony orientation. Then, seven university professors and researchers who are familiar with Chinese culture and Western management theory were invited to serve as judges to evaluate the content (face) validity of these statements. Three inappropriate statements were deleted in this process, resulting in 35 useful statements. This set of statements was then used in a pilot study in which 23 senior business executives attending a seminar on joint ventures in China participated. Ten statements with presumed low reliability were subsequently eliminated, resulting in 25 statements that were used in the survey to measure harmony orientation. Respondents in the main study were asked to indicate their agreement or disagreement with these statements on a 6-point Likert scale.

Item analysis and factor analysis of the harmony orientation statements

In order to assess the internal consistency of the 25 statements on harmony orientation before item analysis and factor analysis, correlation analysis was first conducted. No statement with an insignificant item – total correlation coefficient was detected, hence, all the statements were used for further analysis. Item analysis, which tests the discriminatory power of each item by comparing the means of the first and fourth quartiles of the respondents, was performed. As a result, two items were deleted. Then, a principal component factor analysis with varimax rotation was applied to determine possible underlying dimensions of harmony orientation in China. Out of the 23 statements, a five-factor solution was obtained using the scree test. It had 20 statements with 74.1 percent of the total variance explained. Three statements with relatively low commonality were eliminated.

Table 2.1 shows the emerging harmony orientation dimensions with their factor loadings. Following a close inspection of the item loading of each factor, the five factors were labelled Enrichment, Leading, Bridging, Synchronizing and Imitation.

Using Cronbach's alpha coefficient, the reliabilities of these five factors were found to be 0.881, 0.863, 0.864, 0.850 and 0.902. Nunnally (1978) has suggested that in the early stages of research, modest reliability in the range of 0.50 to 0.60 will suffice. Since this study is one of the earliest on Chinese harmony orientation, the reliability of the scales is considered as acceptable for further analysis.

Construct validity: confirmatory factor analysis model

To examine the construct validity of the scale for harmony orientation, the result of the exploratory factor analysis was subjected to confirmatory factor analysis (CFA). Figure 2.2 shows the confirmatory model for examining harmony orientation together with the parameter estimates and test statistics. Latent variables are represented by ellipses, while observed variables are represented as rectangles (Schumacker and Lomax, 1996; Arbuckle and Wothke, 1999). The observed variables are connected to the latent variables by arrows, signifying that these measurements are theoretically attributed to the latent variables. The values next to the arrows connecting the latent variables to the observed variables are factor loadings and serve as regression coefficients. The values pointing to the observed variables are the response errors of the measurement items, and the curve lines connecting pairs of factors indicate covariances between the factors of HO.

This CFA model yielded an χ^2 of 400.82 with 152 degrees of freedom (df) ($p = 0.00$). The χ^2/df of 2.637 (<3.0), the GFI (0.927), the AGFI (0.900), and the RMR (0.028) all indicate acceptable goodness-of-fit between the hypothesized model and the data. The results suggest that this five-factor

Table 2.1: Summary of factor analysis results and reliabilities of factors

Item	Factor Loading	Item-total Correlation
Enrichment (17.7% variance, α = 0.8812)		
a. We try hard to provide assistance to our partner to make up for their shortcomings.	0.793	0.721
b. When one party cannot solve a problem on its own, the other party will help to settle the problem. on behalf of the partner	0.770	0.764
c. We will consider the opinion of our partner and make up for their shortcomings so that our plans will better suit the market conditions.	0.673	0.731
d. We assist our partner in solving their problems	0.733	0.754
Leading (12.3% variance, α = 0.8632)		
e. remove all stumbling blocks and pave the way for our partner to operate smoothly.	0.451	0.659
f. make arrangements with appropriate government organizations to bring the strength of our partner into play.	0.777	0.726
g. We take initiative to link all units to bring the collective advantages of both parties into play.	0.619	0.745
h. We take preventive actions on issues ignored by our partner, allowing them to avoid mistakes in implementation.	0.696	0.719
Bridging (12.7% variance, α = 0.8645)		
i. We pave the way for our partner to operate smoothly.	0.715	0.680
j. We are well matched and well coordinated.	0.590	0.715
k. We contact the appropriate government organizations, make connections and pave the way for our partner to effectively implement their plan.	0.737	0.749
l. We maintain a close relationship and coordinate well with each other.	0.684	0.710

(Continued)

Table 2.1: (Continued)

Item	Factor Loading	Item-total Correlation
Synchronizing (15.5% variance, α = 0.8502)		
m. We help each other whole-heartedly and progress side by side.	0.680	0.741
n. In making important decisions, both parties will stand for the overall benefits of the joint venture.	0.798	0.717
o. We strive to obtain unanimous agreement in our decisions	0.745	0.682
p. Delegates of the Chinese and foreign partners often meet to discuss and make decisions.	0.651	0.641
Imitation (15.9% variance, α = 0.9022)		
q. We follow the way our partner conducts business to the best of our ability.	0.895	0.808
r. We follow our partner's way of doing things to the best of our ability and adjust our own organization and management to match theirs.	0.920	0.846
s. In making decisions, we consider the standpoint of our partner.	0.848	0.754
t. We adjust our expectations of the joint venture in order to follow the lead of our partner.	0.826	0.718
Whole scale: α = 0.9229		

Note: the following three statements with relatively low commonality were excluded:
1. We support each other, using one's strength to make up for the shortcomings of the other.
2. We intensify our communications so that our works can be well coordinated.
3. Both parties will bear responsibility no matter which partner makes a mistake.

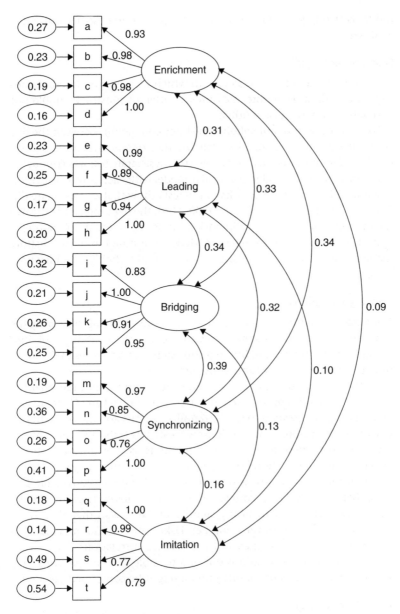

Figure 2.2:   Confirmatory factor analysis model

model is strongly supported. This allows performing further restrictive analyses.

Discriminant validity

Discriminant validity is the degree to which measures of different concepts are distinct. Therefore, measures of different constructs should not correlate highly with each other.

To test for discriminant validity, the inter-correlations between the five components were examined to see whether or not they were significantly different from unity. To achieve this, a separate test was conducted comparing the CFA model to a similar model with each inter-correlation constrained to equal 1.0. Results of the tests show that all *chi*-square differences (χd) are significant at $p < 0.00$. Thus, the hypothesis that the five factors represent the same dimensions must be rejected. Therefore, it appears that the 20 items, when modelled as a function of five distinct factors (true scores), achieve discriminant validity (Phillips and Bagozzi, 1986).

Convergent validity

Convergent validity is the degree to which multiple items measuring the same concept are in agreement. Tests for convergent validity look into the unidimensionality and internal consistency of responses to the items designed to measure the same construct.

Convergent validity can be assessed using a multi-trait multi-method (MTMM) matrix (Campbell and Fiske, 1959). To conduct an MTMM matrix analysis, it is necessary to have both multiple traits and methods. In this case, the dimensions of the scale were treated as traits and the items as methods, as there were no common methods used in the study. It was expected that correlations between items under the same dimension would be higher than those with items under other dimensions (Table 2.2). Note that all the 'validity' correlations between items on the same dimension were high and statistically significant. Note also that there were only a few violations of the Campbell-Fiske criterion that no cross construct correlations should exceed the validity correlations. There were, however, only three violations out of a possible 160 comparisons, suggesting that convergent validity criteria might be considered satisfied.

Predictive validity

To assess the predictive validity of the HO scale, four regression analyses were conducted. In each of the four regression equations, the five dimensions of the HO scale served as independent variables. Since the

Table 2.2: MTMM matrix of correlations

	Enrichment				Leading				Bridging				Synchronizing				Imitation			
	a	b	c	d	e	f	g	h	i	j	k	l	m	n	o	p	q	r	s	t
a	1.00																			
b	0.68**	1.00																		
c	0.60**	0.64**	1.00																	
d	0.62**	0.67**	0.68**	1.00																
e	0.56**	0.58**	0.61**	0.68**	1.00															
f	0.41**	0.49**	0.58**	0.52**	0.56**	1.00														
g	0.56**	0.54**	0.58**	0.55**	0.59**	0.68**	1.00													
h	0.45**	0.48**	0.56**	0.57**	0.58**	0.63**	0.64**	1.00												
i	0.41**	0.44**	0.51**	0.49**	0.47**	0.54**	0.54**	0.55**	1.00											
j	0.48**	0.56**	0.54**	0.54**	0.49**	0.54**	0.58**	0.59**	0.57**	1.00										
k	0.43**	0.52**	0.48**	0.49**	0.55**	0.55**	0.58**	0.57**	0.66**	0.62**	1.00									
l	0.49**	0.55**	0.54**	0.52**	0.53**	0.46**	0.55**	0.46**	0.55**	0.65**	0.63**	1.00								
m	0.55**	0.58**	0.58**	0.59**	0.49**	0.48**	0.60**	0.54**	0.45**	0.61**	0.50**	0.62**	1.00							
n	0.44**	0.50**	0.47**	0.51**	0.42**	0.46**	0.50**	0.45**	0.35**	0.53**	0.43**	0.46**	0.67**	1.00						
o	0.45**	0.43**	0.50**	0.50**	0.48**	0.44**	0.48**	0.48**	0.38**	0.56**	0.48**	0.54**	0.59**	0.65**	1.00					
p	0.44**	0.47**	0.44**	0.44**	0.44**	0.41**	0.48**	0.46**	0.41**	0.51**	0.45**	0.49**	0.62**	0.53**	0.53**	1.00				
q	0.08	0.13**	0.10*	0.17*	0.16**	0.12*	0.09*	0.10*	0.21**	0.14**	0.15**	0.15**	0.16**	0.12**	0.07	0.23**	1.00			
r	0.08	0.10*	0.03	0.11**	0.12**	0.13*	0.10*	0.08	0.17**	0.11*	0.13**	0.11**	0.16**	0.11**	0.07	0.23**	0.86**	1.00		
s	0.13**	0.14**	0.08	0.16**	0.15**	0.14**	0.10*	0.11*	0.18**	0.16**	0.14**	0.20**	0.21**	0.14**	0.11**	0.29**	0.68**	0.69**	1.00	
t	0.12**	0.13**	0.09**	0.11**	0.13**	0.16**	0.13**	0.13**	0.16**	0.15**	0.14**	0.14**	0.18**	0.14**	0.13**	0.25**	0.62**	0.68**	0.67**	1.00

Note: Correlation is significant at the 0.01 level (2-tailed); correlation is significant at the 0.05 level (2-tailed).

Table 2.3:   Results of regression analyses evaluating the predictive validity of the scales

Independent Variables	Dependent Variables			
	(1) *Sales Revenue*	*(2)* *New Product Development*	*(3)* *Operating Cost*	*(4)* *Overall Satisfaction*
Enrichment	0.221***	0.225***	0.188***	0.297***
Leading	0.117***	0.161***	0.087**	0.143***
Bridging	0.157***	0.186***	0.145***	0.222***
Synchronizing	0.263***	0.212***	0.295***	0.398***
Imitation	0.072*	0.119***	0.071*	0.066*
R^2	0.161	0.173	0.160	0.320

*Significance: ***$p < 0.01$; **$p < 0.05$; * $p < 0.10$.*

five components of HO are closely related, the factor scores were used as independent variables to eliminate the possible multi-colinearity effects. The following measurements were selected as the dependent variables: (1) sales revenue, (2) new product/service development, (3) operating cost, (4) overall satisfaction. The first three dependent variables were measured using a 6-point Lickert scale ranging from 1 (strongly disagree) to 6 (strongly agree), and the last one was a composite score.

In the four equations, all five dimensions of the HO scale were found statistically significant and in the right direction. In particular, enrichment and synchronizing were found to have relatively greater impact on all four dependent variables. The effect of imitation on sales revenue, operating cost and overall satisfaction was found to be weak, although statistically significant (at $p < 0.10$). One notable difference was that imitation had a more significant impact on 'new product/service development' as compared with its effects on the other dependent variables.

Overall, the results shown by the four equations were consistent with those reported in the literature. Dimensions that measured harmony orientation were able to predict satisfaction with joint venture performance.

Conclusions and future extensions

This was an exploratory study developing and validating a measure of harmony orientation. The HO scale developed was found to demonstrate reliability and validity. The importance of harmony orientation has not yet been recognized and tested in the business environment. This seems to have been the first study to provide a comprehensive, psychometrically sound and operationally valid measure of the HO of Chinese-foreign joint ventures.

Research and managerial implications

The results of this study are relevant both to business academicians and to practitioners. From the theoretical perspective, it demonstrates the successful development of a harmony-orientation scale. Five dimensions of HO in Chinese-foreign joint ventures were revealed in this study. The HO scale developed in this study not only helps to enrich the content and meaning of the construct, but it also helps to enhance our understanding of the importance of harmony in business ventures in general and in the Chinese business environment in particular. Of course, it would be inappropriate to advance generalizations based on one exploratory study, and the dimensions of harmony orientation proposed in this study may be particularly appropriate to Chinese-foreign joint ventures. Future studies should be conducted to examine the validity of this scale in other cultural contexts.

For researchers, this study also signals that there are important implications for future research in emerging or transitional economies. Many scholars have argued that transitional economies such as China 'offer fascinating grounds to refine and test existing theories and develop new ones' (Nee and Matthews, 1996; Peng and Heath, 1996; Sin, Ho and So, 2000). Moreover, because China shares an important legacy with other countries currently or formerly practising communism, the Chinese experience can help to shed light on the evolution of the business system and the emergence of new venture markets in the post-Soviet republics and Eastern Europe. Of course, the generalizability of the research findings of this study to these countries has to be tested in future studies. Comparative research in different cultural settings may further enhance our understanding of the relationship between harmony orientation and joint venture performance.

From the managerial perspective, this study provides empirical support for the importance of harmony in conducting business in China, and has significant implications for international marketers. When formulating new venture strategies in the greater China market, the scale developed in this study can help to gauge the degree of HO held by IJV partners. In addition, the findings indicate that differences in performance were also found to be related to the five dimensions of HO. International marketers should proceed with caution when choosing to adopt a common strategy for the greater China market.

Limitations and future research

Since this is a pioneering study on harmony orientation in a Chinese context, the present findings are indicative rather than conclusive. However, some promising research directions are suggested by this study. First, one limitation of this study is its cross-sectional nature, which cannot track changes in harmony orientation. Time-series data should be collected in future studies. Second, the samples used for analysis were drawn from Chinese-foreign joint ventures only. Future research, therefore, can expand on the present study by gathering data from joint ventures in other countries so as to track the generalizability of the HO scale. In addition, future research should also apply the scale to other non-joint-venture-related research to enhance the construct validity of the scale. For example, the relationship between HO and work values, as well as the impact of HO on conflict resolution in cross-cultural decision making would be interesting topics to consider in future studies.

Notes

1.   The authors gratefully acknowledge the assistance and funding granted by the Unit for Chinese Management Development, Department of Marketing, City University of Hong Kong to support this study.
     The original article was in *Asia Pacific Management Review*, 10(3), June 2005.

References

Anderson, E. (1990) 'Two firms, one frontier: on assessing joint venture performance', *Sloan Management Review*, Winter, 19–30.

Antoniou, P.H. and K. Whitman (1998) 'Understanding Chinese interpersonal norms and effective management of sino-western joint ventures', *Multinational Business Review* 6(1), 53–62.

Arbuckle, J.L. and W. Wothke (1999) *Amos 4.0 User's Guide* (Chicago, IL: SmallWaters).

Bond, M.H. (ed.) (1993 *The Psychology of Chinese People* (Hong Kong: Oxford).

Campbell, D.T. and D.W. Fiske (1959) 'Convergent and discriminant validation by the multitrait-multimethod matrix', *Psychological Bulletin* 56, 81–105.

Chen, M. (1995) *Asian Management Systems* (London: Routledge).

Chen, M. and W. Pan (1993) *Understanding the Process of Doing Business in China, Taiwan and Hong Kong* (Lewiston, ME: Edwin Mellen).

Chinese Cultural Connection (1987) 'Chinese values and the search for culture-free dimensions of culture', *Journal of Cross-Cultural Psychology* 18, June, 143–64.

Cragg, C. (1995) 'Business in the orient (Chinese business ethics)', *Accountancy Age* 11, 20–22.

DeMonte, B. (1989) *Chinese Etiquette and Ethics in Business* (Lincoln, IL: NTC Business Books).

Ding, D. (1995) *In search of determinants of Chinese conflict management styles in joint ventures: an integrated approach*, Paper presented at the 13 Annual Conference of the Association of Management, Vancouver, Canada.

Hall, E.T. and M.R. Hall, M.R. (1987) *Hidden Differences: Doing Business with the Japanese* (New York: Anchor Books).

Helms, M.M. (1992) 'Taking the single step', *Management Decision* 30(1), 59–64.

Hofstede, G. (1980) *Culture's Consequences: International Differences in Work-related Values* (Beverly Hills, CA: Sage).

Hu, J. (2003) 'China's Inward FDI: A Review of 2002 and an Outlook to 2003', in *Yearbook of China's Foreign Economic Relations and Trade* (Beijing: China Foreign Economic Relations and Trade Publishing House), pp. 41–9.

Kelly, L. and O. Shenkar (1993) *International Business in China* (London: Routledge).

Legge, J. (1967) *Li Chi–Book of Rites. I* (New York: University Books).

Lin, Y.T. (1994) *The Wisdom of Confucius* (New York: Modern Library).

Loo, K.C and K. Lai (1999) 'An Introduction to Accompaniment in Cantonese Opera', in Anonymous, *Commemoration of the Renowned Musician Loo Kah-chi* (Hong Kong: ROI Productions), pp. 161–4.

Nee, V. and R. Matthews (1996) 'Market transition and societal transformation in reforming state socialism', *Annual Review of Sociology* 22, 401–35.

Nunnally, J. (1978) *Psychometric Theory* (2nd edn, New York: McGraw-Hill).

O'Keefe, H. and W.M. O'Keefe (1997) 'Chinese and western behavioural differences: understanding the gaps', *International Journal of Social Economics* 24(1/2/3), 190–96.

Peng, M.W. and P.S. Heath (1996) 'The growth of the firm in planned economies in transition: institutions, organizations, and strategic choice', *Academy of Management Review* 21, 492–528.

Phillips, L. and R. Bagozzi (1986) 'On Measuring Organizational Properties of Distribution Channels: Methodological Issues in the Use of Key Information', in L.P. Bucklin and J.M. Carman (eds) *Research in Marketing* 8, 313–70.

Redding, G.S. (1993) *The Spirit of Chinese Capitalism* (New York: Walter de Gruyter).

Rokeach, M. (1973) *The Nature of Human Values* (New York: Free Press).

Saussy, H. (2002) 'Thunder, rainbows and spicy herbs: the lord of Qi and the tokens of Chineseness', paper presented at the The Disunity of Chinese Science Conference, 10–12 May 2002, University of Chicago.

Schumacker, R.E. and R.G. Lomax (1996) *A Beginner's Guide to Structural Equation Modeling* (Mahwah, NJ: Erlbaum).

Schwartz, S.H. (1992) 'Universals in the content and structure of values: theoretical advances and empirical tests in 20 countries', *Advances in Experimental Social Psychology* 24, 1–65.

Selmer, J. (1996) 'What expatriate managers know about the work values of their subordinates: Swedish executives in Thailand', *Management International Review* 36, 231–43.

Sin, L., S.C. Ho and S. So (2000) 'An assessment of theoretical and methodological development in advertising research on mainland China: A twenty-year review', *Journal of Current Issues and Research in Advertising* 22(2), 53–69.

Sparks, D. (1999) 'Partners', *Business Week* 25(October).

Sulej, J.C. (1998) 'UK international equity joint ventures in technology and innovation: an analysis of patterns of activity and distribution', *European Business Review* 98(1), 56.

Wang, Z.M. (1994) 'Culture, economic reform, and the role of industrial and organizational psychology in China', in H.C. Triandis *et al.* (eds) *Handbook of Industrial and Organizational Psychology* (2nd edn, Palo Alto, CA: Consulting Psychologist Press), pp. 4, 689–725.

Wong, Y.Y. (1995) 'Succeeding in China in the 21st century', *S.A.M. Advanced Management Journal* 60(3), 4–6.

Yau, O.H.M. (1994) *Consumer Behaviour in China: Customer Satisfaction and Cultural Values* (London: Routledge).

3
Economic Reform and its Gendered Impacts in China Today

Sharon Moore and Julie Jie Wen

Introduction

China is changing dramatically from a tightly controlled communist regime, established in October 1949 when the People's Republic of China (PRC) was declared in Beijing, to a much more laissez-faire giant pursuing 'socialism with Chinese characteristics', a process that started in 1978 with the 'open door' policy of economic reform (Wen and Tisdell, 2001). While it is generally agreed that women's social status improves when a society becomes more affluent, as in China, whether the gap in career opportunities between male and female remains, needs to be explored.

Women at work in both paid and unpaid roles is an increasingly popular research area internationally, but has not been regarded as a significant area for academic research in Asia, particularly in China. North American and European feminist studies have been in mainly two areas: in leadership research, and in exploring the barriers women face in paid employment (Bass and Avolio, 1997; Kouzes and Ponser, 1997). Such studies attempt to find reasons in society, organizational structures and at the individual level, for women's continuing under-representation in paid work, particularly in leadership and executive positions. Little such knowledge has been gained in the Chinese context to date, and this study is an attempt to review current knowledge about changes in women's employment and extend analysis through ongoing empirical research in southern China.

We contend that social forces are continuing to shape the gender identity of Chinese women, and that this is exacerbated by the current era of economic growth. Women are still regarded as inferior to men, psychologically weak and intellectually undeveloped according to feudal traditions. Deeply rooted in the culture, this belief is still held by many, even among professional women. The socialist tradition stipulates that women have equal rights under the constitution. Equal work and equal pay is a primary right, protected by Chinese law. Equal rights are also problematic in contemporary China. Equal rights were granted by the state, but not through women's liberation struggles as in many Western economies. Also at the time equality was written in the law, it was part of an acknowledgement that equality had been achieved for both men and women.

The economic reforms currently transforming China are the final major force shaping employment and equity agendas. This is a central theme of our research. The economic reforms are accompanied by social reforms and changes in social ideology. The media promotes two competing, contradictory and ambiguous concepts of the ideal Chinese women; one in which they are depicted as strong and capable workers, the other as nurturing wives and mothers (Kerr *et al.*, 1996; Thakur, 1997). This apparent ambiguity leads to the paradoxical gender identity of women in China today.

The chapter begins with a historical analysis of women's social status in China. After briefly analysing women's status in rural areas, the authors researched educated executive women in urban areas, the group that is normally considered to include the most privileged women in China. The study includes surveys, interviews and focus group data collected in Guangzhou in 2003–04, which analyse the attitudes and aspirations of middle to senior executive men and women. Four case studies are then discussed to shed light on specific examples of business women. The research concludes that although the overall social status of women continues to rise in China today, the gap in career opportunities available for men and women shows no sign of narrowing, but rather is growing as women continue to have to contribute more than their male colleagues for the same level of family and public success and recognition.

Historical perspective of gender equity in China

China experienced almost two millennia of Confucian culture and patriarchy, during which women were definitely regarded to be 'the other', and inferior. They were to stay home, following orders from their fathers, husbands, and then their sons. This long 'misery' is the first stage in women's social status in China, where women had little social respect or political rights, and the gap between the two genders was vast (Wen and Tisdell, 2001).

The second stage started with the establishment of the People's Republic of China in 1949, when the Chinese Communist party vowed to eliminate social differences between men and women. During the Maoist era, from 1949 to 1978, China upheld the slogan that 'women hold half of the sky', and encouraged women to work by equal pay across genders supported by free childcare offered by work units. Women's participation in political life was encouraged by laws to promote gender equality (Shreve, 2000), and mandatory quotas of women representatives at different levels of legislature (Tong, 2003). Sexuality and gender difference was minimized in public, and women took pride in the fact that they dressed like men.

The third stage, sometimes referred to as the post-Mao era or the reform era, commenced in 1978. One of the major themes of economic reform has been to foster market mechanisms and encourage entrepreneurship. Consequently, some areas with better access to factors of production have been growing faster than other areas, and the economic disparity between the east coast and inland China, between professions, and that between urban and rural area has expanded disproportionately (Wen and Tisdell, 2001). Although gender issues and the status of women have received unprecedented government and public attention, and China has hosted the Fourth World Conference on Women, gender equality, although clearly stipulated as an official goal in China, is being acutely threatened by the economic and social development of the nation (Kwok *et al.*, 2003).

The traditional view that the woman's place is in the home, while never raised explicitly, has been reinforced alongside the economic reforms from the late 1970s (Tong, 2003). Alongside the progress of economic reform, many Chinese women experience that their lives are going backwards, because the rules to protect them are no longer being followed. The first sign of this deteriorating status was when women were being more affected by labour retrenchment required to reform the ailing state sector, which resulted in a higher rate of women's unemployment and forced early retirement compared with men (Appleton *et al.*, 2002: 13). While state ideology was that the individual's well-being is to be sacrificed for the state, women were clearly at the forefront of the sacrifice. Discrimination against women is also being reflected in recruitment and human resource management policies, and it has been demonstrated that China's economic reform has led to the continued marginalization of women in paid employment (Crompton and Sanderson, 1990).

In a society where men are still viewed as superior to women (Chan, 1995), and economic reform has undercut women's status by withdrawing state assistance in welfare, recruitment and employment (Rosen, 1995), it is not surprising to find persistent gender differences in China. Kwok *et al.* (2003) argue that the 50 years of socialist transformation in China has not changed the traditional caring ideology, which considers women as the main care-givers in their families. Economic reform has altered the mode of welfare provision in such a way that it deters women from using community services to ease their caring burden. As a result, according to Tong (2003), males are scoring significantly higher than women on media attention, political knowledge, interest, internal and external efficacy, and non-electoral participation. In addition, women's relative economic position has deteriorated with more males engaging in higher paying careers that are often regarded as not secure or desirable for women to entertain. Although reform in China has provided more opportunities for career advancement, women do not appear to have benefited as much as their male counterparts, and it is reasonable to assume that the gender gap in career opportunity may have actually widened.

In order to further validate this argument, the chapter focuses mainly on the experiences of urban women. Successful career women in urban centres clearly enjoy much high social recognition and better access to career development and employment opportunities than their rural sisters. The role of women in Chinese urban households has changed from 'hiding behind' the male to taking the responsibility of the family. This change is exemplified to a great extent by the proportion of women identifying themselves as household heads during national censuses (Li and Zax, 2003). With increasing job opportunities and social status for urban women, it is important to have a closer look at the gender gap.

Job security

There are significant problems related to labour market reform policy. For example, job security has disappeared, and there are serious inequities emerging in workplace arrangements. While economic reform has profoundly changed China's labour market since 1978, the process of change has been gradual and incremental in nature but it has had enormous impacts at the societal and individual worker level. While in the West women have been among the first social groups to be displaced in economic restructuring (Crompton and Sanderson, 1990), women in China suffer similar marginalization as a result of economic reforms.

Leung and Nann (1996: 172) contend that over 60 percent of displaced workers were female. As many as 11 percent of urban workers have been retrenched, and 53 percent of these remained unemployed (Appleton *et al.*, 2002). The risk of retrenchment was higher for women, the less educated, the low skilled, the middle-aged, and those employed by local government or urban collectives. Re-employment rates are low and imply that unemployment will be long term (Ibid.). Calls for employed women to return to their families so as to make way for their younger counterparts have been noted in different studies (Chan, 1995; Leung and Nann, 1996).

Equal pay for equal work?

Women were paid substantially less in pre-socialist China (Maurer-Fazio and Hughes, 2002). Although reform has undoubtedly increased national wealth of China, as from the late 1970s to the early 1990s, per capita gross domestic product (GDP) more than quadrupled in China (SSB, 2000), there is little study on whether Chinese women have benefited proportionately more or less than men. However, there is substantial evidence of increasing disparities between men's and women's incomes in China (Li and Gustafsson, 1999; Maurer-Fazio *et al.*, 1999).

The architects of the reform strategy contend that Chinese workers have gained the freedom to choose where and for whom they work. This has also been accompanied by a movement towards more decentralized economic development, a productivity-determined remuneration system, and a growing private sector in which managers alone decide the size and composition of the work force. In this scenario, women are experiencing an increasing gender-based wage gap in urban China, and the gaps appear largest in the sectors with the most market influence (Li and Gustafsson, 1999; Maurer-Fazio and Hughes, 2002). If this trend continues, the wage gap between men and women may continue to expand.

Lower salary levels for female managers was also evident. Statistics in 2004 reveal that male executive salaries are usually 10 percent higher rising to 30 percent in some industries, including telecommunications, real estate and information technology (Yang and Zhang, 2004). In Beijing, female salaries are often up to 40 percent lower than those of male colleagues in similar roles. In comparison, in Shanghai female managers typically earn 11 percent less, a significant reduction while in Guangzhou women executives earn on average 23 percent less than their male counterparts (Yang and Zhang, 2004).

Political participation

Studies on political behaviour overall reported a gender gap in political participation in nations with widely different political structure and stage of economic growth, including the United States (Baxter and Lansing, 1983), the UK, Switzerland (Mottier, 1995), Japan, Nigeria, and India

(Verba *et al.*, 1971). Women were less participatory than men in such activities as voting, campaigning, communal activities, political knowledge, interest, and membership in social organization. Gender differences are reflected in the political behaviour and attitudes of the economic elite as well as middle- and working-class populations. The same pattern can be observed in China, where it can be argued, women traditionally have been more passive towards public achievements, more accommodating in conflict situations, and had a higher preference for traditional authority (Tong, 2003).

In conclusion, reforms in China since 1978 have resulted in a macro environment in which women have lost state or public support for their careers' while there may be a slow process to bolster a women's movement through its gentler and kinder policies towards civil society and collective action (Wang, 2004). However, at present, its results are insignificant and the gaps in career opportunity between male and female have actually expanded in the post-Mao era. The following section uses empirical data collected from Guangzhou, China, to further validate this view.

Career challenges facing Chinese managers

Empirical studies were conducted with managers undertaking MBA studies at the Sydney Graduate School of Management joint venture with Kingold Education Centre, located in Guangzhou, southern China. 316 surveys have been collected in 2003–04. Among the subjects, 231 were males, and 85 were females. Sampling was voluntary with over a 90 percent response rate. A brief analysis of the survey data follows.

Demographic data of the samples

Age distribution

Twenty percent of the respondents were aged between 25 to 30 years, 33 percent 31 to 35 years, 23 percent 36 to 40 years, and 20 percent gave no answer. Although the average age of the managers in the sample was around 35, a significant number did not complete this item. During more detailed discussions, the researchers were given many examples of the ageism in recruitment and promotion, resulting in fear of indicating their age.

Gender distribution of respondents

Women comprise only 26.9 percent of the total samples. The skewed nature of the gender distribution in the surveys reflects the focus towards gender difference, and the significance of the issues raised in the sample for women managers. This is in dramatic contrast to the decreasing numbers of women entry into MBA programmes in China (Cai, 2004). In fact in the UWS-Kingold MBA programme, the proportion of women in the programme has fallen from approximately 50 percent in intake one in 2001 to less than 20 percent in intake seven in 2004.

Their industry and roles

The sample reflects significant changes in industrial production in China. For example, the proportion of managers from manufacturing fell from 32 percent in the survey conducted in 2003, to 20 percent in the survey in June 2004, reaching an average of 25 percent across all surveys. Contrasting trends occurred in the finance, information technology, and services and sales industries, where significant increases occurred in this very short period. Traditionally, state-owned enterprises (SOEs) and the public sector have supported equal opportunity policies and programmes much more actively than the private sector, reflecting a global pattern. For this reason, the burgeoning Chinese private sector, dominated by transnational companies, appears to be less active in supporting women managers.

When asked about industry background and ownership patterns, dramatic shifts in ownership patterns can also be observed in this brief period. The proportion of samples from SOEs dropped markedly (from 50 to 30 percent), so did those from joint ventures (down to 22 percent), while samples from solely foreign-owned and transnational companies rose sharply (22 percent). This may indicate the declining economic power of the state sector, and the shift from joint ventures to solely foreign-owned ventures when foreign direct investment (FDI) adjusts its entry criteria in China.

Traditionally, SOEs and the public sector have supported equity and human resource management programmes much more actively than the private sector, reflecting a global pattern. For this reason, the burgeoning Chinese private sector dominated by transnational companies appears to be less active in supporting the employees and business executives. For example, the emerging glass ceiling for female business executives in China is a result of the economic changes towards privatization, and growing dominance of transnational companies, with the corresponding lack of support for equal opportunity in employment.

The dominant proportion of line managers in the sample (45 percent) reflects two factors. First, a shift from systemic company support (paying for the tuition and time allowance), to a more individually focused position (functional and line managers paying for their studies to advance their careers to more strategic and general management roles). Second, a more competitive market, and pressure to strive for better qualifications in order to adapt to more demanding jobs and short-term roles.

Occupational mobility

In response to the question about occupational mobility, a decrease in average length of employment with the same organization was apparent, and was supported by numerous examples from the subjects. The researchers were told that the average time spent in an organization has decreased from six to eight to two to five years, with younger managers being more likely to move more frequently. However, women and older managers were likely to be less mobile.

This also reflects the decrease significance of managers from state-owned enterprises (SOEs) in the sample. Traditionally, SOEs have been long-term employers with significant budgets for training and career development.

Reform and career pressures

When asked whether reform has made business executives' situation more difficult, most men and women respondents regarded reform has improved their career opportunity. This reflects the general overall improvement in economic life and opportunities across China, particularly in the cities of southern China.

A surprisingly high 'Yes' response (over 53 percent) for the question on whether increasing demand on employees has made business executives' lives generally more difficult, reflects the common feeling of rising pressure on male and female business executives.

With women still being responsible for undertaking most of unpaid work at home for child and elder care, it is unfortunately evident that most of the women respondents admitted in this research that their life was becoming more difficult with commercialization of education, decreasing social and family support for home based care, and the continued reluctance of men's recognition of sharing family care duties in today's China.

Lack of career advancement and promotional opportunities

Most male and female business executives in the sample were successful in their career because of their skill levels and personal qualities, which meant that they were highly regarded by their organizations. However, in response to questions about overseas business experience, they reported that it was sometimes very difficult for Chinese-born business executives to progress beyond middle level and operational management roles. Few

Chinese business executives were CEOs or members of top executive teams in the global enterprises in which they worked particularly in international business roles. This appeared to be a serous concern warranting further attention, particularly as business executives were often outperforming many of their superiors from overseas backgrounds. The lack of opportunity to work internationally is considered a serious career limitation, and few of the respondents had worked overseas.

In responding to the question whether they had career mentoring, it was reported that mentoring was minimal, with formal processes totally absent. Mentoring that was available was informal and inconsistent. Major sources of mentoring included partner, parents, boss, and surprisingly one's self. There was little evidence formal and consistent examples of ongoing professional development and executive leadership training.

Although most of the men and women managers were optimistic about their career opportunities, there were warning signs for their professional advancement. For example, female business executives were particularly working in four management areas, sales and marketing, HR and finance, and administration (Cai, 2004), while men were clustered in IT, operations, and other specialist areas. This means limited opportunities for Chinese women managers to join top executive teams and leadership roles unless they gain more generalist experience in finance, general management, and strategic leadership roles.

The gap widens for women managers

When asked whether reform has made women's situation more difficult, only 11 said 'yes' (10 were females and 1 male), and the rest regarded reform as improving women's life. This reflects the general overall improvement in economic life and opportunities for both genders across China, particularly in the cities of southern China.

However, decreasing social and family support for child rearing, and continued commercialization of education, led to over 40 percent of subjects believing that life for women was becoming more difficult, and almost 80 percent of those agreeing were women. This reflects the reality that Chinese women are responsible for the great majority of unpaid work and family support for children and elder care, and men's reluctance to acknowledge their responsibility to share the caring duties.

A positive response (over 53 percent) from both men and women respondents to the question on whether increasing demand on employees has made women's life more difficult, reflects the common feeling of rising pressure on women, and men chose to agree that the womens' situation was especially vulnerable. The gender gap at work is clearly recognized in the question on who makes decisions at work. Only one female chose women to be the decision maker, and 10 respondents (including three women) felt that both men and women make decisions together. The rest regarded men to be decision makers at work.

Men are still the decision maker at work according to the respondents. This reflects traditional attitude to men's dominant role at the work/place, in both paid and unpaid roles. For example, the sorts of tasks in which men are normally involved, such as working overtime to make an important decision, are viewed as appropriate unpaid work by both genders, while women's unpaid roles at work, including office, social support, organizing facilities, recreation, etc., are not seen as visible or real unpaid work. This reflects the general trend to discount or not to acknowledge women's unpaid contribution at work.

Chinese women executives for the new millennium – interview and focus group data

As part of the research, 85 women were interviewed individually and in focus groups, with interview and focus group questions relating to the Chinese economic reform agenda and its effect on business and personal life. In particular, the research explored impacts for female business executives, in terms of career progression, work-life challenges and issues of organizational climate and workplace culture.

Of the 85 women in the sample, the majority were married or part-nered, their ages ranged from the mid 20s to late the 40s with most falling in the 30–35 years category. Most of those who were married had one child. More than one half worked for large international companies, mainly European or North American, with the remainder employed in SOEs undergoing major economic reform and partial privatization. The subjects were asked questions about their industry, their position and role, what was important to them about their work, and their aspir-ations both personally and professionally. The research was also inter-ested to explore work-life balance issues as well as child and elderly care responsibilities.

The women subjects were delightfully open and informative; all were extremely committed to their work and professional development. In fact, the MBA they were studying required them to complete 1 core unit per month over 12 months, with attendance at lectures over two week-ends (Friday evening to Sunday evening), an essay due the following weekend and an examination on the fourth weekend of each month. Many commuted to university from outlying regions and cities. Their study commitment was on top of full-time management roles in many of China's leading businesses.

Marital status and accommodation arrangement of the women subjects

Although most women were married and/or mothers, their separation from partners and families was a surprisingly common circumstance, with many in the group living and working in different parts of China from their partners, children and parents. Only 38 percent of the 85 women were living with partner and/or child. This relates to the surprisingly high and growing percentage of women managers living alone and characterizes the extent and nature of personal sacrifice being made in China in pursuit of economic growth and personal career success.

Career opportunities

The women managers reported that women were often successful, particularly in international business, because of their skills, patience and willingness to cooperate. This was compared to their male colleagues, who were described as often being more competitive and less easy for senior foreign managers to work with. However, the women managers also reported that it was very difficult for women to get beyond middle level and operational management roles. No Chinese women were CEOs or members of top executive teams in the enterprises in which they worked, whether these were Chinese or international businesses. This seemed to be a serous concern warranting further attention, particularly as women were outperforming many men in their management studies.

In the meantime, there are other warning signs for women in China. Women were particularly working in four management areas: sales and marketing, human resources, finance, and administration (Cai, 2004). Women were underrepresented in information technology, operations, and general management. This is particularly serious given women's career aspirations, and it is aggravated by the growing trends for employers not to support women's MBA studies in terms of finance or time (Zhang, 2004). As a result there are limited opportunities for women managers to join top executive teams and leadership roles, and reflects the gendered leadership opportunities for Chinese women managers.

Work/life balance

With increasing intensification of work, and the 24/7 phenomenon, most of the women managers said they had little or no balance. They reported that challenges for balancing their professional and personal life were enormous. There were also clear emerging areas of concern in relation to parenting and elderly care responsibilities. This finding may also reflect the traditional Chinese value of commitment and hard work, coupled with the business demand for 110 percent commitment, especially by private and family firms. Transnational companies reflect a different model – that of highly competitive work driven philosophy. It appears that in contrast to Western business, the work-life balance is not promoted or endorsed in Chinese business life.

Employment security

The women subjects agreed that equal pay was not actively pursued in China, despite talk of pay equity. First, salary packages or employment contacts are designed in such a way, including performance based payment and high percentages as being at risk, where women are less advantaged. Second, although there are cases of seemingly equal pay for the same position, women managers are expected to do extra work, have higher expectations than male counterparts, and experience more pressure. Third, there appears to be a different male–female guangxi (relationship), where women spend their time at the desk but men are busy networking. Finally, the lack of explicit transparent human resource policies and programmes means women's experience is hidden. Many women managers respond by disempowering themselves in accepting less pay. In other words, 'the espoused equality and the practical inequality' is the principal mechanism sustaining the inequality between men and women in China (Wang, 2004). Wang also argues that equal rights for Chinese women are based on masculinity as the norm, and there has been little organized effort to dispel negative stereotypes about women.

Half of the women managers experienced sexism at work, particularly from senior executives. Younger women were particularly vulnerable to sexist behaviour and attitudes. Unfortunately, sexism was seen as normal, even natural, in Chinese culture.

Mentoring was minimal, with formal processes totally absent. Mentoring that was available was informal and inconsistent. Major sources of mentoring included partner, parents, boss, and, surprisingly, one's self.

Family support for children and parents

Declining public support for children and parents is common in China. There is no work unit or government support for childcare except in some SOEs. While parents give some support to their grandchildren, this was limited because so many of the managers live far away from their parents and family community, in many cases in a different city or province. Children still saw themselves responsible for their parents, with many contributing financially. However, growing numbers were using private services, including nursing homes.

Career and life goals

The image of Chinese traditional women, with their virtues of being gentle, caring, supportive, and sacrificial, is accelerating through the media and society. The social ideology is changing alongside economic reforms (Wang, 2004). The traditional Chinese value on gender identity does not clearly encourage women to be ambitious and career focused. The media strongly promotes the concept of ideal women as strong and capable workers, as well as nurturing wives and mothers. Women are expected to be independent and hard working to achieve career success, but at the same time, obedient and prepared to sacrifice career success for the sake of their husbands. Thus, women's plans for their work and life include 'achieve work – life balance', 'be happy, have a happy family', 'feel useful to the society and others', 'have a simpler life'. This apparent ambiguity leads to a paradoxical gender identity of women in China, how they treat themselves, and how they are treated in the workplace.

Case studies

The following four case study examples reflect something of the richness and complexities of the interview data and the accompanying focus group discussions. This case approach is added to the more conventional data analysis used in this section in order to convey key issues succinctly and forcefully.

Case 1

Amy is 32, a middle manager in a transnational telecommunications company with headquarters in Europe. With an accounting and economics background, she has worked in this company for 10 years and has steadily progressed during that time. Interestingly, Amy's husband of seven years has worked for a Chinese SOE mining company in Uganda since their marriage. He continues to work in Uganda, returning home every three months for three weeks. Their daughter lives with Amy's parents in a provincial centre some two hours journey by train from Guangzhou.

Amy's job entails substantial amounts of travel within China, for example she goes to either Beijing of Shanghai most weeks. When she is not travelling Amy lives alone in a family-sized modern apartment in the centre of Guangzhou. Her work-home balance is weighted heavily in the direction of work and study. While she misses her daughter, she is only able to visit her monthly and she describes her relationship with her husband as 'very poor'. When he is at home, she describes him as watching television and expecting her to wait on him after her long day at the office. The effect of him working in a male-only work group in Uganda for long periods appears to have severely reduced their ability to communicate and have a quality relationship. Amy's social life is very restricted, although she tries to do nice things for herself regularly, for example, meet friends, have manicures and so on.

While ambitious and capable, Amy turned down the opportunity to work at the company headquarters in Europe because she did not want to be separated from family and friends; a year later she gave birth to her daughter, which curtailed both her ambitions and the opportunity to work internationally, as well as her social networks.

Case 2

Stella, 28, also has a partner who works overseas – in Canada. They are not married, although they have been together for 10 years, because they are waiting for a marriage licence to be issued. Licensing is a regional government responsibility, and exemplifies the social and economic control the state still holds over people's life choices in employment, partnerships, travel, etc. Stella has an economics background and works as the financial manager of a new golf course that attracts wealthy Chinese and international business people.

She has worked at the golf club for four years, and sees it as a growth industry and a great place for business connections. Although she has an equal and very positive relationship with her partner, she appears fairly traditional, both in appearance and attitudes. Unlike Amy, she regarded the amount of discretionary time she had, due to not having domestic responsibilities, as offering her great opportunities for socializing and networking. Stella's personality and appearance seem 'Western', at odds with her somewhat traditional attitudes towards home, family and women's role in society.

Case 3

Trina is 38. She is the most senior woman manager in a North American transnational agricultural products company. Her responsibility within the company covers all of southeast China and she has been with the business in a professional role more than 10 years. Within the group studied, Trina was one of the more outspoken and passionate feminists. She appeared to have a very realistic 'take' on her workplace, stating that after 10 years of positioning herself and working extraordinarily hard, she was now at the point where she could 'let up', not push herself so hard and work on the next stage of her career development.

Trina is single, and concerned about her ageing parents who live in northern China. She is interested in developing a career in elderly care or healthcare, partly in response to her own life issues and perceived needs. For example, she is concerned about her parents' health and recreational support needs, and sees them as reflecting a growing trend in the new China. Trina impresses as extremely competent and confident, and clearly has leadership as well as management qualities. She appears to reflect a typical Western business career trajectory, conveying to us the 'substance plus style' of many successful executive women in our own society.

Case 4

Fleur, 42, is a medical doctor by training who currently works in the pharmaceutical/healthcare industry. She is also single and, like Stella, appears to have a more traditional Chinese style and outlook than the other three. While modest and keeping a low profile within the group, Fleur seems to have remarkable focus and determination in relation to her career and business development opportunities. She also has ageing parents with growing support needs, and is keen to pursue business interests in care of the aged. 'My parents need more in their lives than Mahjong and Tai Chi.' Fleur, like many of the other women interviewed, seems to demonstrates a discernible general trend for business managers in China to be highly focused and driving, enjoying little non-work time (six days work per week the norm) coupled with very long working hours and management education commitments. This seemed to us to be very different form the current Western preoccupation with managing for work, family and 'the self'.

To conclude the case analysis, it is evident that the privatization of formerly provided state social care provision has caused a radical shift in thinking about care and caring. The ideology of care is now incorporating private care models for both elderly and childcare, resulting in new challenges in terms of who pays and who are the carers. Quality education and training for carers is on the policy agenda, alongside a strong continuing commitment to family based care provision. In this way, China has adopted Western care models in less than a decade in many parts of the country. Carers are being imported from rural and less-industrialized areas to support the careers of working professionals and to meet the needs of industrialization.

The research indicates that to advance a more equitable and sustainable balance between industrial production and social reproduction, including quality elderly care and childcare, several factors need to be recognized at policy levels in China today. There is a clear role for centralized planning in terms of accompanying industrial development with social development, particularly at regional and local government level (Wang, 2004). The current polity shift to a more balanced score card approach to planning involving resourcing rural and less developed regions is a welcome initiative.

Employment policy also needs to include social as well as economic development. Healthcare, the education industry, and childcare and care of the elderly, are all key elements and are benchmarks of a civil society. At industry policy and programme levels, the research recommends that gender neutrality be replaced by gender-sensitive policies and practices which acknowledge important gender differences and economic realities. These include upgrading labour laws to cover the services sector, particularly community services, to better protect the rights and interests of women workers in casual jobs, to ensure workplace safety and so on.

Conclusions and implications

China is increasingly viewed as a dominant component in the world's economic future. What social and business models is it building on? It seems that many of the experiences observed in China are reminiscent of earlier eras of Western culture. As well as gender differences, there was an almost complete absence of environmental consciousness, and Chinese businesses were just starting to attend to concerns about social equity. By 2004, however, the government's focus on growth through reliance on foreign direct investment (FDI) and gross domestic product (GDP) had been accompanied by moves towards a more balanced approach. In particular, value creation through integration of financial, social and environmental considerations was being promoted through changes of direction. For example, resources were directed toward the less-developed regional areas in western China, and helping the agricultural sector to re-equip itself for a more important role. Full entry into the world Trade Organization (WTO) and international exposure partly assisted by Beijing being awarded the Olympic Games in 2008, have clearly influenced this strategic direction.

The research proposes three stages of women's status from historical analysis. Since successful career women in urban areas are regarded as women in the most prestigious situation in China in the 21st century, by focusing on opinions on gender gap among successful managers in Guangzhou, the research may be able to describe the emerging gender gap more accurately. The research reveals that the gap between male and female managers in the cities continues to expand with the progress of economic reform in China. This view has been validated from different angles by opinions from both male and female managers in China, through data from surveys, interviews, and focus group discussion.

In relation to economic and class differences, the women managers included in the research represent the emergence of a new executive class of Chinese women. Further, Chinese society is rapidly constructing a set of economic and social relationships almost identical to the business and family experiences of Western business over the past quarter century. Women are moving away from more than 50 years of state socialism towards a more economically 'liberal' but not necessarily 'liberating' future.

At an organizational level, there are business case benefits from including work-life balance issues as well as care of the elderly and childcare in human resource policies. International best practice involves many leading examples of both corporations and smaller enterprises that have become 'employers of choice' directly as a result of commitment to family and community issues. Productive diversity, valuing the contributions of all employees, means that women workers are encouraged to contribute their experience and skills and given appropriate support and recognition. A corporate culture that is inclusive, and values the contribution of all employees, is more likely to be a leading business model for its role as a responsible corporate citizen.

At a personal, individual and family level in China, there is a clear need to 'share the care'. While Chinese women are still carrying the major load at home and work, gender equity is remains an illusion, in theory but not in practice. Younger women and men who are more equity-conscious and gender-aware, may need to promote alternative models of working and living, working and caring. Given the challenges and opportunities in China today, the resilience and flexibility of the Chinese population cannot be underestimated. Both Western and Chinese models offer valuable contributions to the success of this task.

While gaining a foothold in the new economy and international business, executive women are clearly experiencing some negative impacts of China's economic reform. The one-child policy, for example (also known as 'the little emperor policy'), may result in a sense of loss for some women, and for other working women it may offer economic liberation/opportunity. Similar impacts are evident in changes in consumption patterns of increased wealth and materialism. Unfortunately, the 'trophy wife' phenomenon is also increasingly apparent in Chinese cities and business life.

Chinese women executives face great challenges to the work-life balance, are affected at a very personal level by the intensification of work in global business environments, and are embracing these challenges with gusto. Their lives are very different from those experienced by their mothers who raised their families during the Cultural Revolution, and their grandmothers who grew up in pre-Revolutionary China. The speed at which this is occurring is breathtaking.

There are limitations to these findings from a non-representative sample, and a largely descriptive qualitative study. Statistical analysis was not attempted because of the small size of the sample. The purpose was analytical, attempting to develop issues for future studies. Large-scale study in other provinces will help to substantiate further the findings of the present research. Nevertheless, the gender gap among successful executives in China has so far been addressed in systemic research. This research, while exploratory and empirical, may serve to provide valuable insights for policy-making and human resource strategy in China, and encourage other research on the costs as well as benefits of the current reform strategy.

References

Appleton, S., J. Knight, L. Song and Q. Xia (2002) 'Labor retrenchment in China, determinants and consequences', *China Economic Review* 13(2–3), 252–75.

Bass, B.M. and B.J. Avolio (1997) 'Shatter the Glass Ceiling: Women May Make Better Managers', in K. Grint (ed.), *Leadership: Classical, Contemporary, and Critical Approaches* (New York: Oxford University Press), pp. 199–210.

Baxter, S. and M. Lansing (1983) *Women and Politics: the Visible Majority* (Ann Arbor: University of Michigan Press).

Cai, Z. (2004) 'Analysis of Chinese women in joint ventures', available at <www.people.com.an/GB/Shenghuo/200>.

Chan, C.L.W. (1995) 'Gender Issues in Market Socialism', in L. Wong and S. MacPherson (eds), *Social Change and Social Policy in Contemporary China* (Hong Kong: City University of Hong Kong), pp. 188–215.

Crompton, R. and K. Sanderson (1990) *Gendered Job and Social Change* (London: Unwin Hyman).

Kerr, J., J. Delahanty and K. Humpage (1996) *Gender and Jobs in China's New Economy* (Ottawa: North–South Institute).

Kouzes, J.M. and B.Z. Ponser (1997) *The Leadership Challenge: How to Keep Getting Extraordinary Things done in Organization* (San Francisco: Jossey-Bass).

Kwok, K.F., Y. Agnes and M.L. Kim (2003) 'Women and community service in Beijing – limited support?', *Women's Studies International Forum* 26(3), 265–76.

Leung, J.C.B. and R. Nann (1996) *Authority & Benevolence: Social Welfare in China* (Hong Kong: Chinese University of Hong Kong).

Li, S. and B. Gustafsson (1999) 'Zhongguo Chengzhen Zhigong shouru de xingbei chayi fenxi (An Analysis of Gender Difference in Urban Employees in China), in Renwei Zhao *et al.* (eds), *Zhongguo Jumin Shouru Fenpei Zai Yanjiu: Jingji Gaige He Fazhan Zhong De Shouru Fenpei* (Further Research on the Income Distribution of Chinese Residents: Income Distribution in Economic Reform and Development), (Beijing: China Finance and Economics Publishing House), pp. 556–93.

Li, H.Z. and J.S. Zax (2003) 'Labor supply in urban China', *Journal of Comparative Economics* 31(4), 795–817.

Maurer-Fazio, M. and J. Hughes (2002) 'The effects of market liberalization on the relative earnings of Chinese women', *Journal of Comparative Economics* 30(4), 709–31.

Maurer-Fazio, M., T. Rawski and W. Zhang (1999) 'Inequality in the rewards for holding up half the sky: gender wage gaps in China's urban labour market, 1988–1994', *China Journal* 41: 55–88.

Mottier, V. (1995) 'Citizenship and gender division in the Swiss direct democracy: from structure to political action', *West European Politics* 18(1), 161–72.

Rosen, S. (1995) 'Women and political participation in China', *Pacific Affairs* 68(3).

Shreve, C. (2000) 'Women in China: a country profile', Book review, *Journal of Government Information* 27(1), 92–5.

SSB (State Statistics Bureau) (2000) *Zhongguo Tongji Nianjian* (Statistical Yearbook of China), (Beijing: China Statistical Publishing House).

Thakur, R. (1997) *Rewriting Gender: Reading Contemporary Chinese Women* (London: Zed).

Tong, J. (2003) 'The gender gap in political culture and participation in China', *Communist and Post-Communist Studies* 36(2), 131–50.

Verba, S., N. Nie and J. Kim (1971) 'The Modes of Democratic Participation: a Cross National Analysis, *Professional Papers in Comparative Politics*, 2(01–013) (Beverly Hills: Sage).

Wang, Yi (2004) *Gendered Leadership Experience of Chinese Women Managers*, Ontario Institute for Studies in Education, (Toronto : University of Toronto).

Wen, J. and C. Tisdell (2001) *Tourism and China's Economic Development in China* (Singapore: World Scientific Publishing House).

Yang and Zhang (2004) 'Chinese Managers' Salary Trend in 2004', *Executive*, February.

Zhang, Aijing (2004) 'Crisis for Chinese Professional Women', available at <www.people.com.an/GB/Shenghuo/78>.

4
The Road to the Kyoto Protocol: A Harmonious Case of Euro-Chinese Corporate Environmental Behaviour

Lena Croft and Shige Makino

Introduction

While extreme reactions or non-traditional actions to protect the biophysical (natural) environment are labelled as practising radical environmentalism, philosophers continue to look for enlightenment from the natural environment and practitioners carry on their long and hectic journey to fight against environment pollution. Yet, the history of scholarship attention to management of organizations in the natural environment is relatively brief (Starik and Marcus, 2000). The natural environment is being ignored by most in management theory (Hart, 1995).

As a recent scholarly phenomenon, more examinations are conducted to make a connection between natural environments and organizations. Organizational entities have or could have significant impacts, whether positive or negative, real or imagined, on the ecosystems of which they are a part (Starik and Marcus, 2000). While the extant research on natural environment is diversified in terms of its scope and approach, it tends to focus primarily on explaining costs and benefits for organizations to combat environmental issues (e.g., Russo and Fouts, 1997; Guasch and Hahn, 1999; Bohm, 2002; Stoeckl, 2004). Perhaps this is because many firms believe that investment in natural environmental protection makes no, or even negative, direct contributions to firm performance, while acknowledging that such investment may enhance the reputation of the firm as being a socially responsible enterprise. Most important of all, the majority of these studies involving managing organizations in the natural environment rely primarily on the existing management theoretical perspectives (e.g., economics, resource-based, and/or sociological perspectives) to explain the phenomena, yet fail to explain the role that individual, organizational, and societal values play in facilitating or constraining the organization's initiative in protecting the natural environment. Previous studies also fail to identify the specific behaviours that organizations would adopt to protect the natural environment. This study proposes a conceptual framework that explains how organizational values and beliefs influence corporate initiatives in promoting environmental protection, which in this study is called 'corporate environmental behaviour' (CEB).

The study introduces a conceptual framework on CEB. The proposed framework explains how values and beliefs embedded in organizations would shape initiatives in protecting the natural environment. Since organizations have different values and beliefs about the importance of environmental protection and its impact on their economic outcomes, they may have different levels of incentives to engage in CEB. The study provides a case study, which describes the Euro-Chinese interactions under the Clean Development Mechanism (CDM) proposed in the Kyoto Protocol, to explain how CEB plays a role in designing and implementing corporate strategies for environmental protection.

A corporate environmental behavioural framework

Ever-deteriorating environments and sustainability of world resources have drawn much public attention; debates on this pressing issue were highlighted at the United Nations Conference on Environment and Development (UNCED) held in Rio de Janeiro in 1992. More and more researches have been undertaken to address concerns on the continuous exploitation of natural resources (e.g., Levy and Newell, 2000; Bansal and Roth, 2000; Bansal, 2002). Increasing concerns about natural environment protection have now become real business issues that most corporations cannot neglect. On the one hand, corporations with profit-making goals, gradually acknowledge the impact of economic growth on ecosystems. On the other hand, corporations continue to face the challenges of minimizing costs and maximizing profits to achieve sustainable corporate growth. Contrasting responses to the Kyoto Protocol between the US and European governments are typical examples (Levy and Newell, 2000; Hathaway-Zepeda, 2004). To address environmental protection (e.g., pollution prevention) and, at the same time, maintain sustainable corporate growth is seen as paradoxical. While some argue that an incentive-based approach adopted by government bodies that posts heavy penalties – using a 'stick' – to deter any violation suffices to resolve the problem, others advocate that a market-based approach that promotes tradable permits or credits – using a 'carrot' – to encourage corporate innovative can more effectively tackle the problem (Porter and van de Linde, 1995).

While researchers continue to debate on the normative means to tackle these problems, they have started recognizing that values and beliefs that corporations have on environmental protection might play a significant role in promoting CEB, and hence, improving their incentive to protect the natural environment. However, previous studies failed to address and define how such values and beliefs induce and motivate a corporation to adopt CEB and go beyond the compliance of existing regulations in order to achieve better results in environmental protection. To answer this research question, this study presents a conceptual framework that describes how values and beliefs embedded in a corporation guide CEB and explains how firms with high CEB develop strategies that promote protection of natural environment and develop competitive advantage simultaneously (see Figure 4.1).

Corporate environmental values and beliefs

Values and beliefs of an organization lay the foundation for understanding behaviour. Within an organization, a narrow set of values is transmitted; hence it is suggested that very specific values are most relevant in organizations (Meglino and Ravlin, 1998). At an individual level, the study of Stern *et al.* (1999) examined how individuals' value and belief systems are shaped by social norms concerning environmentalism. The study suggests that individual values, and beliefs such as altruism and self-interest, manifest personal norms which might have critical influences on support for environmental protection. The individuals' values and beliefs subsequently affect their behaviour, which in turn, affects their responses to environmental issues. Among these indicators, 'environmental citizenship behaviour' – a personal commitment to learning more about the environment and to taking responsible environmental action has been found to

Figure 4.1:   A conceptual framework on corporate environmental values and beliefs guiding corporate environment behaviours

perform multiple direct effects. The evidence, as Stern *et al.* (1999: 90) indicate, illustrates that environmental citizenship behaviour is a function of variables reflecting a social definition of environmental problems and of individuals' access to resources for social influence. Environmental citizenship encourages individuals, communities and organizations to consider the environmental rights and responsibilities we all have as residents of planet Earth (MacGregor and Szerszynski, 2003: 8). Although the definition of environmental citizenship is yet to gain consensus and subject to debate (Bell, 2004), we do agree that individuals have the rights of, and the responsibilities for being 'citizens' to protect the natural environment.

At a firm level, corporate environmental behaviour is affected by values and beliefs that are embedded in the natural environment where the firm operates. Some firms have clear corporate environmental policy, which explicitly stipulates the values and beliefs that they have on environmental protection. Corporate environmental policy, from a normative perspective, are mandatory under International Organization for Standardization (ISO) 14000 series of environmental management standards, the Economic Management and Audit Scheme, which were developed by the early British initiative and are adopted mostly in the European Union (Graham and Havlick, 1999). From an eco-centric perspective, it is suggested that firms should bear ecological responsibilities, even when the outcomes of their initiative in protecting ecosystems may not be directly accounted for or measured by corporate performance.

To understand the values and beliefs that are to be incorporated into corporate environmental policy statements, we use 237 corporate environmental policies, collected from 20 countries worldwide covering dozens of different industries and ranging from medium to multinational in size and published in Graham and Havlick (1999). Several dimensions are mostly emphasized in corporate environmental policy statements and are identified as follows:

Corporate environmental values and beliefs

(1) Social commitments and ethical responsibilities to protect, restore, reduce risks, minimize exploitation to the environment or sustainable use of natural resources.
(2) Good Citizenship to employees, stakeholders and the communities
(3) Compliance of existing regulations, agreements and standards
(4) Product and service innovation to achieve efficiency
(5) Continuous improvement
(6) Happier human through sustainable development

(7) Openness to the public through communication and information
(8) Accountability

   To realize and execute corporate environmental values and beliefs, firms are believed to act and behave with certain salient characteristics depicted as corporate environmental behaviour (CEB). The proposed conceptual framework describes the relationship between these two constructs.

Corporate environmental behaviour

Upon identification of corporate environmental values and beliefs, we posit that it is these values and beliefs that motivate a firm to eco-centrically act toward the common good of the natural environment in addition to achieving economic goals. Previous studies demonstrate how environmental performance would be linked to economic performance as productivity and innovation (Porter, 1991; Gore, 1992; Russo and Fouts, 1997). Yet, no studies have convincingly explained how corporate values and beliefs motivate CEB, going beyond the premise of profit maximization as primacy dominating modern corporate governance (Friedman, 1970).
   Corporate environmental behaviour is defined in this study as the proactive corporate behaviours to explore capabilities beyond economic activities and the existing institutional requirements. The concept is crucial in explaining why some organizations are more willing than others to engage in activities to improve the natural environment. The concept of CEB is akin to that of organizational citizenship behaviour (OCB) articulated in the seminal work of Organ (1988: 4). This represents a behaviour performed by an individual that is discretionary, not directly or explicitly recognized by the formal reward system, and that in the aggregate promotes the effective functioning of the organization. This individual-level behavioural construct has intensively been explored to enrich our knowledge in understanding why an individual performs extra-role duties within an organizational context (e.g., Moorman, 1991; Organ and Ryan, 1995; Hui *et al.*, 2000). The importance of the concept is echoed in the belief of Katz (1964) that organizations rely on employee contributions that go beyond the call of duty in order to function effectively (Bolino *et al.*, 2002: 505). This belief is extended to organizational-level study on the effectiveness of different corporate strategic responses.
   Within the domain of organization and the natural environment (ONE) studies, previous research has tended to adopt the perspective of institutional theory (e.g., Levy and Rothenberg, 2002). As Ehrenfeld (2002) underscores the deficiency of the institutional framework in explaining

natural environmental management, social norms mainly relate to satisfaction of the rights or needs of autonomous individuals; the environment relates to survival and sustainability relates to flourishing beyond mere satisfaction. Such complexity cannot be utterly defined and explained solely from the institutional perspective. This study introduces distinct views to explain how corporate values and beliefs explain CEB.

Categorization of organizations based on corporate environmental behaviour

In this study, we posit that it is imperative for firms to foster values and beliefs that transcend an individual-level OCB to a corporate-level CEB to deal with environmental problems. In this study, firms are categorized into four groups based on the nature of CEB they perform.

CEB 1

Firms that focus primarily on profit-maximization activities, no matter whether such activities are against the agreements or regulations for environmental protection, are classified in the category CEB 1. The firms in this category perform CEB below the level of minimum regulatory requirements for environmental protection.

CEB 2

Firms that make a minimum engagement in environmental protection are classified in the category CEB 2. The firms in this category perform CEB only to an extent that they satisfy the legal requirements and the regulations for environmental protection.

CEB 3

Firms that satisfy standards set by stakeholders in a society for environmental protection are classified in the category CEB 3. The firms in this category perform CEB going beyond the minimum legal requirement and regulations up to the point at which they satisfy social norms for environmental protection.

CEB 4

Firms that proactively act for environmental protection beyond legal and normative requirements are classified in the category CEB 4. Firms in this category proactively perform CEB going beyond the minimum legal requirement and regulations as well as social norms for environmental protection.

Dynamic patterns of corporate environmental behaviour

As organizations respond to existing regulatory constraints that vary from time to time, country to country, and industry to industry, this bottom-line of compliance varies according to the spatial and temporal dimensions so stated. Generalizability to explain behaviour due to these variances can thus be extended. Hunt and Auster (1990) classify firms according to their responses to environmental constraints. In this study, we argue that corporate values and beliefs regarding environmental protection are reflected in corporate environmental policies. This reflection is then realized through CEB. Thus, we argue that CEB would emerge through dynamic interactions of firms' value and belief formation, policy development, and implementation and that, through the process of these interactions, the indigenous firms become a driving force of transforming the society (country, industry, etc.) from that where only minimal CEB are performed to that where a greater level of CEB are performed by these firms (see Figure 4.2).

Taxonomy of CEB

In defining scope of activities for organizational activities in pursuing CEB, Hoffman (2001: 14) specifically pinpoints that there is no such thing as 'a green company'. The best one can do is to describe the progression of how companies are 'going green'. This argument emphasizes CEB as an evolutionary process involving corporate activities in environmental protection rather than an ultimate goal of an organization. The conceptualization by seeing greening as a process implies the variances in the degree of greening and emphases in components among different

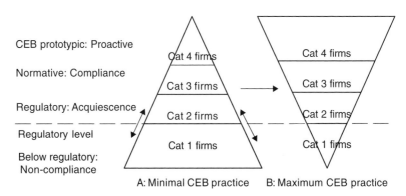

Figure 4.2:   A corporate environmental behaviour evolutionary path

organizations (Forber and Jermier, 2002). Taxonomy of CEB would be based on how a firm acts in relation to environmental protection in order to benefit the community and realize its values and beliefs.

The first facet of CEB is voluntarism. This is based on the principle of relying voluntary action of firms to proactively act towards environmental protection rather than compulsion. While regulatory constraints are defined, there will be no further legal obligation for firms to act beyond existing legislative requirements. Hence, high CEB firms are those that willingly pursue environmental protection beyond existing regulatory control.

With ethical obligations and social responsibilities of a firm defined in the corporate environmental policy statement, a firm would have to act beyond compliance on existing regulatory constraints and requirements in order to achieve beliefs embedded in the firm. Due to concerns of economic costs posted on firms and the support of market-based economy, there are situations where governments do not impose legislation or simply set a low standard on certain environmental controls. A responsible firm would then act to lobby for legislation or meet standards that are acceptable up to international norms or requirements. Going beyond compliance becomes the act of a firm to proceed further than simply comply with current requirements.

The third facet of CEB is incentives. Other than taking environmental protection beyond compliance, firms with high CEB would also like to see their ideas spreading across and warmly received by others. To promote this idea, incentives such as promotional campaigns, educational programmes, open budget on research and development, and training activities are offered in order to communicate the values to the communities and encourage employees to participate in realizing corporate values and beliefs.

The last facet of CEB is initiative. With firms voluntarily performing CEB, it is also necessary for firms to initiate ideas and incentives so as to realize values and beliefs in environmental protection.

Corporate environmental behaviour at a macro level

Once categorization is done and taxonomy on CEB is proposed, we extend this newly identified construct to a macro-level: the Kyoto Protocol – a cross-country agreement – to examine how the concept of CEB helps explain firms' distinct responses to the Protocol, which has widely been debated due to conflicting values of different nations, and achieve harmonious results.

The Kyoto Protocol

Aiming at stabilizing greenhouse gas (GHG) emissions at a level that would minimize anthropogenic impact, the United Nations Framework Convention on Climate Change (UNFCCC) adopted a framework in 1992. The UNFCCC has been in operation in March 1994 and 126 countries are involved. The Kyoto Protocol (KP) was reached after the third meeting of the Conference of Parties (COP) held in Kyoto, Japan, in December 1997.

During the conference, COPs agreed that parties under Annex I, namely industrialized countries, of the Protocol will commit to reduce the GHG emissions by at least 5 percent below 1990 levels between the periods of 2008–12 with targets varying from country to country. Six GHGs are defined under Annex A of the KP.[1] Three mechanisms are set to reduce GHG effectively:

  (i) Joint Implementation (JI) –
      Jointly reducing GHG emissions with other Annex I countries; Ratification to the KP is necessary among participants;
 (ii) Clean Development Mechanism (CDM) –
      Investing in projects to reduce GHG emissions in non-Annex I countries, namely developing countries; and
(iii) International Emission Trading –
      Through certification and accreditation, emission allowances from Annex I countries can be bought and sold on an international carbon trading market.

The CDM is defined under Article 12 of the Kyoto Protocol to the UNFCCC, in which participation in a CDM project activity is voluntary, and that a designated national authority is necessary. Despite sceptic criticism on the viability of the Kyoto Protocol without the support of the country of highest emission – the United States – support mainly in financial terms are seen from the World Bank under the Prototype Carbon Fund (PCF), and the Clean Development Mechanism Facility from the Asian Development Bank (Asian Development Bank, 2003).

In order for the instruments to complete, a firm from Annex I countries would submit a proposal to the executive board of the UNFCCC. A designated operational entity (DOE), as approved by the United Nations (UN) on specific sectoral scopes, will perform the validation duties on the proposed CDM project activities. Currently, there are only four firms with the UN approval worldwide.

Clean development mechanism in China

China is a fast-growing economy in transition from planned economy to market economy. A 'no regret' policy to support economic growth has created much concern that China, as the world's second largest greenhouse gas emitter, would surpass the United States within the next decade. Sheer support of economic growth may lead to a neglect or even exploitation of the natural environment. In view of the possible catastrophic impact to the natural environment as a result of the actions of the fast-growing economy, the World Bank launched the National Strategy Study Programme (NSSP) in 1997 in collaboration with the government of Switzerland (World Bank, 2004). Other sovereign states including Germany, Italy, Finland and Australia joined later. Potentials on CDM projects in China are explored with an agreement reached among the World Bank, the German Technical Cooperation Unit (GTZ), and the Chinese Ministry of Science and Technology, on behalf of the government of the People's Republic of China, and funded by the governments of Switzerland and Germany. Six cases are currently investigated on the potentials of developing commercially viable certified emission reductions (CERs) that are tradable in the future (see Appendix I for project briefs).

Case study – Euro-Chinese corporate environmental behaviours

TÜV Rheinland Group

The TÜV Rheinland Group (TÜV) is a German-based company engaged in worldwide corporate inspection services including certification of ISO14000 for the development and implementation of an environmental management system, product testing, system assessment and other training and educational programmes. Evolved from an industrial self-initiated steam-boiler inspection organization to ensure safety of production facilities since 1872 and as a company from Annex I countries committed to reduce greenhouse gas emissions in the Kyoto Protocol, TÜV observed the opportunities in relation to accreditation services of GHG reduction modalities in China and other developing countries. The company became one of the four UN-approved designated operation entities to offer accreditation services.

Seeing China as a signatory party of the Kyoto Protocol without any constraints tied to GHGs reduction, TÜV is actively engaging in potential CDM projects in China. Environmental problems at this situation become an opportunity for TÜV, which proactively promotes and responds to the

Protocol. With the support of the German government, seminars with expert contributions are organized to initiate discussions and debates relating to the topics. Interactions and communications are frequently exchanged among international chambers of commerce to arrive norms and consensus within the industry. Research and development is conducted to realize potentials of CDM projects in developing countries. All of these activities have demonstrated that TÜV performs the third facet of CEB, by giving incentives to stakeholders to participate in realizing the corporate values and beliefs.

As for China, the historical and political background as a socialist country with most significant activities planned or orchestrated by the central government, corporate environment behaviour is not widely practised. Yet, in line with the practice of opening sectors for foreign participation, the central government adopts a gradual process to implement reforms. Taking a proactive and sustainable pilot-case approach is the latest policy of the Clean Development Mechanism in China (World bank, 2004). With financial and technological support from the governments of Switzerland and Germany, CDM potentials, in particular the assessment of feasible methodologies to reduce GHGs, will be evaluated and explored through 2010. Based on the study of the World Bank (2004), the market share of China in the CDM market is around 50 percent. Although the concluding remarks to the study is that CDM implementation will have no significant effect on gross domestic product growth, the move will be beneficial for energy project proponents and relevant stakeholders in China.

Limitations, contributions and directions for future research

This study contributes to theoretical development by introducing a conceptual framework to depict how corporate environmental values and beliefs as judgemental elements for firms to act beyond the purpose of a firm – profit maximization – relate to a newly identified firm-level construct – corporate environmental behaviour. The proposed construct advances existing knowledge by further deriving categorization, dynamic patterns of categorization and taxonomy of CEB suggesting the future direction of study within the area of organization and the natural environment. Through the exploration of the new construct, this study intends to generate new debates that lead to the enrichment of theoretical development to a relatively new area in the natural environment that is pressing, and practitioners are still adopting a 'learning-by-doing' attitude to tackle the complicated issue.

Although the case is limited to a German company and six pilot cases in China, generalization to other situations is possible by extending the empirically testable construct to other fields or situations. Future research includes exploring the possible causal relation of CEB with organizational outcomes, that is, organizational performance.

Conclusions

This study first introduces a conceptual framework in environmental protection within the organizational context, attempting to explain why firms go beyond the primacy of maximizing shareholders' profits. The arguments are based on two premises. First, at corporate level, there are constant debates in the history of firm as to whether a firm should solely look after shareholders' values or be viewed as an entity that is separate from its shareholders, and performs citizenship responsibilities. Second, at an individual level within the organizational context, individual constructs – organizational citizenship behaviour and environmental citizenship – were previously developed to explain why individuals perform discretionary extra-role or self-initiated ethical behaviours so as to enhance organizational efficiency. With these two premises in mind, this study argues that it is the values and beliefs embedded in the organizations that promote and motivate a firm to perform extra-role duties – to go beyond compliance – within existing institutional constraints. Subsequently, a new construct – corporate environmental behaviour – is introduced.

A case study on the hotly debated international agreement, the Kyoto Protocol, of which disagreements among sovereign countries remain, is used to examine the applicability of the conceptual framework. These disagreements, despite the joint forces of over 100 nations for more than one decade, have demonstrated the difficulties in achieving consensus among nations where different values and beliefs are held. These differences in beliefs and interests are claimed to have contributed to the recent intense levels of turbulence, such as the war in Iraq, September 11 terrorist attacks and the continuous trade wars in international platforms. Yet, this case study demonstrates how a German company interacts with China. The findings illustrate how parties of apparent conflicting values could achieve consensus in combating environmental pollution. On the one hand, developed countries with relatively sounded economic achievements have gradually expressed their concerns on the existing or potential deterioration of the global natural environment in addition to acquiring better economic performance. On the other hand, economic growth continues to be a main priority for most developing countries.

As a result, the natural environment in developing countries, very often, has to be sacrificed as an excuse to sustain economic growth. This study demonstrates how conflicting values and beliefs among firms could eventually transform into converging corporate behaviour to achieve harmonious results.

Appendix I

Clean Development Mechanism pilot cases in China

Case 1: Huaneng-Qinbei Supercritical Coal-fired Power Project (Phase II).
Case 2: Beijing Dianzicheng Gas-fired Combined Cycle Tri-generation Project.
Case 3: Gas-steam Combined Cycle Power Project (Phase II) in Beijing No. 3 Thermal Power Plant.
Case 4: Shanghai Wind Farm Project (Phase II).
Case 5: Anaerobic Treatment of Effluent and Power Generation in Taicang Xin Tai Alcohol Co. Ltd.
Case 6: Landfill Gas Recovery Power Generation Project in Zhuhai, Guangdong Province.
(*Source*: World Bank, 2004: 6)

Notes

1. Six greenhouse gases are carbon dioxide (CO_2), methane (CH_4), nitrous oxide (N_2O), hydrofluorocarbons (HFCs), perfluorocarbons (PFCs), and sulphur hexaflouride (SF_6).

References

Asian Development Bank (2003) *Clean Development Mechanism Facility Paper*, available at <www.adb.org> (accessed 7 July 2004).
Bansal, P. (2002) 'The corporate challenges of sustainable development', *Academy of Management Executive* 18(2), 122–31.
Bansal, P. and K. Roth (2000) 'Why companies go green: a model of ecological responsiveness', *Academy of Management Journal* 43(4), 717–36.
Bell, D.R. (2004) *Liberal Environmental Citizenship*, Paper presented at the 'Citizenship and the Environment' Workshop, European Consortium for Political Research (ECPR) Uppsala, April 2004, available at <www.essex.ac.uk/ecpr/events/jointsessions/paperarchive/uppsala/ws5/Bell.pdf> (accessed 21 July 2004).
Bohm, P. (2002) 'Improving cost-effectiveness and facilitating participation of developing countries in international emission trading', *International Environmental Agreements: Politics, Law and Economics* 3, 261–75.
Bolino, M.C., W.H. Turnley and J.M. Bloodgood (2002) 'Citizenship behaviour and the creation of social capital in organisations', *Academy of Management Review* 27(4), 505–22.

Ehrenfeld, J.R. (2002) 'Environmental Management: New Opportunities for Institutional Theory', in J. Hoffman Andrew and J. Ventresca Marc (eds), *Organisations, Policy, and the Natural Environment: Institutional and Strategic Perspectives* (Stanford: Stanford University Press, pp. 436–50).

Forbes, L.C. and J.M. Jermier (2002) 'The Institutionalisation of Voluntary Organisational Greening and the Ideals of Environmentalism: Lessons About Official Culture from Symbolic Organisation Theory', in J. Hoffman Andrew and J. Ventresca Marc (eds), *Organisations, Policy, and the Natural Environment: Institutional and Strategic Perspectives*, (Stanford: Stanford University Press), pp. 194–213.

Friedman, M. (1970) 'The social responsibility of business is to increase its profits', *New York Times Magazine* 13 September: 32–3, 122, 124, 126.

Gore, A. (1992) *Earth in the Balance: Ecology and the Human Spirit* (Boston: Houghton-Mifflin).

Graham, J.W. and W.C. Havlick (1999) *Corporate Environmental Policies* (MD: Lanham, Scarecrow Press).

Guasch, J.L. and R.W. Hahn (1999) 'The costs and benefits of regulation: implications for developing countries', *World Bank Research Observer* 14(1), 137–58.

Hart, S.L. (1995) 'A natural-resource-based view of the firm', *Academy of Management Review* 20(4), 986–1014.

Hathaway-Zepeda, T. (2004) 'Qualifying the kyoto', *Harvard International Review* 26(1), 30–33.

Hoffman, A.J. (2001) *From Heresy to Dogma* (Stanford: Stanford University Press).

Hui, C., S.K. Lam and K.S. Law (2000) 'Instrumental values of organisational citizenship behaviour for promotion: a field quasi-experiment', *Journal of Applied Psychology* 85, 822–8.

Hunt, C.B. and E.R. Auster (1990) 'Proactive environmental management: avoiding toxic trap', *Sloan Management Review* 31(2), 7–18.

Katz, D. (1964) 'The motivational basis of organisational behaviour', *Behavioural Science* 9, 131–3.

Levy, D.L. and P. Newell (2000) 'Oceans apart? business responses to global environmental issues in Europe and the United States', *Environment* 42(9), 8–20.

Levy, D.L. and S. Rothenberg (2002) 'Heterogeneity and Change in Environmental Strategy: Technological and Political Responses to Climate Change in the Global Automobile Industry', in J. Hoffman Andrew and J. Ventresca Marc (eds), *Organisations, Policy, and the Natural Environment: Institutional and Strategic Perspectives* (Stanford: Stanford University Press), pp. 173–93.

MacGregor, S. and B. Szerszynski (2003) *Environmental Citizenship and the Administration of Life*, paper presented at 'Citizenship and the Environment' Workshop, University of Newcastle , 4–6 September 2003, Newcastle.

Meglino, B.M. and E.C. Ravlin (1998) 'Individual values in organisations', *Journal of Management* 24(3), 351–89.

Moorman, R.H. (1991) 'Relationship between organisational justice and organisational citizenship behaviours: do fairness perceptions influence employee citizenship?', *Journal of Applied Psychology* 76, 845–55.

Organ, D.W. (1988) *Organisational Citizenship Behaviour: The Good Soldier Syndrome* (Lexington, MA: Lexington Books).

Organ, D.W. and K. Ryan (1995) 'A meta-analytic review of a attitudinal and dispositional predictors organisational citizenship behaviour', *Personnel Psychology* 48, 775–802.

Porter, M.E. (1991) 'America's green strategy', *Scientific American*, April 264, 168.

Porter, M.E. and C. van der Linde (1995) 'Toward a new conception of the environment-competitiveness relationship', *Journal of Economic Perspectives* 9(4), 97–118.

Russo, M.V. and P.A. Fouts (1997) 'A resource-based perspective on corporate environmental performance and profitability', *Academy of Management Journal* 40(3), 534–59.

Starik, M. and A.A. Marcus (2000) 'Introduction to the special research forum on the management of organizations in the natural environment: a field emerging from multiple paths, with many challenges ahead', *Academy of Management Journal* 43(4), 539–46.

Stern, P., T. Dietz, T. Abel, G.A. Guagnano and L. Kalof (1999) 'A value-belief-norm theory of support for social movements: the case of environmentalism', *Human Ecology Review* 6(2), 81–97.

Stoeckl, N. (2004) 'The private costs and benefits of environmental self-regulation: which firms have most to gain?', *Business Strategy and the Environment* 13, 135–55.

World Bank (2004) *Clean Development Mechanism in China: Taking a Proactive and Sustainable Approach*, available at <http://www.gtz.de/climate/download/projects/2096_01_title_content.pdf> (accessed 22 July 2004).

5
The Role of Trust in Knowledge Management

Leo Leung and K.F. Lau

Introduction

From an economic development perspective, the transition from an industrial society to a post-industrial society (Bell, 1973) is mainly characterized by an information-intensive environment. Globalization and digitization with connectivity are two major forces that shape the recent knowledge-based competitive arena (Lang, 2001). Knowledge management in terms of creating and sharing knowledge is essential to fostering innovation and is the key challenge in a knowledge-based economy (Kim and Mauborgne, 2003). But, managing knowledge work is different from managing other factors of production such as labour, land and capital. Knowledge as a resource is difficult to be forced out of people. This is especially evident for tacit knowledge, which is socially constructed and is based on experience (Newell *et al.*, 2002: 107). It has been widely accepted that trust can lead to cooperative behaviour (e.g., Axelrod, 1984). Kim and Mauborgne (2003) thus propose that mangers need to build trust as a coordinating mechanism in facilitating knowledge creation and transfer among people in an organization. The argument is simple. When industrial production and scientific management are the predominant modes of managerial practices, the factory model based on codified knowledge can be operated under low-trust environments (Cohen and Prusak, 2001: 51; Newell *et al.*, 2002: 8). But, the knowledge economy today is characterized by interdependence of works, cross-functional teams and network structures (Granovetter, 1985; Achrol, 1997), cooperation and collaboration among individuals or groups are important to capture the needed capabilities and competences for competitive advantages (Cravens, 2000: 3–18; McEvily, Perrone and Zaheer, 2003). Trusts among individuals or groups reduce the perceived level of risks and uncertainty and hence facilitate cooperative behaviour in knowledge creation and transfer (Roberts, 2000; Newell *et al.*, 2002: 56–9). Knowledge intensive organizations are built on trusts. It is thus an interesting research question to explore how trust may enhance knowledge creation and transfer among people within and between organizations.

A preliminary review shows that the research question is a complex one. On the one hand, trust is an elusive concept that is difficulty to define and measure. Various attempts have been tried to summarize the previous researches on trust. For example, Khalil (2003) classifies three major research areas for trust: trust as strategy, trust as taste and trust as trait. Alder (2001) identifies four important dimensions on the study of trust: sources, mechanisms, objects and bases of trust. On the other hand, the role of trust in knowledge management is contingent upon the type of knowledge (tacit versus explicit, individual versus collective etc. (e.g., see Newell *et al.*, 2002: 2–8)), the knowledge creation processes (e.g., the process of socialization, externalization, internalization and combination as proposed by Nonaka (1994)), the knowledge management strategy adopted (e.g., codification versus personalization as suggested by Hansen *et al.* (1999)), the organizational structures and the cultural conditions that shape the social situations for knowledge creation and transfer (e.g., see Newell *et al.*, 2002: 23–35), and lastly the level upon which the concept of trust is operated (e.g. between individuals or between organizations as examined by Alder (2002)). For example, Roberts (2000) demonstrates that information and communication technologies (ICTs) may be used favorably in codified knowledge transfer. But, the ICTs approach may find shortcomings in tacit knowledge transfer that requires the process of face-to-face social interactions among individuals. It is the establishment of trust that enables mutual understandings and sharing of knowledge. However, what are the differences in the role trust in various processes of knowledge creation, for example externalization versus internalization? Are there any differences in the role of trust in knowledge transfer in various organizational structures, for example hierarchy versus network? How may the various sources and bases of trust enhance knowledge management? These questions seem remained unanswered.

It is perhaps beyond the scope of this chapter to map out a comprehensive framework to encompass all the issues involved. Through literature review, this chapter attempts to understand some conceptual foundations of how trust may enhance cooperative behavior and what antecedents are important to building trust. As the operation of trust involves at least two parties, the chapter distinguishes the differences between trust operating at interpersonal level and at inter-organizational level (i.e., between individuals versus between groups). The following discussion first gives an overview of how knowledge is defined and what knowledge management is. Next, the concept of trust is reviewed. Then, the focus is on the role of trust in knowledge creation and dissemination at interpersonal level versus that at inter-organizational level, the empirical evidences found and finally the strategies for trust building is discussed at the end of the chapter.

The concept of knowledge management

Knowledge management is one of the hottest subjects in the new millennium and not without reason. The market is changing so fast. New products and services may become obsolete when they are introduced into the market. To remain competitive, firms have to emerge from individual level to network level (Kothandaraman and Wilson, 2001). Closer buyer–seller relationships, partnerships and strategic alliances are not theoretical frameworks but are in actual practice. The effective transfer and sharing of knowledge among the partnering firms governs the key to success. Before an attempt to manage it, we need to understand what knowledge is. Among the many arguments as to what constitutes knowledge, in this chapter we wish to confine knowledge as a corporate intellectual asset that is stored in the individual brain or encoded in organizational processes, documents, products, services, facilities and systems. Knowledge could be explicit (anything that can be documented, archived and codified) and tacit (know-how contained in the people's heads). Managing it, is to recognize, generate, transfer, share and learn knowledge in a structured manner.

Some people may have confused knowledge with information (Clarke and Rollo, 2001). We therefore try to distinguish data, information, knowledge and wisdom here, using Ackoff's classification (1989) and the definitions are drawn mainly from Standards Australia (2001: 18) in the knowledge management framework.

Data are sets of discrete objective facts, presented without judgement or context. It is just a meaningless point in space and time, without reference to either space or time. A collection of data is not information. It becomes information when it is categorized, analysed, summarized and placed in context, becoming intelligible to the recipient.

Information is data endowed with relevance and purpose. It entails an understanding of the relations between data. It generally does not provide a foundation for why the data are what they are, nor an indication as to how the data are likely to change over time. A collection of information is not knowledge. It develops into knowledge when it is used to make comparisons, assess consequences, establish connections and engage in dialogue.

Knowledge can be seen as information that comes with insights, framed experience, intuition, judgement, and values. It is the body of understanding and skills that is mentally constructed by people. It is increased through interaction with information. It comprises strategy, practice, method, and approach. While information is on *what, who, when* and *where*, knowledge tells the *how*.

Wisdom arises when one understands the foundational principles responsible for the patterns representing knowledge being what they are. It embodies principle, insight, moral, or archetype. It is the *why*.

According to Davenport and Prusak (1998 p. 5),

> . . . knowledge is a fluid mix of framed experiences, values, contextual information, and expert insight that provides a framework for evaluating and incorporating new experiences and information. It originates and is applied in the minds of knowers. In organizations, it often becomes embedded not only in documents or repositories but also in organizational routines, processes, practices and norms.

Knowledge management is therefore a systematic and structured process in which individuals and firms would analyse the situation, identify the source of knowledge, plan for the transfer, execute and control the activities. An effective use of knowledge management may even bring in the positive side of inter-organizational conflicts in highly complex environment such as creativity and innovations enhancement (Vaaland and Hakansson, 2002).

The concept of trust

Drawing upon the various views expressed in a special topic forum on trust, Rousseau *et al.* (1998) identify two critical components of trust: confident expectations and willingness to be vulnerable. Newell *et al.* (2002) review different ways of defining trust in the literature and conclude similarly that two issues are central to defining trust: dealing with risk/uncertainty and accepting vulnerability. Rousseau *et al.* (1998: 395) thus define trust as follows: 'Trust is a psychological state comprising the intention to accept vulnerability based upon positive expectations of the intentions of behaviour of another.'

Ford (2003: 557) examines the targets of trust and draws the distinction between interpersonal trust (essentially the form of trust defined by Rousseau *et al.* (1998)) and group/organizational trust (the willingness of one person to increase his/her vulnerability to the actions of a group of people/a feeling of confidence and support in an employer).

Based on the various sources of trust, Rousseau *et al.* (1998: 398) identify the following forms of trust:

- Deterrence-based trust – based on utilitarian considerations that enable one party to believe that another will be trustworthy, because the costly sanctions in place of bleach of trust exceeds any potential benefits from opportunistic behaviour.
- Calculus-based trust – based on rational choice, that is, characteristic of interactions based upon economic exchange (e.g., credible information regarding the intentions or competence of another.
- Relational trust – derived from repeated interactions over time between trustor and trustee.
- Institution-based trust – derived from *ex ante* deterrents that promote trust at the organizational level (e.g., teamwork culture) or societal level through such cultural supports as legal systems that protect individual rights and property.

Using similar bases of trust, Newell *et al.* (2002: 58) distinguish the following forms of trust:

- Companion trust – based on judgements of goodwill or personal friendships.
- Competence trust – based on perception of the others' competence to carry the tasks that need to be performed and will be important where the skills needed to perform a task are not able to be found within one person.
- Commitment trust – stemmed from the contractual agreements between the parties.

By focusing on a process view of how trust is developed and maintained, Zucker (in Newell *et al.*, 2002: 57) depicts three central mechanisms of trust production:

- Process-based – based on reciprocal recurring exchange
- Characteristic-based – based on social similarity
- Institution-based – based on expectations embedded in social norms and structures

It seems that some form of trust may be stronger that the other and may be developed preceding the development of other form of trust. Take an example, while relational trust may provide a stronger bonding between the two parties concerned than calculus-based trust, calculus-based trust may first be developed followed by relational trust after continuing rounds of interactions when companion trust or characteristic-based trust emerges through acquaintance with each other overtime.

Perhaps, regarding knowledge creating and sharing process at different stages, various forms of trust will come into play depending on time pressure, capabilities possessed, organizational structures and cultures, and the systems of institutions defining the social situation for interactions.

The role of trust in knowledge management at interpersonal level

One conceptual foundation to investigate the interpersonal interactions is rooted in social exchange theory (e.g., Chadwick-Jones, 1976). Using the perspective of symbolic interactionism, an application of the social exchange theory to study how two or more parties interact in a social encounter and mutually develop and negotiate a definition of the social situation for the encounter, Jones and George (1998) examine how trust is evolved and changed over time. Taking trust as an expression of confidence between parties in an exchange of some kind that depends on perceived values, attitudes and moods and emotions of the parties involved, Jones and George (1998: 535) distinguish between conditional and unconditional trust. Conditional trust is a state of trust at the early stage of a social encounter that both parties are 'willing to transact with each other, as long as each behaves appropriately, uses a similar interpretive scheme to define the situation, and can take the role of the other'. This may be interpreted as a form of calculus-based trust or competence trust or even some form of commitment trust. Unconditional trust is more enduring and is based on shared values and mutual understandings. It is backed up by 'empirical evidence derived from repeated behavioral interactions', that is, a form of companion trust, process-based or characteristic-based trust. It is the development of unconditional trust that leads to interpersonal cooperation and synergistic teamwork and enhances knowledge creation and sharing through the following effects (Jones and George, 1998: 540):

- Broad role definitions
- Communal relationships
- High confidence in others
- Help-seeking behaviour
- Free exchange of knowledge and information
- Subjugation of personal needs and ego for the greater common good
- High involvement

Jones and George emphasize that unconditional trust is particularly important for tacit knowledge creation and transfer. The development of unconditional trust over time depends on whether an organization could provide an appropriate environment or a favourable setting. It is however not without costs – costs in terms of time, effort and resources.

According to the model of trust proposed by Jones and George, the development of unconditional trust is an evolutionary process during which various forms of trust may emerge. The social interactions enhance shared values, mutual understandings and evaluation of trustworthiness – the prerequisites for knowledge sharing and creation (Chatzkel, 2003). In fact, a study shows that an increase in communication frequency between the trustor and the trustee may moderate the perceived trustworthiness of each party (Becerra and Gupta, 2003).

The role of trust in knowledge management at inter-organizational level

Employing the transaction cost theory as the conceptual foundation (e.g., Williamson, 1975;1985), Adler (2001) proposes community/trust as the third mode of organizational forms in addition to market/price and hierarchy/authority, especially for knowledge-intensive organizations. In using hierarchy/authority as an organization form, knowledge is treated as a scare resource and will be concentrated in specialized functional units. However, the hierarchy/authority mechanism could mandate free availability of knowledge when needed and thus outperform the market/price mechanism in knowledge dissemination. But, the hierarchy/authority mechanism provides no incentives for innovation and creates difficulty for knowledge generation and creation. On the other hand, while market/price mechanism encourages knowledge innovation, the transfer of knowledge would be much more costly especially when the knowledge is of a tacit kind. Adler (2001) therefore concludes that neither market nor hierarchy could solve the dilemma and meet the challenges of the modern knowledge economy.

In fact, a number of scholars (e.g., Granovetter, 1985; Achrol, 1997) have advanced the network paradigm as an alternative organizational form to supplement the shortcomings of either market or hierarchy in explaining the emergence of various organizational forms. Following this tradition of research, Adler (2001) suggests that community/trust is the third coordinating mechanism for knowledge-intensive organizations. The term 'community' is interpreted as the notion of 'informal' organization with in which the members (including both intra- and inter-organizational relations) constitute a 'community'. Perceived trust among members undermines risk/uncertainty through increased shared values/mutual understandings and thus enhances both knowledge creation and dissemination. This reduces transaction costs and improves performance that neither market nor hierarchy could achieve. However, the three coordinating mechanisms, i.e. market/price, hierarchy/authority and community/trust, are not discrete alternatives that an organization could choose only one among them. An organization might select the right combination among the three mechanisms in organizing the intra- and inter-organizational relations. The high trust hybrids could be found in various network forms of organizational structures and provide a precondition for effective knowledge generation and transfer per se. Adler (2001) therefore put forward the hypothesis of a trend towards the use of community/trust as a third mode of coordinating mechanisms together with market or hierarchy as a hybrid organization form in a knowledge intensive economy.

The high trust hybrid form of organization is not without problems (Alder, 2002: 36–7). First, it is argued that trust can never be a stable and dominant mechanism because there is always a free-rider problem and the betrayal is often more profitable! Second, when trust is based on familiarity or norms, this mechanism makes only a typical 'clan' like organization and it is doubtful whether this type of organization is suitable for knowledge creation and transfer. Third, the overall dominance of market mechanism in a capitalist society tends to corrode the foundations of trust. The market mechanism discourages sources of trust based on institutions and familiarity and promotes calculative sources of trust which makes the development of unconditional trust difficult. Hence, there is a trend towards the development of such trust as competence based, process based and commitment based.

This poses an interesting research question of how various forms of trust may affect knowledge creation and transfer within and between organizations. Ford (2003) examines how interpersonal trust and organization trust may interplay with each other to assist knowledge management. In general, organization trust based on deterrence or institutions and interpersonal trust based on identification and relations enhance more knowledge creation and transfer. But, organization trust seems to have a stronger effect than interpersonal trust in knowledge transfer.

Empirical evidences

It is not surprising to find only a few empirical researches that investigate the role of trust in knowledge management, not to mention the inherent difficulty in measuring trust, in measuring knowledge and in obtaining dyad data, in which there is still a lack of a conceptual framework to summarize the relationships among trust, knowledge, organizational structure/culture and performance. But, a handful of researches could be found in the literature to provide some insights into on the relationships between trust and knowledge creation and dissemination.

The role of trust at interpersonal level

Based on in-depth interviews with managers and teams of several new product development projects in various industries, Madhavan and Grover (1998) found that trust in team orientation, trust in technical competence and rich personal interaction were important to effective and efficient knowledge creation. Using graduate students as a sample, Wang and Rubenstein-Montano (2003) conducted an experiment to investigate relationships between different levels of trust and knowledge sharing. They confirm that the increase in trust levels does increase the benefits from knowledge sharing.

The role of trust at inter-organizational level

Carson *et al.* (2003) attempted to investigate the effectiveness of trust-based governance in inter-firm research and development (R&D) collaboration. They conducted a survey on a sample of 573 qualified informants from several selected firms and found a positive trust-task performance relationship. The effectiveness of the trust-based governance was further moderated by the information processing capabilities of the participating firms to assess their partners' trustworthiness. The task performance in terms of knowledge creation and sharing will increase with the increase of the firms' information processing capabilities to read and learn the partners' behaviours.

Dyer and Chu (2003) examined how the trust between suppliers and buyers might reduce transaction costs and enhance knowledge sharing. They chose a cross-national setting for the study and conducted a survey on a sample of Japanese firms (characterized by high trust environment) and US firms (characterized by low trust environment). The regression analysis showed that higher levels of trust did reduce transaction costs and increase information sharing.

The strategies for trust building

Taking trust building as a strategy for knowledge management, the previous discussion implies that the process for building trust requires time, costs and commitment of resources. An appropriate organizational setting coupled with open communication channels is important to fostering perceived trust among members in a community. Various forms of trust may be needed at different stages of the knowledge management process and for different types of knowledge. Calculus-based trust may be more important at the initial stage while commitment-based trust and institution-based trust are more important at a later stage. However, for tacit knowledge creation and transfer, it might be more critical for building deterrence-based trust and institution-based trust at the initial stage when there is lack of interpersonal trust. In other words, it is also important to build organization trust based on identification, competence or commitment when either party is not familiar with the other at the initial encounter. To promote trust among team members, Robbins and Finley (2000: 160–67) recommend the following strategies:

- Have clear, consistent goals
- Be open, fair and willing to listen
- Be decisive and make explicit how the decisions are made
- Support all other team members
- Take responsibility for team actions
- Give credits to team members
- Be sensitive to the needs of team members
- Respect the opinions of others
- Empower team members to act

Some empirical researches have shown that increasing interactions among team members enhances shared values and mutual understandings and hence promotes trust (e.g., Madhavan and Grover, 1998; Carson *et al.*, 2003). Gibson and Manuel (2003: 72–5) suggest the following communication strategies for trust building:

- Build a supportive communication climate – for example active listening to members' concerns and ideas, proactive information exchanges, explicit verbalization of commitment, etc.
- Adopt framing to avoid miscommunication – that is, always consider the other party's frame of reference. This is critical in intercultural communications.
- Follow up to get feedback and to reconcile differences among members

Risk and vulnerability are two critical components of trust. Risk creates an opportunity for trust and risk up to a certain level and necessitates the use of trust. However, too much risk may be detrimental (Gibson and Manuel, 2003: 62). This is particularly acute in multicultural communications. It is therefore necessary for a manager to be sensitive to the level of risk involved and decide what type of trust needed to be promoted to reduce the perceived risk and thus enhance cooperative behaviours.

Conclusion

In a knowledge intensive environment, knowledge management in terms of new knowledge creation and knowledge transfer is important in gaining competitive advantages. Trust is then advanced a coordinating mechanism for enhancing knowledge generation and dissemination. The foregoing discussion attempts to understand the role of trust in knowledge management at interpersonal level and at inter-organizational level. In general, it is believed that trust promotes share values, mutual understandings and reduces transaction costs, perceived risk, etc. Different forms of trust may emerge at various stages of the knowledge process. Developing unconditional trust is not without costs, time and resources. Various problems that occur with developing trust warrant further research – the problem of free riding, betrayal and conflicts with the dominant modes of organization settings such as market price. Although some researches have shown the positive relationships between trust and knowledge generation/dissemination, there is still a lack of theoretical framework to depict the antecedents and consequences of trust in knowledge management. There are more questions unanswered than answered.

References

Achrol, R.S. (1997), 'Changes in the theory of interorganizational relations in marketing: toward a network paradigm', *Journal of the Academy of Marketing Science*, 25(1), 56–71.

Ackoff, R.L. (1989), 'From data to wisdom', *Journal of Applied Systems Analysis*, 16, 3–9.

Adler, P.S. (2001), 'Market, Hierarchy, and Trust', in C.W. Choo and B. Nick (eds), *The Strategic Management of Intellectual Capital and Organizational Knowledge* (Oxford: Oxford University Press), pp. 23–46.

Axelrod, R. (1984), *The Evolution of Cooperation* (New York: Basic Books).

Becerra, M. and A.K. Gupta (2003), 'Perceived trustworthiness within the organization: the moderating impact of communication frequency on trustor and trustee effects', *Organization Science*, 14(1), 32–44.

Bell, D. (1973) *The Coming of Post-Industrial Society: A Venture in Social Forecasting* (New York: Basic Books).

Carson, S.J., A. Madhok, R. Varman and G. John (2003) 'Information processing moderators of the effectiveness of trust-based governance in interfirm R&D collaboration', *Organization Science* 14(1), 45–56.

Chadwick-Jones, J.K. (1976) *Social Exchange Theory: Its Structure and Influence in Social Psychology* (London: Academic Press).

Chatzkel, J.L. (2003) *Knowledge Capital* (Oxford: Oxford University Press), pp. 203–23

Clarke, T. and C. Rollo (2001) 'Corporate initiatives in knowledge management', *Education & Training* 43(4/5), 206–14.

Cohen, D. and L. Prusak (2001) *In Good Company: How Social Capital Makes Organizations Work* (Boston, Mass.: Harvard Business School Press), pp. 27–51.

Cravens, D.W. (2000) *Strategic Marketing* (6th edn, Boston, Mass.: Irwin/McGraw-Hill).

Davenport, T.H. and Prusak, L. (1998), *Working Knowledge: How Organizations Manage What They Know* (Boston, Mass.: Harvard Business School Press), pp. I–24.

Dyer, J.H. and Wujin Chu (2003) 'The role of trustworthiness in reducing transaction costs and improving performance: empirical evidence from the United States, Japan and Korea', *Organization Science* 14(1), 57–68.

Ford, D.P. (2003), 'Trust and Knowledge Management', in C.W. Holsapple, Springer (eds), *Handbook of Knowledge Management*, Vol. 1, (New York: Springes), pp. 553–75.

Gibson, C.B. and J.A. Manuel (2003) 'Building Trust: Effective Multicultural Communication Processes in Virtual Teams', in C.B. Gibson and S.G. Cohen (eds), *Virtual Teams that Work: Creating Conditions for Virtual Team Effectiveness*, (San Francisco, California: Jossey-Bass) pp. 59–86.

Granovetter, M. (1985) 'Economic action and social structure: the problem of embeddedness', *American Journal of Sociology* 91(3), 481–509.

Hansen, M.T., N. Nohria and J.T. Tierney (1999) 'What's your strategy for managing knowledge', *Harvard Business Review*, March–April, 106–15.

Jones, G.R., and J.M. George (1998) 'The experience and evolution of trust: implications for cooperation and teamwork', *Academy of Management Review* 23(3), 531–46.

Khalil, E.L. (2003) 'Why Does Trustworthiness Pay? Three Answers', in E.L. Khalil, *Turst*, An Elgar Reference Collection (Cheltenham: Edward Elgar), pp. 13–32.

Kim, W.C. and R. Mauborgne (2003) 'Fair process: management in the knowledge economy', *Harvard Business Review*, January–February, 127–38.

Kothandaraman, P. and D.T. Wilson (2001) 'The future of competition', *Industrial Marketing Management* 30, 379–89.

Lang, J.C. (2001) 'Managing in knowledge-based competition', *Journal of Organizational Change Management* 14(6), 539–53.

Madhavan, R. and R. Grover (1998) 'From embedded knowledge to embodied knowledge: new product development as knowledge management', *Journal of Marketing* 62(4), 1–12.

McEvily, B., V. Perrone and A. Zaheer (2003) 'Introduction to the special issue on trust in an organizational context', *Organization Science* 14(1), 1–4.

Newell, S., M. Robertson, H. Scarbrough and J. Swan (2002) *Managing Knowledge Work*, (Basingstoke: Palgrave Macmillan).

Nonaka, I. (1994) 'A dynamic theory of organizational knowledge creation', *Organization Science* 5(1), 14–37.

Robbins, H.A. and M. Finley (2000) *Why Teams Don't Work: What goes Wrong and How to Make It Right* (San Francisco, California: Berbert-Koehler) pp. 157–72.

Roberts, J. (2000) 'From know-how to show-how? questioning the role of information and communication technologies in knowledge transfer', *Technology Analysis & Strategic Management* 12(4), 429–43.

Rousseau, D.M., S.B. Sitkin, R.S. Burt and C. Camerer (1998) 'Not So different after all: a cross-discipline view of trust', *Academy of Management Review* 23(3), 339–404.

Standards Australia (2001) *Knowledge Management: A Framework for Succeeding in the Knowledge Economy* (Sydney: Standards Australia).

Vaaland, T.I. and H. Hakansson (2002) 'Exploring interorganizational conflict in complex projects', *Industrial Marketing Management* 32, 127–38.

Wang, R. and B. Rubenstein-Montano (2003) 'The Value of Trust in Knowledge Sharing', in E. Coakes, *Knowledge Management: Current Issues and Challenges* (Hershey: IRM Press), pp. 116–30.

Williamson, O.E. (1975) *Markets and Hierarchies: Analysis and Antirust Implications*, New York: Free Press.

Williamson, O.E. (1985) *The Economic Institutions of Capitalism* (New York: Free Press).

Zucker, L.G. (2002) 'Production of Trust: Institutional Sources of Economic Structure', *Research in Organizational Behavior*, in Newell *et al.* (eds), *Managing Knowledge Work* (Basingstoke: Palgrove Macmillan), p. 57.

6

Trust One's Alliance Partner? Maybe – Maybe Not! Preliminary Results of Recent Research in China

John Kidd and Xue Li

Introduction

The act of forming an alliance implies a need to be stronger in unison and that there is some common agreement between the parties – they have shared goals for instance. In the commercial world, however, this simple definition needs to be broadened as alliances are created for many reasons, some of which are anti-competitive. In this chapter, we concentrate on alliances that cross national boundaries, and are (presumably) set up to be of benefit to each party so as to increase their reach in one or more aspects of their joint business: specifically they will be alliances in mainland China, located in the southwest region.

Often the international joint venture (IJV) is created so as one party – in this case a Chinese firm – can acquire new technology and know-how. The other party – from overseas – has this technology and wishes to reach a wider market for its products: notably, the 1.3 billion people in China which represent an attractive market. This is a theme mentioned by many, and is recalled constantly throughout the book *Mr China* (Clissold, 2004). Of course we know that not all the people in China will be interested in the given output of the IJV – it may after all be a sub-component of a consumer product to be assembled by yet another firm, so this IJV would be operating within a supply chain. Furthermore, while many people in China are still classified as 'rural poor', there is a rapidly growing more-affluent urban population who purchase international brands in preference to home brands, although their reasoning and buying habits are changing. Consequently, Chinese firms are able and willing to act as manufacturers and/or distributors for these outside brands and become an IJV. As the Chinese labour force accepts very cheap wages (when compared to most outside labour rates), and as there may be a tariff barrier against imports, it behoves the outsider to source parts in China (if possible) and to assemble in China. For example, General Motor's profits are US$ 145/car in the United States, but their Chinese cars each pull in US$ 1,132 (*BusinessWeek*, 21 June 2004). There is often a profitable bottom line for the IJV – as well a burgeoning marketplace – although by no means are all IJV happy in China, nor are all profitable: there is simply a business necessity to 'be represented' there.

Joint ventures (JV) take a while to set up (unless it is a pre-emptive strike designed to spoil market sentiment: in which case a fast-formed alliance need not necessarily be a working alliance): and IJV take longer to set up as laws in the host country, as well as attitudes and expectations have to be understood by the incoming party. In Asia, IJV are particularly difficult for the Occidental as there are gross differences in expectations and in actual operations vis-à-vis 'capitalisms' and 'business rationale' (Whitley, 1999; Redding, 2002). Also, in China in particular, we find the historicism of culture shapes individual expectations, developing a 'them and us' attitude (Fukuyama, 1996; Kidd *et al.*, 2003). Nor do the Chinese trust people who are outside their direct family: though they are not unique in this respect as the Brazilians and the Russians also strongly align to 'family' (Fukuyama, 1996; Hutchings and Michailova, 2004). The Chinese government presents attitudes predicated on their past decisions and we find that senior Chinese officials, being long-time Confucians as well as one-time Marxists, hold attitudes that are in sharp contrast to those of the openly capitalist Occidentals. And naturally the supporting institutions and their bureaucratic mechanisms are also different – especially the often silent but the still omnipresent Communist Party cadre. Nevertheless, there are many IJV in China, and because of a better understanding between the parties involved through more exposure to information and general experience, the process of creating an IJV is becoming easier. At one time this was not the case (Kidd and Zhao, 1996).

However, even routine operations in an IJV are not straightforward. Both sides often accuse the other of obfuscation, and attempting to gain over the other – one wants larger market share fast, the other needs new technology quickly and a full range of training; and each side may be perceived to wish to break away and be a competitor. Sometimes third parties may intervene, such as customs officials, who refuse to allow the import of upgrades against the officially sanctioned contract items (Kidd and Li, 1999). So both sides of the IJV become annoyed, although they exhibit this annoyance differently. Once there was the General Agreement on Tariffs and Trade (GATT), and now there are the World Trade Organization (WTO) rulings pushing for the reduction of tariffs, and for free trade – in turn this dynamically alters strategic business plans, demanding a subtle understanding between the insider and the outsider staff because parent companies' staff may hold rather different views on 'trade' than the CEO and managers in the IJV. The nuances of the WTO are important to understand, since both sides of the IVJ whose headquarters are located in China, and let us say, the United States, have to grasp what the 'faceless ones' of the WTO in Geneva are formulating and making into binding international law.

In this chapter, we have chosen to describe the Chinese managers as 'insiders' and the overseas managers as 'outsiders'. This is not meant to be pejorative, but simply to reflect a fact of life in China. We quote from Chen (2004: 71):

> . . . According to Confucian ethics, 'family' is the most fundamental revenue and expenditure unit, within which every member contributes his of her income to the common family fund while each one has the right to obtain a portion of it, with the rest belonging to the family as a whole. The interests of the family take precedence over those of society and of other society members . . . Under the influence of this concept, the business owner tends to regard the business as the private property of the core family, and thereby is reluctant to share ownership with others.

Chen also states that Chinese society is a high ritual society (ibid.: 24) but, as the members of the society have been brought up under this pattern since birth, they do not realize how much it influences their behaviour.

In China, being a member of an in-group affects all daily events, and the in-group is inextricably linked to trust (Chen *et al.*, 2003; Sheer and Chen, 2003). Those who fall out of such a personal group are regarded as having lost 'face' and can not share in group networking (Chen, 2004: 52). The in-group is the source of identity, protection and loyalty: and knowledge can be expected to be shared within the group and withheld from those considered as 'outsiders'. In many ways, this insider aspect is tied to the Chinese concept of *guanxi* – a major integrating force within interpersonal networks that may be described as the mutual exchange of services and the acceptance of abstract debt obligations. The nurturing of the personal *guanxi* network is time and resource consuming, maybe taking up to 20 percent of ones disposable income (Schramm and Taube, 2003: 278); and the delicate gift-giving ritual between members is complex to understand (Nojonen, 2003), but once mastered will serve one well to secure negotiations – provided one is Chinese (Fang, 2004).

Schramm and Taube note that Hong Kong businessmen may have spent up to 5 percent of their investment in China on gifts and *guanxi* maintenance; yet elsewhere, in a long report to the Hong Kong Chamber of Commerce, Child warns against outsiders attempting to work as though an 'insider' in *guanxi* environments 'as they do not understand it' (Child and Faulkner 1998).

It is against this background we research in southwest China. We review the attitudes (towards trust) held early in the IJV life, and note if these change as the parties get to know each other better over the passage of time.

Methodology

The overall research, partially reported here, is to look at the concept of trust in joint alliance relationships in China and how this construct may change over time as both parties get to know each other better. The data collection supporting the research is based upon a questionnaire and on data culled from semi-structured interviews (which were often, but not always, tape-recorded for subsequent transcription and analysis). It is an early analysis of the quantitative data from the questionnaires that supports this chapter.

It is our opinion that we ought not to ignore simple quantitative analyses (means, standard deviations, correlations and regression models) in favour of the more complex quantitative models: but the latter, in the form of multivariate and non-linear methods can yield subtle answers to research questions. Similarly the basic use of grounded theory (Glaser and Strauss, 1967) provides an introduction to the qualitative analysis of the data: here again, modern qualitative methods supported by software packages, such as QSR's Nvivo, allow more subtle framing of the exploratory research. The conceptual approaches of qualitative analysis may seem simple, yet in practice considerable care has to be exercised in using grounded theory (Locke, 2002) – even though 10 years ago it was described as 'the most widely used interpretive framework in the social sciences today' (Denzin, 1994: 513).

As may be perceived, the research plan will engage in a mixed mode of analysis – partially quantitative, and partly qualitative. The former mode will eventually be based on SPSS cross-tabs and factor analysis and so on; and the latter on the use of software from QSR (for instance, NUD*IST or Nvivo) once the interview tapes are transcribed and coded. We recognize that social science researchers in recent years have more easily applied mixed methodologies in the same research project looking to combine the advantages of quantitative and qualitative methods while avoiding their shortcomings (Brannen, 1992; Creswell, 1995; Tashakkori and Teddlie, 1998). This is despite a some concern over the incompatibility of the qualitative and quantitative paradigms and thus, when combined, the 'lack of purity in the research'.

Conceptual framework relating to trust (and learning)

It is impossible to work within grounded theory without some guiding principles to help orientate the theoretical perspectives. These may take many forms – Pettigrew (1990) used contextualism for guidance, but the greatest support comes from symbolic interactionism – conceived by Blummer (1969), who stated first, that meaning is central to social behaviour; second, people interpret the meaning of objects around them and then take action based on their interpretation; and third, a meaning is not fixed or stable, but is modified over time as new perceptions arise. These tenets apply both to those researched upon and to the researchers – so there is constant flux in interpretation as the research progresses. Initially, a symbolic map needs to be expressed by the researcher, and according to Crossan *et al.* (1999) a good framework has several requirements. First, it should identify the phenomenon of interest. Second, the key premises or assumptions underlying the framework need to be stated (Bacharach, 1989, cited by Crossan *et al.*, 1999). Third, the relationships among the elements of the framework need to be described (Sutton and Staw, 1995), which is indeed similar to the requirement to express symbolic interactions in the development of grounded theory.

We have mentioned 'learning' at this time because we are not interested in trust as an abstraction, but related to the development of an environment conducive to organizational learning (OL) and knowledge management (KM). Yet we will not be researching directly upon OL or KM, except insofar as our respondents are business people, and we presume them to be interested ultimately in OL and KM in their daily interactions in their international joint alliance frameworks.

We all exist within socially embedded systems – it is where we grew up, went to school and college, and it upholds our workplace behaviour: it represents the framework of our society and we find it differs as we cross boundaries – to the 'next village' as it were, and especially if we cross national boundaries. We assume that 'trust' – as we understand it – only exists within socially embedded systems, and this in turn can be broken down to 'early' and 'late' trust. The former relies upon a calculus, and the latter relies more on the relationships between the partners. Also, in general, there is a degree of interdependence and behavioural similarity between the partners. So, in turn, 'trust' links in a feed-forwards (-backwards) manner to (organizational) learning and knowledge sharing.

The development of our supporting research framework has been informed by an extensive literature search. Initially, this was through a reading of the joint venture literature, and second, as we became more convinced that 'trust' was a fundamental factor in the joint ventures' well-being, the trust literature had to be perused. We briefly note some aspects of each, commencing with the IJV literature.

Views upon joint ventures

The study of joint ventures goes back a long time – in truth to the commencement of trade whereby one person had to accept the help of another as each had skills – recognized by the other – as pertinent to the goals of both, and together they were stronger than if working separately. As trade and commerce intensified after the Industrial Revolution in Europe from the mid-1800s, studies were undertaken into how better to operate jointly. In modern times, one might note Child and Faulkner (1998), who presented several disciplinary perspectives (economics, strategy, organization theory), and they offered numerous examples from the corporate world wherein firms have alliances both within their own countries, and overseas with foreign partners. Foreign investors in China may now choose between three modes of entry: equity joint ventures, contractual joint ventures, or wholly foreign-owned enterprises – which all vary considerably in their legal forms, risk characteristics, resource commitments, and investment motivations. Often IJV research looks only to large firms, for a variety of reasons, not least being the relative ease of access to data and for discussions. Gatignon and Anderson (1988) found that US-based manufacturing companies tended to use equity entry modes when entering markets in which environmental uncertainty was low, but tended to prefer non-equity modes in parts of the world that they perceived as being 'more uncertain'. Erramilli and Rao (1993) also found that US service firms perceiving high country risk opted for less equity-intensive entry modes. Nakos and Brouthers (2004) reviewed the entry mode of small and medium enterprises (SME) and found that their decisions were able to be mapped against the tradition of transaction cost analysis (TCA). They found that, by and large, if the firm is thinking about doing business in a country where the economic, political, and social system is relatively stable and certain, equity modes of entry should be preferred. When there is volatility in the economic, political, and/or social environment, non-equity modes may provide a more effective way of dealing with these uncertainties. What this hints at is while the venturing firm is considering joining with another 'over there . . .' the 'distance between the firms' may be perceived by the managers as an issue to be addressed explicitly.

The argument that 'distance in business operations matters' is as old as business itself. Adam Smith noted over 200 years ago that – 'if there were no . . . communication between . . . two places, ... there could be little or no commerce of any kind between distant parts of the world' (Smith, 1976 [1776]: 22–3). And, in trading with distant parts, one has to overcome the differences inherent in working with others holding different concepts and mores – the more distant, generally the more different. Distance, and its intrinsic notion of location sensitivity in business transactions became a theoretical underpinning in the international business literature after the concept was explicitly introduced by Beckerman (1956). His findings showed that not only do countries often concentrate their trade initially in close neighbouring countries, but that a country's location itself, that is, its relative distance to other regions of economic activity, does matter. Nowadays, this aspect of distance – geographic distance – is the location pillar in Dunning's Eclectic Paradigm (Dunning, 2000), and in international trade theory (Krugman, 1990; Markusen and Venables, 2000). However, the distance concept incorporates more than a simple spatial dimension – Vahlne and Wiedersheim-Paul (1973) reintroduced Beckermann's relatively unspecified term 'psychic distance', stating that firms begin trading with neighbouring countries or those that are comparatively well known and similar according to various factors, such as their economic development, political system, culture, business habits, legal environment, religion, language and education. They suggested that firms initially enter markets with minimal levels of psychic distance and gradually enter markets with successively greater levels, noting that distance between business parties increases the costs of conducting business. In this research, we consider differences between business partners rather than differences at the aggregate level, for example, differences at the country level. The greater these differences, the more difficult it becomes for business partners to communicate, because successful communication (e.g., achieving a sale) depends on an exchange of mutually understood symbols and values (Conway and Swift, 2000).

There are other views relating to 'external' or 'internal' measures of distance: external distance involves the rather objective evaluation of cultural, economic and geographic distance, while internal distance encompasses the subjective individual assessment of psychic distance by the decision makers in the firm, both of which are influenced by legal, political, economical, technological, and social globalization forces. In other words, one cannot avoid the viewpoints of the 'social embeddedness' literature. Here, as we said earlier, we can be described as the products of our background and our early learning, and we have to become aware of the social milieu in which we find our self in order to operate and live. In terms of the IJV, controlling foreign operations is a special skill that requires time to develop and refine (Anderson and Gatignon, 1986) but often in these ventures we do not have long enough to acculturate and absorb the local ways of working. Nor do the locals necessarily feel they have to accommodate the foreign party, as it is the latter that are the outsiders. Both parties in fact must learn to trust each other in their business climate, and in the more social relations that inevitably accompany an overseas venture.

Views upon trust

The study of 'trust' has a long history, but somewhat recently it has achieved a greater prominence: one needs only to peruse Fukuyama (1996) to glean its conceptual breadth. Our research frame has many supporting literatures – too many to cite – yet one of importance is Child (2001) in which he offers a form of summary of his earlier work. He notes the changeable nature of 'trust' as the context moves from early stages of a relationship to the later stages. In the first instance, the trustor is more calculating of the others' likely actions; in the latter stages he/she is more embedded in relationship maintenance. We note also that Lewicki and Bunker's three-stage model suggests a 'stage-wise evolution of trust' (Lewicki and Bunker, 1996: 124), in which trust develops gradually as the parties move from one stage to another. They argue that trust first starts on the basis of a market-oriented, economic calculation whose value is derived by determining the outcomes resulting from creating and sustaining the relationship relative to the costs of maintaining or severing it. Williamson (1993) also describes trust as calculative, personal and institutional. He argues that calculative trust is a rational form of trust fostered by mutual hostages and other economic commitments. He notes that institutional trust is calculative as well, which derives from social and organizational embeddedness.

In this research we define *early trust* as the rational consideration of self-interest between interdependent parties whose agreement is ensured by mutual hostages and other economic commitments including systems of penalty and rewards. In other words, party A confidently enters into a vulnerable situation because it is in party B's rational self-interest to behave in a way that is consistent with party A's welfare. Research suggests that many business and legal relationships start and stop in this calculative stage. Trust, based on calculation, clearly depends on the avail-ability of relevant information of the other, and in practice there may be significant limits to this, so it may be the only form of trust that can apply to arm's length, and hence impersonal, economic exchange (Child, 1998).

Within a developmental process, the calculative trust activity provides a confirmation of the validity of trust, though it is partial and quite fragile (Lewicki and Bunker, 1996): if this is negated by facts, the relationship fails. Early trust allows relative unfamiliar firms to become sufficiently relaxed to begin further interaction and develop their relationship into a higher-state trust – that is, late trust. *Late trust* then is about pre-dictability – knowing the other sufficiently well so that the others' behaviour may be anticipated. Late trust emphasizes information that accumulates over time through repeated interactions, making the par-ties' behaviours more predictable. It is developed through frequent con-tact and communication that facilitates an understanding of each other's needs, choices and preferences; and also by sharing some of the same needs, choices and preferences as one's own. This social embedded-ness serves and provides the information during regular communication – so courtship enhances trust.

When the parties' mutual understanding is developed to the point that each can effectively act for the other, this permits one party to serve as the other's agent and substitute for the other in interpersonal transac-tions (Deutsch, 1962, cited in Lewicki and Bunker, 1996), When this stage of trust develops further, the parties would 'think like' the other, 'feel like' the other, and 'respond' like the other. There is thus a collective identity – the sharing of needs, preferences, thoughts, and behaviour patterns (Lewicki and Bunker, 1996: 123). Late trust shares some aspects of what McAllister (1995a) has termed 'affect-based trust' where emo-tion affects the relationships through frequent, long-term interaction.

In the background of this research, these points are extended into testable propositions, but we do not show them here, since, we reiterate, this chapter reports only on an initial analysis of the data.

The formulation of the research design

Readings of Miles and Huberman (1994), (Fink, 1995) and Yin (2003) and other works, shaped the general thrust of the research programme, and the research of Lewicki and McAllister formed the detailed base for the development of the questionnaire used in this study (see citations, but in addition there were personal communications with Li). The resulting 32 questions were grouped with respect to trust (in general), early/late aspects, predictability (of the partner), etc., and even *guanxi*. The English language questionnaire was translated into Mandarin and back translated: it was also piloted in the UK for comprehension and sense making (with Chinese managers). For a detailed exposition of the items' development one should contact Li.

We split the time-frame of the research arbitrarily to below and above four years – categorizing data which derive from the first four years of IJV operations as 'early', and after four years as 'late'. It was an arbitrary choice to create a split time-frame at four years. Following advice in creating Lickert-type scales, we know that working with too fine a granularity causes dithering on the part of the respondents, even if we offered three periods relating to early, mid term and long term. Further, from 'critical incidents' research, we know that mental recall is quite difficult, and looking for several incidents is taxing, especially over a long timeframe. So we settled on just two time periods – the 'early' and the 'late'. The start-up date of the operation of the IJV is a pretty obvious 'critical incident', so this defined the 'early' time period. The selection of the 'four year' boundary to delineate the 'late' period was subjective, and yet it was practical (a) to allow enough time to elapse, so allowing any 'critical' changes in working practices to develop, and (b) not be so long a time as to fall beyond the lifespan of the IJV.

It was hoped initially that the questionnaires would have been sent to firms targeted before the data gathering and interview visit. But this did not occur: in part, because Xue Li was not in the *guanxi* network of the Shenzhen researcher with whom she was in e-mail and fax contact. At a distance, she was marginalized. Instead, the questionnaire was taken to firms directly by Xue Li, and selected senior personnel filled in the forms directly, while the semi-structured interviews (with the top managers) took place. The acquisition of firms in the survey became a matter of 'snowballing' to achieve samples through personal contacts. Though obviously inclined to bias, this mode has been accepted as one of 'best practice' in these circumstances (von Glinow *et al.*, 2002: 150).

The responding firms of this survey were from the electronics, telecommunications, automotive and agriculture sectors located in southwest China (in Guangdong and Guangxi provinces). As the firms wish to remain anonymous, and as it is difficult to break promises, we can say only that the 'outsider' firms come from the UK (4), United States (2), Japan (2), and one each from Thailand and Singapore.

As far as this chapter is concerned we investigate a simple proposition:

- When firms join in an IJV, they ought to be inclined to work with each other although there may be some issues of concern, but . . .

• Over time, if they are working well together, they ought to harbour very few (or zero) issues of concern. That is, they should be even closer to each others' thoughts and wishes than they were originally.

Results

We investigate the proposition above by reviewing the responses expressed in the questionnaire by the Chinese and by the expatriate managers. We search for the differences, rather than similarities, as the critical criteria of the 'development' of trust over time. After all, if managers initially agreed with their partners (and why not, as they voluntarily entered the IJV?) they ought to proffer responses similar to their partners in the 'early' phase. If they continue to be happy with their partners, we ought to find many similarities in their responses. It is only if they drift apart (or come together from divergent stances) that we will find differences in their responses 'early to late'.

The data upon 32 questions have been entered into an Excel spreadsheet and averages to each question have been extracted for the early and late responses split into 'insider' (Chinese respondents $N_I = 58$), and 'outsider' (all outsiders, from the UK, United States, Japan, etc., $N_O = 14$). The gross changes in responses have been elicited to investigate how each side 'moved' their perception of each question's focus over time. We note only 'significant' shifts – but it has to be said that 'significant' is used in a non-statistical, subjective manner, especially as we have a distinctly unbalanced data set. In the future, detailed comparisons within and between nationalities will be investigated before data aggregation. This quick analysis uses aggregate data.

Respondents were told, for each question, to tick the box which best reflected their opinion – from 'strongly disagree' [box 1] to 'strongly agree' [box 7], with [box 4] being the 'neutral or don't know' response. Following our computations, the absolute differences of the insider–outsider [early to late] response for each question are plotted in Figure 6.1 (ranked from maximum to minimum change) with the relevant question number marked above each column.

It is not meaningful to discuss all 32 responses, when clearly many show a minimal difference in the change from the 'early to late' over the 'insider–outsider' viewpoint, and only a few questions indicated strong differences in perceptions between the parties. Therefore, in Figure 6.1, we determined 'significant' against 'insignificant' differences by applying a subjective test akin to the scree test (the determination of the most

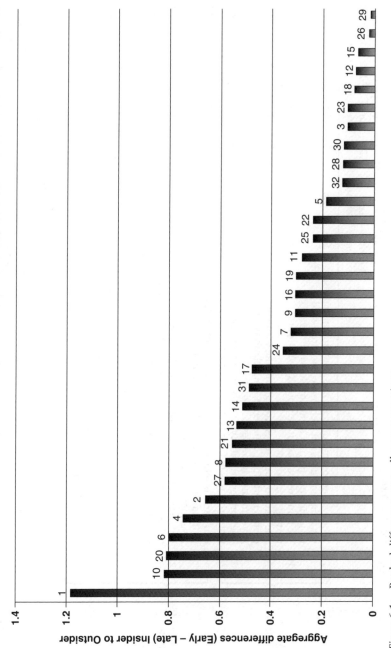

Figure 6.1: Ranked differences over all survey questions

Table 6.1: Detail of the most important differences

	Q	Question text	Insider			Outsider		
			Early Average	Late Average	Shift	Early Average	Late Average	Shift
About Partners	1	When we encounter difficult and new circumstances, my company does not feel worried or threatened by letting our partner company do what it wants	5.0	4.5	-0.5	3.5	4.2	0.7
	10	We think we can accurately predict what our partner firm will do.	3.8	3.3	-0.5	3.1	3.5	0.4
	20	The foreign party relies strongly on the Chinese party's marketing, experience, and relations with government's resources.	4.8	4.6	-0.2	4.7	5.2	0.5
	6	The partner firm always stands by its word even when this was not the best interest for it.	4.6	4.2	-0.4	4.3	4.7	0.4
About our firm	4	Our party is reluctant to make resource commitment to the alliance when specifications in the alliance agreement are ambiguous	5.1	5.4	0.3	5.2	4.7	-0.5
	2	My company is familiar with the patterns of behaviour our partner company has established, and we can rely on them to behave in certain ways.	4.7	4.5	-0.2	4.4	4.9	0.5
	27	We plan to document all aspects of our negotiations with our partner	5.5	5.6	0.1	5.1	5.8	0.7
Both firms	8	Both parties in our alliance can rely on each other to abide by the alliance management agreement	5.5	5.2	-0.4	4.9	5.3	0.4
	21	Together we have invested a great deal in building up our joint business.	5.4	4.9	-0.5	5.3	5.3	0

	1	2	3	4	5	6	7
Question scales	Strongly disagree	Disagree	Slightly disagree	Neutral	Slightly agree	Agree	Strongly agree

Table 6.2: Text of significant questions subjectively rewritten according to the response ranges

	Insider (Early to Late)	Outsider (Early to Late)
1	5.0 − 4.5 = −0.5 We agreed initially when we encountered difficult and new circumstances, we did not feel worried or threatened by letting our partner company do what it wanted. Now we are more neutral.	3.5 − 4.2 = 0.7 Initially when we encountered difficult and new circumstances, we did feel worried & threatened by letting our partner company do what it wanted. Later we felt more neutral on this point.
10	3.8 − 3.3 = −0.5 Initially a bit unsure we could accurately predict what the partner firm will do: later, more sure we cannot predict their behaviour.	3.1 − 3.5 = 0.4 We could not accurately predict what the partner firm would do initially: later, still unsure about our ability to predict their behaviour.
20	4.8 − 4.6 = −0.2 Initially agreed somewhat that the foreign party relies strongly on the Chinese party's marketing, experience, and relations with government's resources: now we are more neutral.	4.7 − 5.2 = 0.5 Initially agreed somewhat that we relied strongly on the Chinese party's marketing, experience, and relations with government's resources: more sure later.
6	4.6 − 4.2 = −0.4 We agree a bit that the partner firm always stands by its word even when this was not the best interest for it: later we are slightly more inclined to disagree.	4.3 − 4.7 = 0.4 Initially were neutral that the partner firm always stands by its word even when this was not the best interest for it: later to later we are still neutral in our views.

About partners

(Continued)

Table 6.2: (Continued)

	Insider (Early to Late)	Outsider (Early to Late)
About our firm	**4** 5.1 − 5.4 = 0.3 We were reluctant to make resource commitment to the alliance when specifications in the alliance agreement is ambiguous: now we are more reluctant	5.2 − 4.7 = −0.5 We were reluctant to make resource commitment to the alliance when specifications in the alliance agreement is ambiguous: but over time we became more willing to invest.
	2 4.7 − 4.5 = −0.2 We agreed we were a bit familiar with the patterns of behaviour our partner company has established, and we can rely on them to behave in certain ways: later we are neutral.	4.4 − 4.9 = 0.5 We were not very familiar with the patterns of behaviour our partner company has established, and we think we were neutral about relying on them to behave in certain ways: later we become more familiar and more able to be reliant on them.
	27 5.5 − 5.6 = 0.1 We planed to document all aspects of our negotiations with our partner and we continue more strongly with this resolve.	5.1 − 5.8 = 0.7 We planed to document all aspects of our negotiations with our partner: later this resolve grew.
Both firms	**8** 5.5 − 5.2 = −0.4 Initially we thought we could rely on each other to abide by the alliance management agreement: later we were a bit less confident.	4.9 − 5.3 = 0.4 We thought we could rely on each other to abide by the alliance management agreement: later we were more sure of this view.
	21 5.4 − 4.9 = −0.5 Initially we thought we had invested a great deal in building up our joint business: later we think we have invested a bit less than we thought originally.	5.3 − 5.3 = 00 We have not changed our views over time: we have invested a great deal in building up our joint business.

Question scales

1 Strongly disagree	2 Disagree	3 Slightly disagree	4 Neutral	5 Slightly agree	6 Agree	7 Strongly agree

significant eigenvectors in factor analysis). This resulted in four questions being placed in group 1, three in group 2, and two in group 3. The rest, having difference scores below 0.5, were ignored (for the purposes of this chapter). Table 6.1 shows the relevant data for these nine, most important, highlighted questions.

Interestingly we find that each group seems to have different 'drivers':

Group 1:   Is about our views of our partner.
Group 2:   Is about our views of ourselves primarily: 'we', 'our', etc.
Group 3:   Is about our alliance 'togetherness' with the partner.

Table 6.2 restates the questions of Table 6.1 – but reworded by us in a subjective manner according to the aggregate replies of the respondents. Herein we note what the respondent *might have been* saying to him/herself given the observed changes in levels (early to late). We do this for the insider (Chinese) and for the outsider (UK, United States, etc.) respondents. We suggest the reader may also wish to interpret the data according to their own bias, thereby guarding against our interpretative bias.

Notwithstanding the interpretations given in Table 6.2, we may see from Table 6.1 that the belief level differences 'early to late' between 'insider and outsider' across all questions show only one response with a large difference, namely Q1:

The Chinese are more neutral nowadays in letting the partner resolve new difficulties and doing what it wants than formerly, when they were not greatly worried. But the Outsider is growing in confidence (from 'worried' towards 'neutral') about letting the Chinese partner do what it wants. The Chinese have shifted 'backwards' while the Outsider has shifted 'forwards' from their Early to Late levels of response to the question.

And we must not lose sight of our focus on trust for this chapter, and note the response in particular to Q27:

Here the Insider (Chinese) has said that they plan to document, and even increases slightly that urge towards documentation in the 'late' stage of the alliance: the Outsider is even stronger in this resolve as time progresses.

What might this mean? In a trusting society, there is little need to document agreements, but conversely, if partners are worried each about the other, they need to be clear about the limits of their agreement, so must document everything. Perhaps, we see here that the trust in each other is asymmetric – with the insider (Chinese) moving less strongly towards greater documentation than the outsider. Could this mean the outsider is becoming less trusting over time?

Discussion

Many decision systems rely on trust between the partners – and 'trust' is said to be perhaps the most fundamental relationship (Child, 2001). However, in many basic relationships we have to act autonomously – just as we do not consciously monitor our heart rate, our breathing, or the control of our muscles as they act in autonomic unison to keep us balanced – we cannot delve deeply into the reasoning and analysis of the data that leads our partners to their decisions. This is not to say that we must abrogate our existence to the whims of others. We must work in concert to question some of the data and some of the decisions some of the time: but an analysis of the mass of data and decisions surrounding us, for lack of time and/or competence on our part, has to be left to others. We must trust them, and thus we must live our personal as well as our public lives almost 100 percent autonomously.

Trust exists in context and is shaped by dynamics specific to particular social settings and networks – which in this study refer to the natural work networks of IJV in China. In a transitional economic situation, IJVs have more interaction with the foreign parent(s) than with their own parent firms, and knowledge is often transferred from the foreign parent to the joint venture (Tsang, 2002). Yet despite legal contracts drawing the boundaries of a partner's commitment in these relationships, socially embedded relationships in the natural work network surpass these contracts and are evidenced by characteristics, such as trust, fine-grained information transfer, and joint problem-solving arrangements (Uzzi, 1997). Furthermore, trust is path-dependent – it is a socially constructed variable that evolves over time depending on the social, institutional and national [cultural] context. International collaboration is also path dependent and is continuously changing over time. Therefore, trust is a dynamic and continuous variable, which can vary substantially both within and across relationships, as well as over time (Schindler and Thomas, 1993).

'Distrust' is a different construct that is time-consuming to manage and costly to society. This is not a simple absence of trust, but a set of cognitive and affective factors that inhibit cooperation and coordination between different partners (McAllister, 1995a; 1995b). Fukuyama (1996) notes that societies may be split into high trust and low trust groupings – and that people in the low trust societies will be more suspicious and questioning of the motives of others. Hutchings and Michailova (2004) state that the Chinese and Russians (like the Japanese, as well as some Italians and South Americans) are naturally highly distrustful of others not in the 'family'. This hinders voluntary data exchange and slows down organizational learning since one thinks the other is 'milking one' to take an early profit.

Lewicki *et al.* (1998) suggest that we need to consider simultaneous measures of trust and distrust with respect to our partner in our dyadic alliance relationships. There may be no real reason for us to think ill of the other person – after all, in our daily interaction they may have 'delivered the goods as agreed' – but conversations with third parties may give one cause for alarm, hence one might also carry a degree of distrust in this dyadic relationship. Remember, organizations are composed of individuals, and it is the peer-wise linking of these who exchange data. Later, it is their meaningful knowledge exchange that will nurture (or hinder) the alliance between the firms. In Figure 6.2, we have noted that the least intimate interaction is in cell 1, where only professional courtesy is exchanged, 'we do not trust the other, yet neither do we distrust,

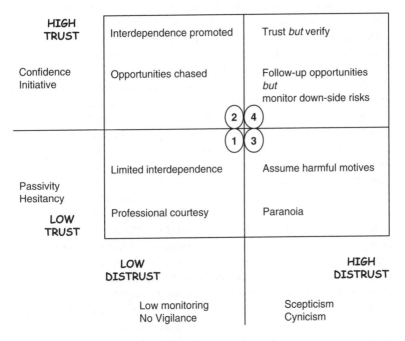

Figure 6.2:   An example of the multi-dimensionality of trust
Note: Following Lewicki *et al.* (1998).

since there is no perceived need to distrust'. If the alliance depends on this form of dyadic relationship alone, the alliance will eventually atrophy. Moving on to cell 3, it is obvious that the alliance will fail, as there is little to nurture the relationship given each assumes the worst of the other. In cell 2, there is euphoria, as high trust is combined with low distrust and there is free rein to consider all initiatives and not to doubt the other side. But the more realistic case is cell 4. Here, high trust is tinged with the need to verify and monitor the other – not so strongly as to question motives and thus engender distrust in the partnership, but enough to maintain a critical awareness of downside costs.

These alternatives and dimensions of trust and distrust link together when it is clear that opportunities exist for the relationships of the alliance parties to fall into a 'state of anomie' (Durkheim, 1933; Fukuyama, 1996: 6), or to think one side is 'milking' the other (Inkpen, 1996). Kidd (2003) – when discussing the work of Larsson *et al.* (1999) – suggest when insufficient care is taken to absorb cultural complexity in the alliance, an unwillingness to collaborate develops, and we do not volunteer data to the other side. Lewicki *et al.* would assert that if there is distrust evident there will be a natural unwillingness to proffer data, and thus individuals will not voluntarily engage in peer-wise organizational learning.

Of course, we must recognize that an alliance is an arrangement between two parties for mutual gain and these will not be charitable arrangements (Burton, 1995; Richter, 2000). In such circumstances, we say that firms should strive for a 'win-win' situation where they would both become more successful in the long term – they must learn to play the 'Prisoner's Dilemma' correctly (Inkpen, 1996; Khanna *et al.*, 1998). Partnership should not be a one-way process, but a long-term relationship carried by mutual trust, and here it is important to note the Japanese *kyosei* – which means 'symbiotic interaction with the surrounding companies' (Murakami, 1992; Teramoto, 1993). Further, there is self-interest in Japan, which lies in *hateke zukuri* (ploughing the field) against future eventualities – since you never know when you may have to become indebted to others (*osewa ni naru*). This is similar to *guanxi* in China (Luo, 2000). Since *kyosei* aims for the co-evolution of the cooperating companies, we may envisage a learning model that focuses on 'a profit' for all participating companies. Yet 'profit' in financial terms is not the ultimate driver in all circumstances. Generally, we ought to strive to raise the levels of social capital, which in turn will raise our intellectual capital and knowledge capital. We might refer to Figure 6.3, in which the dynamics of learning encompass explicit data and rules for its combination (as in databases, the Internet, and organizational rules), as well as the implicit

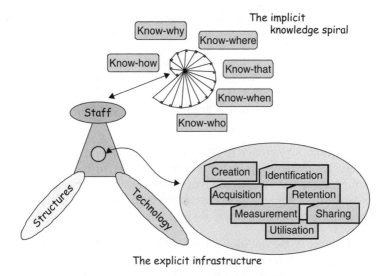

Figure 6.3: The interdependence of explicit and tacit systems of knowledge
Source: Based on Lehaney *et al.* (2004: 11).

(wherein players learn how to conceptualize data to perform better, and travel along a knowledge-learning spiral). In this we see echoes of Nonaka and Takeuchi, 1995; Rao, 2003; Lehaney *et al.*, 2004; Ishikura, 2004 – and importantly we see the need to trust in the others.

In this research, we review only the direct aspects of trust, not anomie, and not distrust. We accept the multi-stage model of Lewicki and Bunker (1996), who suggest that the stages [of trust] move from an initial stage of 'calculative' to a stage wherein the partners are getting to know each other – when they will pass considerable data for the use of the other side – which they call ' knowledge-based trust'. Somewhat later, the partners move into a symbiotic third state which they label 'identification-based trust', which is somewhat akin to *kyosei*. Given that the literature suggests alliances do not all live 'for ever' and that after a period they break up, in our research we have discarded the third stage mentioned above, and we concentrate on the values that may differentiate the stages of 'early' and 'late' trust.

Thoughts on our data

Our analyses suggest a three-tier categorization of the 'significant' differences in the respondents' perceptions over the 32 questions from a visual analysis of Figure 6.1, which resulted in four questions being placed in group 1, three in group 2 and two in group 3 – with the rest of the responses being ignored [for the purposes of this chapter]:

Group 1: About our views of our partner [Qs 1, 10, 20, and 6].
Group 2: About our views of ourselves primarily: 'we', 'our', etc. [Qs 4, 2, and 27].
Group 3: About our alliance 'togetherness' with the partner [Qs 8, and 21].

We will now subjectively re-interpret and consolidate the text of the questions (as presented in Table 6.2) with respect to the strengths of response (on the scale 1–7) in terms of average levels and changes thereof from early to late from the viewpoints of the insider (Chinese) and the outsider (remembering herein there are multiple overseas nationalities).

Group 1 – Over all the questions [1, 10, 20 and 6] the Chinese side weakened their position by about half a scale unit (~ 0.5 to ~ 0.2), while the outsiders strengthened their position by more than half a unit (~ 0.7 to ~ 0.4). Both sides moved their viewpoints of their partners in opposite directions – with the Chinese side becoming a little more unsure of their partner while the outsiders became a little more confident of their relationship.

Group 2 – The Chinese side [on Qs 4, 2 and 27] expressed concerns about ambiguity, a concern which was increasing over the period 'early to late' . . . and they were a bit more reluctant to commit resources, less sure of the partner's behaviour, and wanting to better document the relationship. However, the outsiders seemed happier with the relationship over time, though they wished to better document the relationship.

Group 3 – In their responses [to Qs 8 and 21] the Chinese seem to be pulling back from the relationship over time. The outsiders were becoming more positive of their relationship saying they could better rely on the partner, and had not changed their views on their continued strong investment in the relationship.

This strongly aggregated summary indicates that over time the Insiders and Outsiders tend to move their feelings of the other in opposite directions (except for Q27 when the Chinese moved by + 0.1 and the outsider by + 0.7: both saying they wished to document more strongly in the latter years of their alliance). Overall, there is some indication that each side, over time, is distancing itself from the other.

In each group, the Chinese seem to be backing out of the alliance: in group 1 becoming a little more unsure [of their partner]; in group 2 expressing greater concerns over ambiguity; and in group 3 being less sure of committing their own resources to the alliance. In contrast, the outsiders seemed much more positive about their relationships over all groups. We may re-interpret this to suggest . . . 'the Outsiders are becoming more confident of their operations in China, and could "go it alone" but with the continued help of their alliance partner with whom they have a stronger [positive] relationship'. This sentiment aligns with Vanhonaker who has stated that there are an increasing number of 'unhappy' IJV. In China, when the partners realize this sorry state of their affairs, the nature of Chinese culture makes it hard to dissolve a relationship, however poorly performing, when formed on trust and confidence – no wonder, he continues, that many [outsider] companies have begun to explore the wholly foreign-owned mode (Vanhonaker, 1997).

As mentioned earlier, this is a quick, preliminary, data exploration – we do not address the detailed research propositions that form the basis of the full research programme – only a brief proposition has been posed and analysed at this stage. Later, a detailed multivariate quantitative analysis will be undertaken as well as a detailed qualitative analysis. However, we end this review quoting a memory from the interviews that strengthens our notion of the 'separation of trust between the parties . . .' as time progressed. In one firm we learned that (from the Chinese side):

When the joint venture was initiated all our best technicians came to the joint venture leaving our traditional firm with the 'dross' [our choice of word: Li/Kidd]; and as the international brand began to be sold the customer base for our once successful local brand fell. Over time we have sold more and more of our stockholding to the foreign partner, so they almost wholly own us (ie the IJV), and we feel they want to become independent. If that takes place, we will still be able to return to our original host firm, but it is a weak shell now, with few sales of our original brand, and weaker staff. We thus trust our partners less than we did initially as we are uncertain of our future.

Conclusions

Alliances are set up (and dissolved) for myriad reasons. Research by others has noted that during the life of the alliance the growth of mutual dependency (on trust, and in learning to be open and to share data) is slow to mature. In that case, organizational learning is also slow to mature and may never take off – thereby hastening the demise of the alliance, as one partner may accuse the other of attempting to 'milk the alliance' and gain an unbalanced advantage in the short term.

In the research reported here, albeit based only on an initial data analysis, we accept that inter-partner trust is not simple to define. From the data, we find each side of the partnership displaying opposite tendencies – the Chinese becoming more hesitant, and less trusting of aspects of their joint alliance as time progresses. The outsiders, over the same time frame, are becoming more trusting it seems: but we may interpret this as 'being more confident of their situation in China'. We might infer that over time there is a change in trust, as 'calculative' moves to 'knowledge based', yet in fact the theoretically desirable *kyosei* is not taking place – rather it is an alteration of ownership status from joint to wholly owned that is hinted at.

The research is focused upon trust so we cannot infer anything about organizational learning, nor about knowledge management. However, later, within the qualitative analysis of the interview data, we will be careful to note any issues that depend on trust, such as KM and OL. All we may reiterate at this time is that KM is difficult to initiate in joint alliances, and it is said that OL will proceed only if trust is present, nurtured, and strengthened. Our conclusion suggests that trust, if not decreasing between the partners over time, is altering in its nature. Consequently we assume their OL must be affected, probably being resisted.

Of course these findings impact on today's alliance managers. It is clear that once the excitement and euphoria of the new alliance has calmed down and managers settle into a routine, they are able to assess their peers. They will find differences they do not necessarily like, but initially will compromise for the sake of the alliance; and if they are magnanimous, they might expect to learn a bit more of their peers and hope to work better with them in the future thereby obviating the need to compromise. But if the differences continue, or are magnified over time, individuals may innovate to avoid conflict – and in so doing find new ways of working that removes the need to confer with peers. Of course, decreasing peer contact will decrease OL, but maybe by having a 'work around' leads the manager into a new realm of greater direct contact with the world outside the IJV to better achieve a strategic goal. But this is conjecture based on the findings from the initial data analysis.

Until the full analysis is done, we suggest all of the IJV staff must become aware of 'the needs of the other party' and to be attentive to subtle changes in both their (and the others') attitudes and expectancy as the alliance matures. Such attention might obviate the need to break up the alliance prematurely (though a lack of awareness of the other partners' needs); or conversely, it may allow the dissolution of the alliance without recrimination through the recognition of the [valid] needs of the other party.

References

Anderson, E. and H. Gatignon (1986) 'Modes of foreign entry: a transaction cost analysis and propositions', *Journal of International Business Studies* 17(3), 1–26.

Bacharach, S. (1989) 'Organisational theories: some criteria for evaluation', *Academy for Management Review* 14, 496–515.

Beckermann, W. (1956) 'Distance and the pattern of intra-European trade', *Review of Economics and Statistics* 38, 31–40.

Blummer, H. (1969) *Symbolic Interactionism: Perspective and method* (Upper Saddle River, NJ: Prentice-Hall).

Brannen, J. (ed) (1992) *Mixing Methods: Qualitative and Quantitative research* (Brookfield, VT: Ashgate).

Burton, J. (1995) 'Partnering with the Japanese: threat or opportunity for European businesses?', *European Management Journal* 13, 304–16.

Chen, C., M. Peng and P. Saparito (2003) 'Individualism, collectivism, and opportunism: a cultural perspective on transactional cost economics', *Journal of Management* 28(4), 567–83.

Chen, M. (2004) *Asian Management Systems: Chinese, Japanese and Korean styles of business* (2nd edn, London: Thompson Learning).

Child, J. (1998) 'Trust and International Strategic Alliances: The Case of Sino-foreign Joint Ventures', in C. Lane and R. Bachmann (eds), *Trust Within and Between Organisations* (Oxford: Oxford University Press).

Child, J. (2001) 'Trust – the fundamental bond in global collaboration'. *Organizational Dynamics* 29(4), 274–88.

Child, J. and D. Faulkner (1998) *Strategies of Cooperation: Managing Alliances, Networks, and Joint Ventures* (Oxford: Oxford University Press).

Clissold, T. (2004) *Mr China* (London: Robinson).

Conway, T. and J.S. Swift (2000) 'International relationship marketing: the importance of psychic distance', *European Journal of Marketing* 34(11/12), 1391–413.

Creswell, J.W. (1995) *Research Design: Quantitative and qualitative approaches* (Thousand Oaks, CA: Sage).

Crossan, M.M., H.W. Lane and R.E. White (1999) 'An organisational learning framework: from intuition to institution', *Academy of Management Review* 24(3), 522–37.

Denzin, N. (1994) 'The Art and Politics of Interpretation', in N. Denzin and Y.S. Lincoln (eds), *Handbook of Qualitative Research* (Thousand Oaks, CA: Sage), pp. 500–19.

Deutsch, M. (1962) *The Resolution of Conflict* (New Haven, CT: Yale University Press).

Dunning, J.H. (2000) 'The eclectic paradigm as an envelope for economic and business theories of MNE activity', *International Business Review* 9(2), 163–90.

Durkheim, E. (1933) *The Division of Labour in Society* (New York: Macmillan).

Erramilli, M.K. and C.P. Rao (1993) 'Service firms' international entry-mode choice: a modified transaction-cost analysis approach', *Journal of Marketing* 57(3), 19–38.

Fang, T. (2004) 'The 'Co-op Comp' Chinese Negotiation Strategy', in J.B. Kidd and F.J. Richter (eds), *Trust and Antitrust in Asian Business Alliances: Historical roots and current practices* (London, Palgrave Macmillan), pp. 121–50.

Fink, A. (1995) (Series Editor) *The Survey Kit* (Thousand Oaks, CA: Sage).

Fukuyama, F. (1996) *Trust: The Social Virtues and the Creation of Prosperity* (New York: Free Press).

Gatignon, H. and E. Anderson (1988) 'The multinational corporation's degree of control over foreign subsidiaries: an empirical test of a transaction cost explanation', *Journal of Law, Economics & Organization* 4(Fall), 305–36.

Glaser, B.G. and A.L. Strauss (1967) *The Discovery of Grounded Theory* (Hawthorne, NY: de Gruyter).

Hutchings, K. and S. Michailova (2004) 'Facilitating knowledge sharing in Russian and Chinese subsidiaries: the role of personal networks', *Journal of Knowledge Management* 8(2), 84–94.

Inkpen, A. (1996) 'Creating knowledge through collaboration', *California Management Review* 39(1), 123–41.

Ishikura, Y. (2004) 'Clusters of 'ba' for Knowledge Management', in J.B. Kidd and F.J. Richter (eds), *Trust and Antitrust in Asian Business Alliances: Historical Roots and Current Practices* (London, Palgrave Macmillan), pp. 290–314.

Khanna, T., R. Gulati and N. Nohria (1998) 'The dynamics of learning alliances: competition, co-operation and scope', *Strategic Management Journal* 19(3), 193–204.

Kidd, J.B. (2003) 'Us and them: obstructing knowledge management in MNEs', *Journal of Knowledge and Process Management* 10(1), 18–28.

Kidd, J.B. and X. Li (1999) 'Eliciting opaque views: a vision through multinational perspectives', *Journal of the International Association for Human Resource Information Management* 3(4), 26–33.

Kidd, J.B. and Q. Zhao (1996) *An expert database for the support of joint venture negotiations*, presentation to the 11th LVMH Conference, INSEAD, Fontainebleau, 14–16 January.

Kidd, J.B., F.-J. Richter and M. Stumm (2003) 'Learning and trust in supply chain management: disintermediation, ethics and cultural pressures in brief dynamic alliances', *International Journal of Logistics Research* 6(4), 259–76.

Krugman, P.R. (1990) *Rethinking International Trade* (Cambridge, MA: MIT Press).

Larsson, R., L. Bengtsson, K. Henricksson and J. Sparks (1999) 'The interorganizational learning dilemma: collective knowledge development in strategic alliances', *Organizational Science* 9(3), 285–306.

Lehaney, B., S. Clarke, E. Coakes and G. Jack (2004) *Beyond Knowledge Management* (Hershey, PA: Idea Group Publishing).

Lewicki, R.J. and B.B. Bunker (1996) 'Developing and Maintaining Trust in Work Relationships', in R.M. Kramer and T.R. Tyler (eds), *Trust in Organisations: Frontiers of Theory and Research* (Thousand Oaks, CA: Sage), pp. 114–39.

Lewicki, R.J., D.J. McAllister and R.J. Bies (1998) 'Trust and distrust: new relationships and realities', *Academy of Management Review* 23, 438–58.

Locke, K. (2002) 'The Grounded Theory Approach to Qualitative Research', in F. Drasgow and N. Schmitt (eds), *Measuring and Analysing Behaviour in Organisations* (San Francisco, CA: Jossey-Bass).

Luo, Y. (2000) *Guanxi and Business* (Singapore: World Scientific Press).

Markusen, J.R. and A.J. Venables (2000) 'The theory of endowment, intra-industry and multi-national trade', *Journal of International Economics* 52, 209–34.

McAllister, D.J. (1995a) 'Affect- and cognition-based trust as foundations for inter-personal cooperation in organisations', *Academy of Management Journal* 38, 24–59.

McAllister, D.J. (1995b) 'Two Faces of Interpersonal Trust', in R.J. Lewicki, R.J. Bies and B.H. Sheppard (eds), *Research on Negotiation in Organisations* 6 (Greenwich, NJ: JAI Press) pp. 87–112.

Miles, M.B. and A.M. Huberman (1994) *Qualitative Data Analysis: A Sourcebook of New Methods* (Newbury Park, CA: Sage).

Murakami, T. (1992) 'Kyosei and the next generation of Japanese-style management', *Nomura Research Institute Quarterly* Winter, 2–27.

Nakos, G. and K.D. Brouthers (2004) 'Entry mode choice of SMEs in central and eastern Europe', *Entrepreneurship Theory and Practice* 27(1), 47–63.

Nojonen, M. (2003) 'The Competitive Advantage with Chinese Characteristics – the Sophisticated Choreograpy of gift-giving', in J.B. Kidd and F.J. Richter (eds), *Corruption and Governance in Asia* (London: Palgrave Macmillan), pp. 107–30.

Nonaka, I. and H. Takeuchi (1995) *The Knowledge-creating Company: How Japanese Companies Create the Dynamics of Innovation* (New York: Oxford University Press).

Pettigrew, A.M. (1990) 'Longitudinal field research on change: theory and practice', *Organizational Science* 1, 267–92.

Rao, M. (2003) *Leading with Knowledge: Knowledge Management Practices in Global Infotech Companies* (New Delhi: Tata McGraw-Hill).

Redding, G. (2002) 'The capitalist business system of China and its rationale', *Asia Pacific Journal of Management* 19, 221–49.

Richter, F.J. (2000) *Strategic Networks: The Art of Japanese Interfirm Co-operation* New York: Haworth Press.

Schindler, P.L. and C.C. Thomas (1993) 'The structure of interpersonal trust in the workplace', *Psychological Reports* 73, 563–73.

Schramm, M. and M. Taube (2003) 'The Institutional Economics of Legal Institutions, Guanxi and Corruption', in J.B. Kidd and F.J. Richter (eds), *Fighting Corruption in Asia: Causes, Effects and Remedies* (Singapore: World Scientific), pp. 271–96.

Sheer, V.C. and L. Chen (2003) 'Successful sino-western business negotiation: participants accounts of national and professional cultures', *Journal for Business Communication* 40(1), 50–85.

Smith, A. (1976 [1776]) *An Inquiry into the Nature and Causes of the Wealth of Nations* (Chicago: University of Chicago Press).

Sutton, R. and B.W. Staw (1995) 'What theory is not', *Administrative Science Quarterly* 40, 371–84.

Tashakkori, A. and C. Teddlie (1998) *Mixed Methodology: Combining Qualitative and Quantitative Approaches* (Thousand Oaks, CA: Sage).

Teramoto, Y. (1993) *Gakushu Suru Soshiki* (The Learning Organization) (Tokyo: Shobunsha).

Tsang, E.W.K. (2002) 'Acquiring knowledge by foreign partners from inter-national joint ventures in a transitional economy: learning-by-doing and learning myopia', *Strategic Management Journal* 23, 835–54.

Uzzi, B. (1997) 'Social structure and competition in interfirm networks: the paradox of embeddedness', *Administrative Science Quarterly* 42, 35–67.

Vahlne, J-E. and F. Wiedersheim-Paul (1973) *Psychic Distance – An Inhibiting Factor in International Trade*, Working Paper Uppsala: (University of Uppsala).

Vanhonaker, W. (1997) 'Entering China: An Unconventional Approach', *Harvard Business Review*, March–April, reprinted in *HBR on Doing Business In China* (Boston: Harvard Business School Press, 2004), pp. 109–21.

von Glinow, M.A., E.A. Drost and M.B. Teagarden (2002) 'Converging on IHRM best practices: lessons learned from a globally distributed consortium on theory and practice', *Asia Pacific Journal of Human resources* 40(1), 146–66.

Whitley, R. (1999) *Divergent Capitalisms: The Social Structuring and Change of Business Systems* (Oxford: Oxford University Press).

Williamson, O.E. (1993) 'Calculativeness, trust and economic organisation', *Journal of Law and Economics* 36(1), 453–86.

Yin, R.K. (2003) *Case Study Research, Design and Methods* (3rd edn, Thousand Oaks, CA: Sage).

7

Global Corporate Cultures: Issues of Shared Goals, Communication and Trust – Empirical Evidence from the Japanese, German and American Units of a Multinational Company

Pamela Yeow and Wolfgang Dorow

Introduction: Culture and globalization

This research, which is a part of the project 'Corporate Cultures in Global Interaction', supported by the Bertelsmann Foundation,[1] is focused on studying intercultural management processes within global companies. The research is keen to investigate comparatively the interaction between the top management of the headquarters and subsidiaries of European, Japanese and US multinationals. Participating multinational companies include BASF, Bertelsmann AG, Deutsche Post World Net (DHL/Danzas), Henkel, Lufthansa, Nestlé, Pfizer, Toyota and Volkswagen.

Key questions include what cultural attributes characterize the interactions in and between different business units with different national backgrounds (cf. parent companies and their subsidiaries).

Specifically, the research concentrates on the following questions:

(1) What sort of corporate cultural design global companies are pursuing?
(2) What is the balance firms are attempting to strike between accepting diverse local cultures on the one hand, and the alignment to a unifying company culture on the other hand?
(3) What cultural frameworks and instruments are being used in global firms for the integration of their different cultures?
(4) What is the effectiveness of the integration instruments?
(5) How can the multinational companies effectively and constructively make use of cultural heterogeneity for economic, political and social gains?

Multinational and transnational enterprises can be identified as essential drivers of globalization, whose importance for the global economy have risen significantly since the 1990s. According to the *World Investment Report* (UNCTAD, 2002), about 65,000 transnational enterprises employed 54 million employees worldwide (1990: 24 million) in 850,000 subsidiary and affiliate companies and attained revenues amounting to US\$ 19 billion in 2001. This corresponds to about one tenth of the gross global product. One of the most important growth drivers of multinational corporations is cross-border mergers and acquisitions (M&A). The way multinational groups deal with the different cultures in their spheres of activity must therefore be seen as an important challenge to the management of global company networks.

There are basically two fundamentally distinct perspectives by which one can view the way multinational corporations handle local cultures. One perspective takes the view of the internal stakeholders, and the other looks to external stakeholder groups of multinational corporations (see Figure 7.1).

From the point of view of the internal stakeholders in the company, the efficient management of culturally heterogeneous interest groups within the organisation is necessary in order to minimize conflict. The creation of global synergies within a multinational organization for example, may require a certain degree of harmonization of leadership

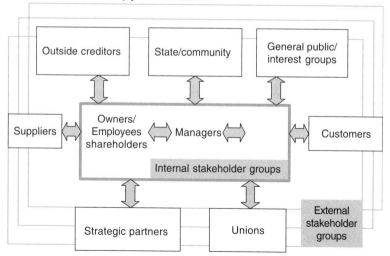

Figure 7.1:   Stakeholders in multinational corporations
Source: Dorow and Blazejewski, (2004).

styles, pay systems or decision-making processes. Effective communication and coordination across national or regional boundaries require clear, shared corporate values and objectives for all subsidiaries and affiliates. In addition, trust between people coming from the most diverse cultural backgrounds would be beneficial. Current research have shown that up to 85percent of all transnational company mergers which are primarily driven by financial and strategic objectives do not yield the success hoped for, due to cultural barriers (Buono and Bowditch, 1989; Sudersanam, 1995). International joint ventures or strategic alliances must often deal with culturally induced misunderstandings and conflicts, reducing the expected positive effects of cooperation between two or more organizations. Brewster (1991), Black *et al.* (1992) and Hendry (1994) reported that a lack of management experience in dealing with cultural differences could cause up to 40 percent of expatriates to terminate their assignments prematurely, creating considerable costs. The average cost of a failed assignment has been estimated to range from US$ 200,000 to US$ 2.1 million (Sanchez, Spector and Cooper, 2000). According to Black *et al.* (1992), 50 percent of expatriates do not meet the expectations of the parent company. Against such findings, there is certainly urgency in identifying efficient methods of handling heterogeneous cultures within multinational companies.

However from the point of view of *external stakeholders*, there are political arguments in discussing issues on culture and globalization. Multinational organizations, often originating from the highly industrialized, affluent countries of the 'West' are often criticized and accused of cultural hegemony and of creating an imbalance when looking at the development of local value systems and traditions, mainly in developing countries (Stiglitz, 2003). By applying measures developed in the West, such organizations end up demanding that their local subsidiaries and partners follow 'their way', and ignore issues that stem from local cultures, patterns and traditions.

Such challenges are thus what modern day multinational organizations face in the globalized and turbulent environment in which they subsist. There is not only the need for internal cultural integration in order to achieve global objectives, but also there is the need to show respect and understanding for local cultural diversities in order to avoid conflicts with both local communities and other stakeholders in their environment.

What is culture?

Culture comprises divergent behaviours, norms and expectations and is fluid across space and time (Ettlinger, 2003) and can be viewed as the patterns of cognitions and behaviour shared by a group which evolve and becomes manifest in continuous processes of social interaction. Globalization of firms and markets involves reorganization and confrontation between cultures, both at the organizational level and the national level (Mattsson, 2003). The need to understand the role of culture in looking at globalizing firms has been highlighted by a number of observers (Mattsson, 2003; Robertson and Crittenden, 2003; Weaver, 2001; Schneider and Barsoux, 2003a, 2003b).

Much work has been done in the importance in considering notions of culture in terms of global organizations, virtual or otherwise (e.g., 1980, 1994; Schein, 1989, 1990; Hampden-Turner and Trompenaars, 1993; Trompenaars, 1993). Hofstede carried out large cross-cultural studies and identified five dimensions of differences or traits between national cultures.[2] Although there been accolades to his work, there have also been many criticisms. One major problem with Hofstede's approach is methodological. Cray and Mallory (1998) write that the use of aggregated national data can be misleading when applying societal characteristics to individual behaviour because there can be considerable variance in the degree to which individuals adhere to any set of values. Others (cf. Goodstein, 1981; Hunt, 1981; Robinson, 1983; Dorfman and Howell, 1988; Sondergaard, 1994) have also criticised his scales in terms of their validity and usefulness of their four dimensions at the individual level of analysis. It was argued that it is not possible to discuss the impact of cultures on organization structures if all the data originates from the same study (Tayeb, 1988) with Hunt (1981: 62) questioning whether Hofstede was 'studying the culture of the Japanese or the French or the British or Malaysian executive or the culture of a multinational firm'.

Culture is a highly complex phenomenon that basically can be differentiated according to the dimensions of depth and focus/breadth (Martin, 2002). According to Schein (1989) cultures are structured by three depth layers (Figure 7.2) reaching from the surface phenomenon artefacts (visible manifestations of culture such as actions, symbols, etc.), espoused values (conscious cognitive and behavioural patterns, expressed, for example, in management guidelines) to the pre-conscious basic cultural assumptions (concerning basic aspects of human life such as good and bad, the nature of fellow human beings).

Regarding the dimension of focus or breadth, multinational corporations are characterized by a variety of cultural segmentations, which reflect the complexity of the phenomenon as such and consequently also the problem of handling different overlaying cultural strata which influence interaction within the organization (Figure 7.3). In a macro perspective,

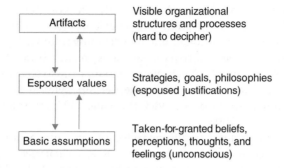

Figure 7.2: Culture model according to E. Schein
Source: *Schein,* (1989).

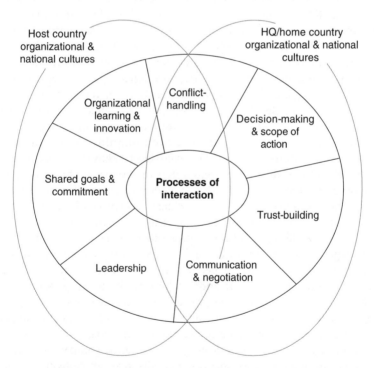

Figure 7.3: Culturally sensitive interaction processes in multinational organizations
Source: Dorow and Blazejewski, (2004).

national and regional cultures have an early effect on the formation of individual patterns of cognition and behaviour, especially through the education system and through imitative learning from family members or other relation groups. International management research has shown that these socio-cultural differences can amount to up to 60 percent of the variance of management values and leadership styles in international comparison (cf. Trompenaars, 1993; Hofstede, 1997, 2001; Reber *et al.*, 2000; House *et al.*, 2002).

A further important determining factor for social interaction in enterprises is the organizational culture, a field of research in its own right which has been developing since the beginning of the 1980s (Deal and Kennedy, 1982; Peters and Waterman, 1982; Smircich, 1983; Allaire and Firsirotu, 1984; Schein, 1989; Martin, 2002). Organizational cultures establish differences in the cognitive and behavioural patterns between enterprises in the same macro-cultural environment. Depending on their characteristics and distinctiveness (e.g., in respect to strength, flexibility, innovativeness), organizational cultures have long been perceived as key corporate success factors (Wilkins and Ouchi, 1983; Denison, 1990). At a macro level, cognitive and behavioural patterns arising from affiliation with different business sectors or professional groups are superimposed over national, regional and organizational cultures. Diversity research (Nkome and Cox, 1997; Sackmann, Bissels and Bissels, 2002) has predominantly been focused on cultural formation arising from religion, ethnic identity and gender, and has developed models for utilizing this cultural diversity productively within enterprises. At a micro level, below the level of organizational cultures, further differentiations materialize within the organization along the lines of division, function or scope of responsibility, hierarchical level or location of subsidiary, which can be described as subcultures. Subcultures, too, develop their own structures of cognitive schemes and action in continuous processes of social interaction, which with regard to other subcultures may behave complementarily or conflictingly. All these different perspectives on culture, from the macro perspective of national or regional culture to the micro-perspective of organizational subcultures overlay each other and are interdependent. In their entirety they constitute the cultural system, which eventually explains and determines the way people interact in multinational corporations.

In shifting the mindset in dealing with domestic companies to international organisations, the degree of complexity increases. Notwithstanding, cultural complexity and diversity increases simultaneously, alongside uncertainties in the external environments in which international companies and their subsidiaries operate. Such multinational organizations thus have to develop and implement efficient processes to deal with and perhaps reduce potential tensions and conflicts that might arise when two or more cultures within parent companies and their subsidiaries meet. In a broader context, organizations that operate at a global level need to consider issues such as trust (building and maintaining), transfer of knowledge, ideas and skills, decision-making processes, communication and negotiation processes, leadership styles and the notion of shared goals and objectives. These issues are important not just within the headquarters of the multinational organization, but also in their interactions with their subsidiaries and affiliates across continents and countries. For example, an organization that comes with an autocratic style of leadership and management would probably clash at all levels if it enters a culture that prefers or utilises a more participative leadership style. Conversely, if a new leader adopts a participative and consultative approach in an organization that is used to an autocratic management system, that new leader might even be ostracized as he/she might be viewed as someone who is unable to make decisions independently!

The main focus of our research is therefore on the cultural differences of types of interaction processes as outlined in Figure 7.3. The formulation and implementation of shared values and goals and the commitment to them by Japanese, German and American top managers, cultural differences of organizational learning and innovation, conflict handling, decision making and demand for scope of action, trust building, and communication and negotiation styles as well as leadership styles are core dimensions of cultural differences in the relationships between these managers. These core dimensions were identified during pilot studies in five multinational companies and reflect the main areas of cultural differences from the perspective of the interviewed management.

Referring to Figure 7.3, we observe that all our participating project companies pursue a strategy of balancing between the acceptance of diverging local cultures and the adaptation of diverging local cultures to the culture of the corporate centre (headquarters) The 'point of balance' is of course company specific and varies between a rather 'laissez-faire' style of accepting a high degree of cultural differences to a strong adaptation of subsidiaries' cultures to the culture of the headquarters. Our findings allow the assumption that these company-specific cultural points of balance have less to do with the product/market strategy and the structure of the company as it is often asserted (Bartlett and Ghoshal, 1989) but more with the intercultural experience of top management. Companies that have a homogeneous national board tend to transfer to a large degree their corporate-centre culture to the subsidiaries, while companies with a long tradition of forming culturally mixed boards strive for merging the cultures. This supports desired global synergies to attain transparent knowledge transfer processes, and the development of innovative learning between organizations. By effectively handling the various differences, management can support its international staff across borders, whether it is to adapt to local cultures, or to build an understanding and open communication between locals and the foreign employee.

In the following section we will present some data from our project regarding the assessment of Japanese, German and American top managers of their company's cultural profile of the dimensions 'shared goals and commitment', 'trust' and 'communication'.

Method

Sample and procedure

The project involved nine multinational organizations across the world, with headquarters and subsidiaries located in Germany, Switzerland, Japan and the United States. The research was conducted in two parts, qualitative in-depth interviews, and quantitative online questionnaires.

Between October 2003 and May 2004, a total of 189 (39 in Japan, 77 in Germany and Switzerland, and 73 in the United States) semi-structured interviews were conducted in German, English and Japanese at top-management level.[3] These lasted between 90 and 120 minutes.

A comprehensive, multi-part online questionnaire was developed and translated/back translated into German, English and Japanese. The final sample size consisted of 286 usable replies, a response rate of 64 percent.

The major reason for using interviews as well as surveys, as is typically the case, is that it allowed the researchers to have subject matter experts discuss the situation in an in-depth manner, rather than simply rely on the information provided by the respondents. Furthermore, it was that it was possible to ensure that the respondents understood what they were being asked, follow-up issues and check any inconsistencies in the information that was being provided. As Miles and Huberman (1994:1) write, qualitative data 'are a source of well-grounded, rich descriptions and explanations of processes in identifiable local contexts'.

As we are in the midst of analysing all of the data from all of the participating companies and subsidiaries, in this chapter, we present certain data and findings from one company (sample total: 66), a German multinational.

Development of questionnaire

To examine the effect of cultural diversity within the multinational companies, the authors interviewed managers and directors of several of the participating companies using a semi-structured approach. This allowed focus on topics of cultural diversity and interactions between parent companies and their subsidiaries. At the same time, this semi-structured style allowed the flexibility of following through on matters of concern and interest to participants. Interviews under taken at this pilot stage were designed so as to generate theories, adopting a broadly grounded theory approach (Glaser and Strauss, 1967). Increasingly, grounded theory methods have proved to be useful for the generation of categories warranting further investigation (Eisenhardt, 1989). Semi-structured interviewing has been recommended in situations where the participant is recognized as the expert on the subject (Smith, 1995).

By doing initial interviews as part of a pilot study, major themes began to emerge. Such themes have enabled more focused and efficient exploration to take place in subsequent phases. These dimensions have been grouped into the following within the questionnaire: shared goals and commitment (18 items); scope of action and decision-making autonomy (14 items); leadership (20 items); conflict handling (21 items); trust (10 items); knowledge management, innovation and flexibility (26 items); communication and negotiation (21 items). There was also a section on biographical and background information to enable a form of statistical control. In this section, each respondent was asked to indicate the organization they worked for; the location; corporate division and function; age; gender; nationality; native language; corporate language; education level; number of years with the global organization; type of contract; management level and managerial function.

Current data

As mentioned earlier, for the purpose of this chapter, we present selected data and findings from one company (sample total: 66), a German multinational. This is because at the time of going to press, the project had only recently ended and we had only then recently started data analysis.

Results

In this chapter, we present and analyse data from one company (sample size: 66). We also discuss only the following three dimensions from the questionnaire: Shared goals and commitment; trust; and communication and negotiation. All dimensions were measured by a 5-point Lickert scale from 1 to 5 (1 = strongly disagree, 2 = disagree, 3 = neither, 4 = agree, 5 = strongly agree).

Table 7.1: Summary of background details

		Frequency	Percentage (%)	Mean	Standard Deviation
Headquarters	Yes	18	27.3	1.64	0.572
	No	45	68.2		
	Not indicated	3	4.5		
Location	Germany	24	36.4	1.85	0.749
	Japan	28	42.4		
	US	14	21.2		
Nationality	German	23	34.8	2.11	1.204
	Japanese	27	40.9		
	American	9	13.6		
	Other	7	10.6		
Gender	Male	56	84.8	1.00	0.392
	Female	5	7.6		
	Not indicated	5	7.6		

Background details

In this sample of 66 respondents, 68.2 percent (45) were from the subsidiary companies and 27.3 percent (18) were from the corporate headquarters in Germany. Four point five percent (3) did not indicate where they were from. Of these, 36.4 percent (24) were located in Germany, 42.4 percent (28) were in Japan and 21.2 percent (14) were working in the United States. In terms of nationality, 34.8 percent (23) were Germans, 40.9 percent (27) were Japanese, 13.6 percent (9) were Americans and 10.6 percent (7) were of other nationalities. Just over 50 percent were senior management and above. See Table 7.1 for the summary. Within each location, there was a mix of both local and expatriate management.

Shared goals and commitment

Table 7.2 summarizes the means and standard deviations of the 'shared goals and commitment' dimension for this German multinational. The F value indicates the significant levels.

It can be seen that in this cultural dimension, in general and on the whole, it appears that Japanese employees of this multinational company do not agree as much as their German and American colleagues that 'there is a clear and consistent set of organizational values and norms that governs the way we do business in this organization', and that 'the organizational values and norms guiding our behaviour are predominantly local'. Although from the in-depth interviews conducted within this company and its subsidiaries, there was a general consensus

Table 7.2: Means and standard deviations of the 'shared goals and commitment' dimension (only selected significant findings are tabled)

Nationality	Q1	Q6	Q12[4]
German	3.86 (0.57)	2.24 (0.70)	3.24 (0.77)
Japanese	2.94 (0.87)	3.06 (0.64)	2.89 (0.76)
American	3.44 (1.01)	2.00 (0.76)	3.25 (0.71)
Other	3.40 (1.34)	2.40 (0.55)	1.80 (0.84)
F-value	3.78*	6.59***	5.22**

Note: $*p < 0.05$, $**p < 0.01$, $***p < 0.001$.
Number in bracket indicates standard deviations. Main number is the mean value.

that identification of Japanese employees with 'their' foreign company, which has traditionally been relatively low, is gradually improving, it was felt that the identification potential of 'belonging to' an international corporation in the consciousness of Japanese employees is nowhere near being fully exploited. Interestingly, there was a significant difference between the way the Japanese seemed to view cultural differences as compared to the Americans or the Germans. For Q12, the Germans and Americans felt that it was more important to tolerate and accept cultural differences than to strive for common values and norms for the entire global corporate group.

The reasons for this must be sought are in the deeper layers of the value system. From a Japanese point of view, quality and customer focus – basic values in Japanese business management – are not given enough weight by foreign corporations.

The difficult management task arising from this is to coordinate this (long-term) Japanese value preference with the (relatively short-term) economic preferences of the foreign management. Carrying out this conflict of values, which in many cases has not been fully articulated, will be one of the most important management tasks.

Trust

Table 7.3 summarizes the means and standard deviations of the 'trust' dimension for this German multinational. The F value indicates the significant levels.

'Trust' was seen as a particularly critical cultural variable in the interaction relationships between local and foreign executives. Within the 'trust' dimension, it was found that in general, the Japanese significantly did not feel that they could rely on their subordinates or superiors, as much as the Germans and Americans (cf. Qs 5, 10, 19). It was also found

Table 7.3:   Means and standard deviations of the 'trust' dimension (only selected significant findings are tabled)

Nationality	Q1	Q5	Q8	Q10	Q19[5]
German	3.13 (1.36)	3.39 (1.27)	2.57 (1.38)	3.52 (1.47)	3.74 (1.54)
Japanese	1.41 (1.50)	1.63 (1.64)	1.37 (1.45)	1.85 (1.90)	1.78 (1.81)
American	2.22 (1.86)	3.00 (1.80)	2.78 (1.72)	3.00 (1.94)	3.33 (2.00)
Other	1.86 (1.46)	2.50 (1.72)	1.57 (1.40)	2.86 (2.04)	2.43 (2.30)
F-value	5.57**	5.65**	3.90*	3.79*	5.33**

Note: $*p < 0.05$, $**p < 0.01$, $***p < 0.001$.
Number in bracket indicates standard deviations. Main number is the mean value.

that the Japanese preferred to have more formalized procedures within the organization, significantly more so than the Germans and the Americans. Shared basic values (e.g., employee and quality focus, long-term thinking) have facilitated the evolution of a culture of trust between European (specifically German) and Japanese executives. However, this trust relationship is at risk from stereotypes that have developed over the past two decades, partially based on short-term deployment practices. The heavily criticized increase in explicit, formal monitoring, which is interpreted as a policy of suspicion, should be reviewed by the parent companies with a view to building trust. Language barriers exacerbate the problem of intercultural trust building by obscuring the authenticity of the communication partner. Trust building is a long-term management task; its advantage lies in reduced monitoring expenses.

Communication and negotiation

Table 7.4 summarizes the means and standard deviations of the 'communication and negotiation' dimension for this German multinational. The F value indicates the significant levels.

Respondents see the intercultural problems in the 'communication and negotiation' dimension as the most difficult to solve. Within this cultural dimension, unlike the other two dimensions, this time it appears that the Germans are slightly different from the Japanese and American managers. The German managers of this company felt significantly that many communications problems within the organization between expatriates and local employees were due to different levels of abstract understanding, different issues at the core of the problem, and different methods and approaches to resolving problems. However, interestingly, there was a significant difference in the way the different nationalities viewed communication between expatriates and locals. The Germans followed by

Table 7.4: Means and standard deviations of the 'communication and negotiation' measure (only selected significant findings are tabled)

Nationality	Q6a	Q6f	Q9b	Q9f	Q19[6]
German	1.90 (0.70)	3.76 (0.54)	2.71 (0.72)	3.50 (0.76)	2.10 (0.70)
Japanese	2.77 (0.44)	3.08 (0.28)	3.57 (0.51)	3.14 (0.36)	3.07 (0.62)
American	2.14 (0.38)	3.71 (0.76)	2.29 (0.49)	3.86 (0.38)	2.43 (1.13)
Other	2.20 (1.10)	4.20 (0.45)	2.60 (0.55)	4.40 (0.55)	2.80 (0.84)
F-value	4.77**	7.66***	8.88***	6.30***	4.82**

Note: $*p < 0.05$, $**p < 0.01$, $***p < 0.001$.
Number in bracket indicates standard deviations. Main number is the mean value.

the Americans and the Japanese felt that face-to-face communication was one of the main ways foreigners communicated with the locals and vice-versa. Also, the Germans were more in agreement than the Japanese and the Americans that negotiation styles were different between the parent company and their subsidiaries. This might be because this is a German organisation and their headquarters is in Germany.

With regards to the Japanese as a culture, permanently anchored basic Japanese values regarding communication style stand in stark contrast to modern trends in formalized communication. The cultural variable-ness of forms of communication bears considerable risks of economic inefficiency, based on the high probability that information will be distorted. As personal communication is increasingly replaced by more formal modes of information exchange (forms, management by e-mail), information is more and more likely to be distorted (through misunderstandings based on language, stereotypes, prejudice) as perceived by the general lack of 'politeness' (from the questionnaires). These distortions are difficult to counteract without personal contact. From the in-depth interviews, a decline in personal, direct contact was very frequently criticized.

It is suggested that there should be a creation of a dialogue or a forum that takes into account Asian communication expectations and styles. This would be a significant contribution to effective intercultural management.

Discussion and further research

This research, supported by the Bertelsmann Foundation, is interested in the interaction between different cultures within the corporate system of multinational companies. In looking at the dimensions of interaction, we are interested in analysing, first, the role of culture in the interaction of these companies within and between the subsidiaries and themselves; and, second, what instruments are effective and useful in integrating the diverse cultures within and between these organizations across borders.

In this chapter, we have looked at a German organization's empirical evidence, across headquarters (in Germany) and at two subsidiary locations (Japan and North America). We looked at three cultural dimensions of shared goals and commitment, communication and negotiation, and trust.

From the findings and in-depth interviews carried out with the top management of this multinational organization, it was found that the Japanese employees of this German company did not agree as much as their German and American counterparts that there were clear organizational goals and values that were transferable from the headquarters to the local subsidiaries. This implies that the Japanese employees feel somewhat that the goals, values and norms that govern them at the Japanese subsidiary do not reflect or are not similar to those held by the headquarters company. The in-depth interviews revealed that although the identification of Japanese employees with their 'foreign'-owned company is gradually improving, it was felt that there was a lot more scope and work that can be done to further accelerate the process of belongingness and identity.

In terms of trust, again perhaps related to the identity issue of Japanese employees within this German firm, the Japanese significantly did not feel that they could rely on or trust their subordinates or superiors, as much as the German and American counterparts. This could be related to the fact that the Japanese preferred a more formalized procedure within the organization, and where this is lacking, it is felt that trust cannot be built.

Within the 'communication and negotiation' dimension, it was identified that the German employees felt (more so than the Japanese or the American colleagues) that many communication problems within expatriates and local employees were due to different understanding of the core problems, different levels of abstract understanding of the problem and different methods and approaches to resolving problems. This can be related to the amount of knowledge sharing that goes on within the companies. If the group of employees tasked to understand and solve the problems have different levels of access or different information sources, then it would lead predictably to different understanding of the core issues. Clearly then, knowledge, learning and information sharing at this point has to be addressed.

One suggestion that has emerged from the questionnaire data and interviews conducted is that perhaps multinational organizations need to consider a different perspective when dealing with employees from a different culture. For example, we might want to consider the Eastern/Asian perspective as opposed to the Western perspective when considering human resource policies, communication, trust and negotiation between employees from different cultures. Miles and Snow (1978), Weick (1985) and Brown (1998) all recognized the close link between culture and strategy and see this link as inevitable, and indeed a crucial element of an organization's success. They argue that the culture of an organisation will determine key strategic elements, including how the environment is perceived and interpreted, how information is analysed and how the main players react. Bartlett, Ghoshal and Birkinshaw (2003:vi) write that in differentiating between domestic companies and multinationals, although within-country local variations exist (in terms of social, political and economic contexts), 'they are nowhere near as diverse or as conflicting as the differences in demands and pressures the MNC faces in its multiple host countries'.

Within this particular company and its subsidiaries, it was decided that the headquarters and their subsidiaries would have a high degree of autonomy, decentralization and delegation. Among other things, this would allow for greater flexibility in local adaptation of products, greater creativity and autonomy. However, this might have led to different perceptions in the transferability of shared values and goals across the organization.

Increasing economic efficiency requires intensive efforts to formulate transparent goals for corporate cultural development, as well as sensitive, communicative management to reach these goals. The goals of cultural change cannot be achieved to the desired extent without intensifying personal exchange. In doing so, the companies in the group must solve various dilemmas of shaping corporate culture. On the one hand, there is the goal of reducing the complexity of intercultural management relationships to accelerate processes. And on the other hand, the goal of keeping information and decision-making processes open for creativity and ideas from a great number of employees from different cultures – whose integration prolongs the process. Another dilemma to be solved is that of general cost cuts caused by global competition on the one hand, and necessary investments in ensuring the progress of international corporations through cost-intensive programmes for developing 'global managers' on the other. Ultimately, striking a balance between cultural differentiation and cultural integration will contribute to reducing and resolving these dilemmas. Schneider and Barsoux (2003b:154) write that in 'examining the degree to which organisations have centralized power, specialized jobs and roles, and formalized rules and procedures, we find distinct patterns of organizing which prevail despite pressures for convergence'.

There are several limitations within this chapter. Clearly this only discusses a selected section of the data from one company, even though the project involved at least nine organizations and their subsidiaries. In the future, more analyses and results will be presented and there will be a more in-depth and clearer understandings of the cultural dimensions at work in multinational organizations. We hope to be able to have the elaborated results in the second half of the year. We also intend to further analyse the kinds of instruments that these organizations utilize and investigate which are more pertinent and effective.

Future papers will investigate the differences within the other nine organizations that participated in this project. We will also compare them, in terms of nationality of employees, and type of industry the organizations' main functions are. With the knowledge gained from this project across borders, multinational companies will be in a better position to exploit the resources that they currently have (in their multinational employees) and through the existence of globally affiliated heterogeneous organizational cultures and subcultures, positively influence the innovation potential of the enterprise as a whole, with effective transcultural communication and knowledge-sharing processes in place.

In developing appropriate instruments that can measure and integrate diverse cultures, far from making all cultures into one global culture, we can help understand better the advantages of each culture. In understanding the diverse cultures of the world, it is the hope that a better utilisation of the already existing functions of these multinationals can be done to foster cultural integration and understanding, and the development of common values and principles among all employees.

Notes

1. Members of the research group are besides the authors of this article, Dr Susanne Blazejewski, European University, Frankfurt/Oder; Prof. Dr Gerhard Reber, Johannes Kepler University Linz, Linz; Prof. Dr Yoshiaki Takahashi, Chuo-University, Tokyo; Prof. Dr Masaru Sakuma, Chuo-University, Tokyo; Prof. Karen Walch, PhD, Thunderbird, The American Graduate School of International Management, Phoenix. Project Manager of Bertelsmann Foundation is Simone Lippisch.
2. These were labelled power-distance, uncertainty avoidance, individualism collectivism, masculinity-femininity and long-term-short-term orientation.
3. The interviewees included people who held positions such as CEO, president, country manager, vice-president, HR-director, divisional manager, marketing manager and operations manager.

4. Q1: There is a clear and consistent set of organizational values and norms that governs the way we do business in this organization; Q6: The values and norms of the global corporate group are hardly applicable to the local situation of this organization; Q12: For this organization, it is more important to tolerate and accept cultural differences than to strive for common values and norms for the entire global corporate group.
5. Q1: In this organization, written directives and formal control procedures between superiors and subordinates are of minor importance. Q5: In this organization, subordinates and superiors can rely on each other. Q8: Cultural distance has a negative impact on the development of trust between the parent company and its subsidiaries. Q10: In this organization, I can trust my superior because I can rely on his/her competences and skills. Q19: In this organization, I can generally trust my subordinates because I can rely on their competences and skills.
6. Q6a: In this organization, communication between expatriates/foreigners and locals is mainly characterized by a high degree of fomalization; Q6f: In this organization, communication between expatriates/foreigners and locals is mainly characterised by a high degree of politeness; Q9b: Communication between the parent company and its subsidiaries is mainly characterized by speed and efficiency; Q9f: Communication between the parent company and its subsidiaries is mainly characterized by politeness; Q19: A compromise as a negotiation outcome reflects weak power bases and inefficient negotiation strategies.

References

Allaire, Y. and M.E. Firsirotu (1984) 'Theories of organizational culture', *Organization Studies*, 5/3.

Bartlett, C.A and S. Goshal (1989) *Managing across Borders: The Transnational Solution* (Boston, MA: Harvard Business School Press).

Bartlett, C.A., S. Ghoshal and J. Birkinshaw (2003) *Transnational Management: Text, Cases and Readings in Cross-Border Management* (Boston: McGraw-Hill).

Black, J.S., H.B. Gregersen and M.E. Mendenhall (1992) *Global Assignments: Successfully Expatriating and Repatriating International Manager* (San Francisco: Jossey-Bass).

Brewster, C. (1991) *The Management of Expatriates* (London: Kogan Page).

Brown, A. (1998) *Organisational Culture* (2nd edn, London: Financial Times Pitman).

Buono, A. and J. Bowditch (1989) *The Human Side of Mergers and Acquisitions* (San Francisco: Jossey-Bass).

Cray, D and G.R. Mallory, G.R. (1998) *Making Sense of Managing Culture* (London: International Thompson Business Press).

Deal, T.E. and A.A. Kennedy (1982) *Corporate Cultures: The Rites and Rituals of Corporate Life* (Reading: Addison-Wesley).

Denison, D.R. (1990) *Corporate Culture and Effectiveness* (New York: Wiley).

Dorfman, P.W. and J.P. Howell (1988) 'Dimensions of national culture and effective leadership patterns: Hofstede revisited', *Advances in International Comparative Management* 3, 127–50.

Dorow, W. and S. Blazejewski (2004) 'Global Corporate Cultures: Management between Cultural Diversity and Cultural Integration', in Bertelsmann Foundation (ed.), *In a Cultural Forum. Corporate Cultures in Global Interaction*, (Bertelsmann Foundation: Guetersloh), pp. 12–29.

Eisenhardt, K.M. (1989) 'Building theories from case study research', *Academy of Management Review* 14, 532–50.

Ettlinger, N. (2003) 'Cultural economic geography and a relational and micro-space approach to trusts, rationalities, networks, and change in collaborative workplaces', *Journal of Economic Geography* 3, 145–71.

Glaser, S., and A.L. Strauss (1967) *The Discovery of Grounded Theory: Strategies for Qualitative Research* (Chicago, IL: Aldine).

Goodstein, L.D. (1981) 'American business values and cultural imperialism', *Organisational Dynamics* 10(1), 49–54.

Hampden-Turner, C. and F. Trompenaars (1993) *The Seven Cultures of Capitalism: Value systems for creating wealth in the United States, Britain, Japan, Germany, France, Sweden, and the Netherlands* (New York: Doubleday).

Hendry, C. (1994) *Human Resource Strategies for International Growth* (London: Routledge).

Hofstede, G.H. (1980) *Culture's Consequences: International Differences in Work-related Values* (London: Sage).

Hofstede, G.H. (1994) *Cultures and Organisations: Intercultural Cooperation and its Importance for Survival* (London: McGraw-Hill).

Hofstede, G.H. (1997) *Cultures and Organizations. Software of the Mind* (New York: McGraw-Hill).

Hofstede, G.H. (2001) *Cultures Consequences: Comparing Values, Behaviors, Institutions and Organizations Across Nations* (Thousand Oaks, CA: Sage).

House, R.J., P.J. Hanges, M. Javidan, P.W. Dorfman, V. Gupta and Globe Associates (eds) (2002) *Cultures, Leadership, and Organizations: Globe: a 62 Nation Study Vol. 1* (Thousand Oaks, CA: Sage).

Hunt, J.W. (1981) 'Applying American behavioural science: some cross-cultural problems', *Organisational Dynamics* 10(1), 55–62.

Martin, J. (2002) *Organizational Culture: Mapping the Terrain* (Thousand Oaks, CA: Sage).

Mattson, L.-G. (2003) 'Reorganisation of distribution in globalisation of markets: the dynamic context of supply chain management', *Supply Chain Management: An International Journal* 8(5), 416–26.

Miles, M.B. and A.M. Huberman (1994) *Qualitative Data Analysis: An expanded Sourcebook* (2nd edn, Thousand Oaks, CA: Sage).

Miles, R.E. and C.C. Snow (1978) *Organisational Strategy, Structure and Process* (London: McGraw-Hill).

Nkome, S.M. and T. Cox (1997) 'Diverse Identities in Organizations', in S.R. Clegg, C. Hardy and W.R. Nord (eds), *Handbook of Organization Studies* (Thousand Oaks, CA: Sage).

Peters, T.J. and R.H. Waterman (1982) *In Search of Excellence* (Reading: Addison-Wesley).

Reber, G., A.G. Jago, W. Auer-Rizzi and E. Szabo (2000) 'Führungsstile in sieben Ländern Europas – Ein interkultureller Vergleich', in E. Regnet and L.M. Hofmann (eds), *Personalmanagement in Europa* (Göttingen: Verlag für Angewandte Psychologie).

Robertson, C.J. and W.F. Crittenden (2003) 'Mapping moral philosophies: strategic implications for multinational firms', *Strategic Management Journal* 24, 385–92.

Robinson, R.V. (1983) 'Geert Hofstede: cultures' consequences: international differences in work-related values', *Work and Occupations* 10, 110–15.
Sackmann, S.A., S. Bissels and T. Bissels (2002) 'Kulturelle vielfalt in organisationen: Ansätze zum Umgang mit einem vernachlässigten Thema der Organisationswissenschaften', *Die Betriebswirtschaft* 62(1).
Sanchez, J., P. Spector and C. Cooper (2000) 'Adapting to a boundaryless world: a developmental expatriate model', *Academy of Management Executive* 14(2), 96–106.
Schein, E.H. (1989) *Organizational Culture and Leadership* (San Francisco: Jossey-Bass).
Schein, E.H. (1990) 'Organizational Culture', *American Psychologist* 45(2), 109–19.
Schneider, S.C. and J.-L. Barsoux (2003a) *Managing Across Cultures* (2nd Edn, Harlow: Financial Times Prentice Hall).
Schneider, S.C. and J.-L. Barsoux (2003b) 'Culture and Organization', in C.A. Bartlett, S. Ghoshal and J. Birkinshaw (eds) (2003) *Transnational Management: Text, Cases and Readings in Cross-Border Management* (Boston: McGraw-Hill).
Smircich, L. (1983) 'Concepts of culture and organizational analysis', *Administrative Science Quarterly* 28.
Smith, J.A. (1995) 'Semi-structured Interviewing and Qualitative Analysis', in J.A. Smith, R. Harre and L. van Langenhove (eds), *Rethinking Methods in Psychology* (London: Sage).
Sondergaard, M. (1994) 'Research note: Hofstede's consequences: a study of reviews, citations and replications', *Organisational Studies* 15, 447–56.
Stiglitz, J.E. (2003) *Globalization and its Discontents*. New York: W.W. Norton & Company).
Sudersanam, P.S. (1995) *The Essence of Mergers and Acquisitions* (London: Prentice Hall).
Tayeb, M. (1988) *Organisations and National Culture* (London: Sage).
Trompenaars, F. (1993) *Riding the Waves of Culture: Understanding Cultural Diversity in Business* (London: Economist Books).
UNCTAD (2002) *World Investment Report: Transnational Corporations and Export Competitiveness* (Geneva: UNCTAD).
Weaver, G.R. (2001) 'Ethics programs in global businesses: culture's role in managing ethics', *Journal of Business Ethics* 30, 3–15.
Weick, K.P. (1985) 'The Significance of Corporate Culture', in P. Frost, L.F. Moore, M.R. Louis, C.C. Lundberg and J. Martins (eds), *Organisational Culture* (CA: Sage), pp. 381–90.
Wilkins, A. and W. Ouchi (1983) 'Efficient cultures: exploring the relationship between culture and organizational performance', *Administrative Science Quarterly* 28.

8

An Empirical Study of Trust, Commitment, Relationship Quality, and Behavioural Consequences for International Tourist Hotels in Taiwan[1]

Che-Jen Su and Cheng-Chien Wang

Introduction

The international tourist hotel industry in Taiwan has been receiving more attention in recent years. According to Tourism Bureau's formal release, the average ratio of occupation in international tourist hotels dropped from 61.62 percent in 2002 to 57.43 percent in 2003. In such highly competitive circumstances, the problem of maintaining customer loyalty has become a critical and strategic issue for practitioners. Previous research advocated attracting, maintaining, and enhancing customer relationships in order to address a problem like this (cf. Berry, 1983). Recently, the focus has been put on a series of transactions which build an awareness of a shared relationship through trust and commitment, among other factors (Morgan and Hunt, 1994).

What interested us most was that past discussions concerning the causality of related constructs were confusing. For example, Garbarino and Johnson (1999) found that overall satisfaction had a direct effect on future intentions for low relational customers who are less involved with personal relationships and anticipation or obligation of future exchanges (Dwyer *et al.*, 1987). For high relational customers, however, it was trust and commitment that directly impacted future intentions rather than satisfaction. Hennig-Thurau *et al.* (2002) found that satisfaction may have a positive impact on commitment. Wong and Sohal's (2002) findings, in contrast, implied the reverse relationship. Moreover, rarely has previous research examined overall associations among trust, commitment, relationship quality, and behavioral consequences. These unknown associations stimulated the authors to clarify or to confirm these connections in the hotel industry.

In the present study, we attempt to examine the roles of trust and commitment on the employee level and tourist hotel level in forming retail relationship quality between hotel employees and guests, and their indirect effects on the customer's behavioral consequences. Following previous research, we integrate these constructs into a model and simultaneously discuss these linkages in the setting of international tourist hotels through analysing data collected in Taiwan.

Background and model development

Relationship quality refers to an overall assessment of the strength of a relationship and the extent to which it meets the needs and expectations of the parties based on a history of successful or unsuccessful encounters or events (Crosby *et al.*, 1990). From a buyer's viewpoint, it is a customer's perceptions of how well the whole relationship fulfils expectations, predictions, goals and desires the customer has concerning the whole relationship (cf. Jarvelin and Lehtinen, 1996). Literature review reached no consensus on the dimensions of relationshp quality, but suggested that they generally include trust (e.g., Crosby *et al.*, 1990; Smith, 1998; Kim and Cha, 2002), commitment (e.g., Smith, 1998), and customer satisfaction (e.g., Crosby *et al.*, 1990; Smith, 1998; Kim and Cha, 2002). Some other researchers, such as Wong and Sohal (2002) in recent studies suggested that trust and comittment are not part of, but are antecedents to relationship quality. Their findings provide empirical support for the proposed model. Unfortunately, Wong and Sohal's contribution failed to explain the impact of relationship quality.

This chapter mainly integrated Wong and Sohal's model with related literature to design an empirical study for the international tourist hotel industry in Taiwan. As shown in Figure 8.1, implicit in our hypotheses is the belief that relationship quality is explained by trust and commitment on the employee level and the hotel level (cf. Wong and Sohal, 2002). While relationship quality simultaneously affects three constructs of behavioral consequence, namely, relationship continuity, word of mouth, and share of purchases (cf. Kim and Cha, 2002).

Our model attempts to solve the problem of controversial roles in customer's satisfaction, trust, and commitment proposed by Garbarino and Johnson (1999). A future-oriented relationship continuity was introduced into the framework causing relationship quality to be the mediator, thus providing a more comprehensive and balanced way of explaining these cause–effect relationships.

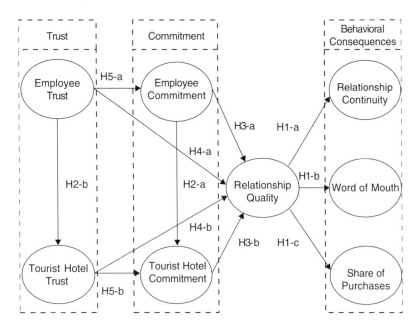

Figure 8.1:   Structural model of relationship quality for tourist hotels

In Wong and Sohal's (2002) study, relationship quality was operationally defined as the overall assessment of the quality of respondents'
relationship with the contact employee and with the company. Their
consideration only met the nature of relationship quality. However, this
abstract construct was supposed to be measured through multi-items
which are more observable rather than using a single-item scale. As we
noted previously, customer satisfaction was one of the well accepted
components of relationship quality (e.g., Crosby *et al.*, 1990; Smith, 1998;
Kim and Cha, 2002). Additionally, past research on industries of hospitality found that customer satisfaction or satisfaction-centered relationship quality is positively related to word of mouth (e.g., Knutson, 1988;
Oh, 1999; Kim *et al.*, 2001; Kim and Cha, 2002), repurchase intention or
relationship continuity (e.g., Oh, 1999; Choi and Chu, 2001; Kim *et al.*,
2001; Kim and Cha, 2002), and additional purchases of products or services (e.g., Kim and Cha, 2002). Based on the above arguments, the following hypotheses related to relationship quality are proposed:

H1-a: Relationship quality will be positively related to relationship
       continuity.
H1-b: Relationship quality will be positively related to word of mouth.
H1-c: Relationship quality will be positively related to share of purchases.

Commitment is defined as an enduring desire to maintain a valued relationship, while trust refers to a willingness to rely on an exchange partner in whom one has confidence (Moorman *et al.*, 1992). Based on the concept of two levels of relationships proposed by Iacobucci and Ostrom (1996), researchers have speculated and confirmed that customer trust in and commitment to the salesperson can be transferred to the firm or the store (cf. Foster and Cadogan, 2000; Wong and Sohal, 2002). For our research purpose of the tourist hotel industry, we hypothesize as with past findings:

H2-a: A customer's commitment to the employee will be positively related to his/her commitment to the tourist hotel.
H2-b: A customer's trust in the employee will be positively related to his/her trust in the tourist hotel.

Wong and Sohal (2002) reviewed the literature and summarized that customers with a high level of commitment or obligation believe that they receive more value from a relationship (cf. Moorman *et al.*, 1992), and thus are willing to make it mutually satisfying (cf. Morgan and Hunt, 1994). Hypotheses stating the positive effect of commitment on relationship quality in Wong and Sohal's model were supported by their findings. Hence, we advance the following hypotheses:

H3-a: A customer's commitment to the employee will be positively related to relationship quality.
H3-b: A customer's commitment to the tourist hotel will be positively related to relationship quality.

Wong and Sohal (2002) argued that trusting relationships between customers, salesperson, and the stores are associated with positive overall outcomes in the retail context. Customers would expect a positive outcome from a reliable partner (cf. Morgan and Hunt, 1994). Especially in service industries, the transaction process should be more risky. Therefore, the customer's trust in service providers or hotels was likely to enhance the benefits or the positive outcomes from their shopping experience in hotels. Wong and Sohal's findings supported the existence of the causality between trust and relationship quality. Accordingly, we hypothesize:

H4-a: A customer's trust in the employee will be positively related to relationship quality.
H4-b: A customer's trust in the tourist hotel will be positively related to relationship quality.

Trusting relationships could be so highly valued that customers will desire to commit themselves to such linkages (cf. Hrebiniak, 1974; Wong and Sohal, 2002). The positive effect of trust on commitment has been generally supported by related research (cf. Morgan and Hunt, 1994; Garbarino and Johnson, 1999; Wong and Sohal, 2002). Hence, the hypotheses appear reasonable for our empirical model:

H5-a: A customer's trust in the employee will be positively related to employee commitment.

H5-b: A customer's trust in the tourist hotel will be positively related to tourist hotel commitment.

Methodology

Sample and data collection procedures

Data on frequent purchases were collected from a sample of the members of the Junior Chamber International, Taiwan and the Rotary International, Taiwan. Most of the potential informants were business tourists and from several dozen firms and non-profit organizations in various sectors. They were asked to choose one international tourist hotel in Taiwan where they had used services most frequently within the past 18 months. These cases meet either of the following minimum criteria: (1) Seven nights in one stay or two stays, (2) Having meals four times in the restaurant, (3) Attending conventions or banquets three times, or (4) Using other services five times. This ensured that they were actively involved in forming relationships with international tourist hotels and their employees, and are thus more likely to be knowledgeable about the information needed.

A total of 750 survey questionnaire packets with personalized letters requesting their participation were mailed to potential informants on the list. The final dataset consisted of 182 usable responses, yielding a 24.3 percent response rate. The estimation procedure of AMOS 4.0 applied here was maximum likelihood estimation (MLE), and the sample size approximated a 'critical sample size' of 200 (Hoelter, 1983). Most of the respondents were males (51.7 percent), college graduates (66.9 percent), 26–30 years old (29.7 percent), and working in service industries (36.5 percent).

Operational measures

The measure of trust and commitment at the employee level (eight items and four items respectively) and tourist hotel level (three items and five items respectively) was suggested by Wong and Sohal (2002) with minor adaptations to conform to the tourist hotel industry context. Combined scales for relationship quality (three items for employee level

Table 8.1:   Summary of item purification

Construct	No. of final item (No. of initial item)	% of variance accounted for	% of accumulated variance accounted for
Employee trust	3 (8)	57.78	57.78
Tourist hotel trust	2 (3)	65.47	65.47
Employee commitment	2 (4)	84.74	84.74
Tourist hotel commitment	2 (5)	85.65	85.65
Relationship quality	3 (7)	68.13	68.13
Behavioural consequences			
Relationship continuity	3 (3)	60.18*	60.18
Word of mouth	1 (2)	14.71	74.89
Share of purchases	1 (2)	11.13	86.12

Note: *based on the repeated principal component analysis.

and four items for tourist hotel level) were developed with reference to the idea of some previous research (cf. Hennig-Thurau *et al.*, 2002; Kim and Cha, 2002). As for the measure of the customer's behavioural consequences, including relationship continuity (three items), word-of-mouth (two items), and share of purchases (two items), we used the scales proposed by Kim and Cha (2002) based on Crosby *et al.* (1990) study.

Informants were asked to report how they perceived their interaction and satisfaction with the specified hotel and their employee(s), and their consequent intention during the past eighteen months on a 5-point scale ranging from (1) 'strongly disagree' to (5) 'strongly agree'.

Development and validation of measures

After the process of a formal survey, we deleted items from their respective scales if doing so increased the reliability of the scale. The final values of Cronbach alpha range from 0.60 to 0.92. Next, we utilized a factor analysis with Promax rotation (due to expected inter-correlations between factors) to purify the remaining items. For employee trust, tourist hotel trust, employee commitment, tourist hotel commitment, and relationship quality, we analysed each construct respectively to find and to eliminate items that failed to load most strongly (below 0.60) on the factor with the highest eigenvalue and weakly on other factors. The factor structure for the consequence items was examined and two items were found to load on the wrong factor or to load on more than one factor. After deleting these items, the remaining five items were reanalysed. The structure matrix did not show mixed loadings and all items loaded strongly on their intended factors.

The reduced set of 17 items was then submitted to a principal component analysis with Promax rotation, setting the number of factors to eight. The findings indicated that all of the eigenvalues were accounted for 83.93 percent of the varience. Furthermore, all the standardized factor loadings were positive and high (>0.70) on the appropriate dimensions to demonstrate convergent validity and weak on other factors to meet the requirements of discriminant validity (Venkatesh *et al.*, 1995). Table 8.1 summarizes the results of item purification. In sum, the evidence suggested that our scale of measurement had adequate properties.

Analysis and findings

Model estimation and fit

Hair *et al.* (1998) suggested that the more preferable minimum ratio of sample size to estimated parameter is 10 for structural equation modelling. Our maintained model contained 28 path parameters to be estimated based on initial measures. The ideal sample size should be 280. Applying a single-indicator approach, the proposed model consisting of 11 path estimates was analysed with a sample of 182, resulting in a ratio of 16.5, which exceeded the recommended ratio of 10. In order to develop single indicators for our model, the items of each construct were submitted to a principal component analysis to form a single indicator respectively. As seen in Table 8.2, the leading factor emerged with an eigenvalue higher than 1.0 and a reliability value above the critical value of 0.7 (cf. Nunnally, 1978) for each multi-item construct with all factor loadings being noticeably high. The adjustment utilized for measurement error and the path from the construct to the indicator was suggested by Sörbom and Jöreskog (1982).

Based on Figure 8.1, we transform the hypothesized model into a path diagram that is tested in this study, as presented in Figure 8.2.

As presented in Table 8.3, the *chi*-square was 13.89 ($df = 10$, $p = 0.178$), and other values of the measures were: (1) GFI, AGFI, NFI, CFI, IFI, and RFI > 0.9, (2) RMR and RMSEA < 0.05. The fit statistics for the proposed model indicated that an ideal match between the model and the data structure was found acceptable.

Hypotheses testing

The relative effects of the individual factors in the model were analysed after model estimation. We applied one-tailed tests of significance to determine the significance of each cause–effect relationship. Table 8.4 provides the structural parameter estimates (standardized path coefficients) of the

Table 8.2:   Items of single indicators

Single indicators and the items	Eigenvalue	Factor loading	% of variance
Employee trust (α = 0.84)	2.27		75.49
1. Hotel employees can be trusted at all times.		0.87	
2. Hotel employees have high integrity.		0.87	
3. Hotel employees are honest.		0.86	
Tourist hotel trust (α = 0.72)	1.56		77.83
1. Tourist hotel understands the customer.		0.88	
2. Tourist hotel can be trusted at all times.		0.88	
Employee commitment (α = 0.82)	1.70		84.74
1. Plan to maintain relationship with hotel employees.		0.92	
2. Care about relationship with hotel employees.		0.92	
Tourist hotel commitment (α = 0.83)	1.71		85.65
1. Commitment to the tourist hotel.		0.93	
2. Intention to continue consuming at the tourist hotel.		0.93	
Relationship quality (α = 0.87)	2.40		79.86
1. I think a service provider is favorable.		0.88	
2. I am pleased with a hotel employee.		0.90	
3. I am satisfied with hotel employees.		0.90	
Relationship continuity (α = 0.85)	2.29		76.38
1. I believe a hotel employee will provide better service in the future.		0.85	
2. I will continue the relationship with this hotel.		0.89	
3. I will visit this hotel again in the future.		0.88	
Word of mouth	NA		NA
1. I want to tell other people good things about this hotel.		NA	
Share of purchases	NA		NA
1. I use other hotel services such F&B outlets and catering.		NA	

Notes: N = 182; Missing observations are omitted while conducting analysis;
Format: 5-point scale ranging from (1) 'strongly disagree' to (5) 'strongly agree';
NA = not applicable.

hypothesized model. Results support all the hypotheses at the 0.01 level of significance, except for H3-a regarding the positive impact of employee commitment on relationship quality ($t = -1.38$, $p > 0.10$) and H4-b stating the relationship between tourist hotel trust and relationship quality

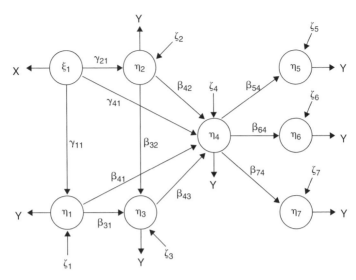

Figure 8.2:   Path diagram of proposed model

Table 8.3:   Overall fit measures of the SEM

Statistic	Acceptable level	Value
Absolute fit measures		
Probability for the chi-square statistic (chi-square = 13.89, df = 10)	>0.05	0.178
Goodness of fit index (GFI)	>0.90	0.981
Root mean square residual (RMR)	<0.05	0.027
Root mean square error of approximation (RMSEA)	<0.08	0.046
Incremental fit measures		
Adjusted goodness of fit index (AGFI)	>0.90	0.932
Normed fit index (NFI)	>0.90	0.980
Comparative fit index (CFI)	>0.90	0.994
Incremental fit index (IFI)	>0.90	0.994
Relative fit index (RFI)	>0.90	0.943

($t = 0.04$, $p > 0.10$). Thus, a customer's plan to maintain or caring about relationship with hotel employees and his or her belief that the hotel is trustworthy appear not to be related to his or her overall assessment of the relationship quality with the contact employee.

As hypothesized in H5-a, H2-b, and H4-a, positive speculations relating employee trust to employee commitment, tourist hotel trust, and relationship quality are supported by our findings when the significant level

Table 8.4: Estimated effects within the SEM

Hypothesis	Parameter	Standardized path coefficient	t-value	Empirical support
H1-a(+)	Relationship quality → relationship continuity	$\beta_{54} = 0.93$	11.90***	Yes
H1-b(+)	Relationship quality →word of mouth	$\beta_{64} = 0.53$	7.43***	Yes
H1-c(+)	Relationship quality →share of purchases	$\beta_{74} = 0.52$	7.38***	Yes
H2-a(+)	Employee commitment → tourist hotel commitment	$\beta_{32} = 0.25$	3.47***	Yes
H2-b(+)	Employee trust →tourist hotel trust	$\gamma_{11} = 0.74$	11.88***	Yes
H3-a(+)	Employee commitment → relationship quality	$\beta_{42} = -0.11$	−1.38	No
H3-b(+)	Tourist hotel commitment → relationship quality	$\beta_{43} = 0.86$	5.43***	Yes
H4-a(+)	Employee trust →relationship quality	$\gamma_{41} = 0.29$	3.28***	Yes
H4-b(+)	Tourist hotel trust →relationship quality	$\beta_{41} = 0.01$	0.04	No
H5-a(+)	Employee trust →employee commitment	$\gamma_{21} = 0.45$	5.98***	Yes
H5-b(+)	Tourist hotel trust →tourist hotel commitment	$\beta_{31} = 0.52$	7.20***	Yes

*: $P < 0.10$(one tailed), **: $P < 0.05$(one tailed), ***: $P < 0.01$(one tailed).

is $0.01(\gamma_{21} = 0.45; \gamma_{11} = 0.74; \gamma_{41} = 0.29$, respectively). Once a customer believes that the employees who provided him or her service are honest and trustworthy, this belief would reinforce his or her desire to maintain a relationship with the hotel employees, a willingness to rely on the hotel he or she consumed at, and pleasure or satisfaction with hotel employees. Furthermore, the intervening role of tourist hotel commitment connecting tourist hotel trust (H5-b) and relationship quality (H3-b) is strongly confirmed ($\beta_{32} = 0.52$; $\beta_{43} = 0.86$), while employee commitment is significantly and positively related to tourist hotel commitment (β_{32} of H2-a = 0.24). This, thus, also verifies the latter's mediating function between employee commitment and relationship quality.

Consistent with H1, the positive effect of quality relationship on behavioural consequences is highly supported by the current data. Relationship quality appears to substantially increase relationship continuity (β_{54} of H1-a = 0.93), word of mouth (β_{64} of H1-b = 0.53), and share of purchases

(β_{74} of H1-c = 0.52). If a customer has been satisfied with the service provider(s), he or she would possibly revisit this hotel in the future to continue this relationship, share favourable information about the hotel with other people, and use other hotel services.

To summarize, in general, the estimated model can explain the dynamics of relationship quality speculated in our model for tourist hotel industry.

Based upon their findings, Wong and Sohal conclude that interpersonal relationships are more essential than individual-to-firm relationships in predicting overall relationship quality. This approach failed to discuss the comprehensive effects in all possible paths and thus should be explained with care. To analyse the whole picture of the findings, the indirect and total impacts of each latent variable on behavioural consequences are included in Table 8.5. We note that tourist hotel commitment appears to play a key role in increasing all behavioral consequences due to strong and statistically significant total effects (0.80 on relationship continuity; 0.45 on word of mouth; 0.46 on share of purchase, respectively). In contrast, the total effects of employee trust, hotel trust, and employee commitment fail to receive full empirical support and are thus more questionable. In addition, relationship quality has been the intervening core connecting the trust-commitment linkages and behavioural consequences in our framework and results prove its prominent direct effect on all consequences. It is crucial to examine the relative effects of trust and commitment on relationship quality. As is indicated in the right column of Table 8.5, tourist hotel commitment also has a more positive impact on the forming of relationship quality than the other antecedents.

Discussion and implications

The authors have attempted to extend Wong and Sohal's model by introducing behavioural consequences derived from literature review. We not only investigated how trust and commitment on the service provider level and the hotel level influence relationship quality directly and indirectly, but also how relationship quality reinforces relationship continuity, word of mouth, and share of purchases. That is, this study expands the knowledge of relationship quality's mediating role in the process of improving behavioural consequences of relational customers in the international tourist hotel industry. A remarkable finding is that commitment to the hotel explains more variance than the other antecedents of relationship quality and behavioural consequences. In testing a theoretical model on the respondents from the Junior Chamber International,

Table 8.5: Determinants of behavioural consequences and relationship quality

Construct	Relationship continuity			Word of mouth			Share of purchases			Relationship quality		
	Direct effect (1)	Indirect effect (2)	Total effect (1) + (2)	Direct effect (1)	Indirect effect (2)	Total effect (1) + (2)	Direct effect (1)	Indirect effect (2)	Total effect (1) + (2)	Direct effect (1)	Indirect effect (2)	Total effect (1) + (2)
Employee Trust	–	0.62†	0.62	–	0.34†	0.34	–	0.35†	0.35	0.29	0.37†	0.66
Tourist hotel Trust	–	0.42†	0.42	–	0.23†	0.23	–	0.24†	0.24	0.01†	0.44	0.45
Employee commitment	–	0.09†	0.09	–	0.05†	0.05	–	0.05†	0.05	−0.11†	0.21	0.10
Tourist hotel commitment	–	0.80	0.80	–	0.45	0.45	–	0.46	0.46	0.86	–	0.86

Note: †not /partially supported when significant level is 0.05.

Taiwan and the Rotary International Taiwan, we found some empirical support for our model, along with some discrepancies.

As is supported by Kim and Cha (2002), acquiring satisfied or pleased customers is likely to substantially facilitate a share of purchases, relationship continuity, and positive word of mouth. These linkages in our model even demonstrate relatively stronger effects than their counterparts in Kim and Cha's findings. Therefore, implementing relationship marketing should now be seen as the key mechanism to create a competitive advantage in the tourist hotel industry across some cultural backgrounds.

Two out of four hypotheses stating the direct effects of trust and commitment on the employee level and the hotel level on relationship quality are supported at the 0.01 level of significance. However, all of the relationships connecting these antecedents are found to be significant at the same level. This implied that organizational trust and employee commitment appear to build and enhance relationship quality more indirectly. In general, outcomes in the current study are consistent with the results and the explanation proposed earlier by Wong and Sohal (2002). The path linking employee trust, tourist hotel trust, tourist hotel commitment, and relationship quality demonstrates positive and strong chain effects in the tourist hotel industry. The present study in some ways interprets Wong and Sohal's model with greater empirical evidence. Specifically, both studies found that store or hotel trust possibly results in relationship quality only by way of reinforcing store or hotel commitment. The processes by which trust is engendered are likely to differ between service providers and the hotels they represent (cf. Wong and Sohal, 2002). This shared result suggests that more comparative studies are needed in the future to identify the relationship or to re-elaborate upon some other possible structures.

Another distinctive and noticeable finding in our study, in contrast to what Wong and Sohal concluded, is that employee commitment might not be useful in developing relationship quality in hotels. Considering unsupported hypotheses suggests that a customer's commitment to a hotel, rather than commitment to service providers, is the key antecedent that leads to pleased or satisfied customers. An interesting implication of our findings, in opposition to Wong and Sohal's conclusion, is that individual-to-firm relationships are more likely to explain or predict overall relationship quality than interpersonal relationships. If we consider the linkages with direct and indirect effects, we can also conclude that tourist hotel commitment actually plays the dominating role in achieving higher levels of relationship quality. Based on total effects, hotel commitment can substantially improve customers' behavioural consequences.

One explanation for this different finding may be that customers in luxury hotels normally focus their preference on brand associations that are unique, favourable, and strong which result from both personal relevance and consistent information over time (cf. Keller, 1998; Moore *et al.*, 2002). Added value cherished by a customer that accrues to an international tourist hotel may be derived from its brand equity rather than attributes of service providers.

As supported by Kim and Cha (2002), the relationship quality of satisfaction orientation in our model appears to improve all customer behavioural consequences, namely, relationship continuity, word of mouth, and share of purchases at the 0.01 level of significance. One point that should be mentioned is that the relative effects of these relationships in Kim and Cha's model were equally low. In contrast, our relationships showed comparably strong impacts of relationship quality in the integrated model. This study provides greater support for past findings in a more comprehensive framework.

Limitations and future consideration

The current study has some limitations that need to be acknowledged and remedied in future research, despite the fact that the authors highlight the dynamics of relationship quality in international tourist hotels. First, there are substantial differences in the measurement of relationship quality among studies, and ours focused on satisfaction with employees only (cf. Wong and Sohal, 2002). This has been a serious problem for researchers to make comparison of previous findings and design advanced research based on literature review. Thus, to integrate further findings of research and prospects from various disciplines, a commonly accepted construct of relationship quality for empirical research should be developed and refined in the future.

Second, our study followed Wong and Sohal's model and thus ignored or simplified some causalities or their directions. For example, researchers suggested that trust and commitment may directly influence future intentions (cf. Morgan and Hunt, 1994; Garbarino and Johnson, 1999; Hennig-Thurau *et al.*, 2002). In addition, relationship quality, customer satisfaction, or overall satisfaction was found to be positively related to commitment or trust in low relational interactions (cf. Garbarino and Johnson, 1999; Kim *et al.*, 2001; Henning-Thurau *et al.*, 2002). It would be rewarding to examine the relative impact of contingent factors, such as culture, on the forming and consequences of relationship quality so that we can better generalize our results across conditions.

Finally, only when the all possible paths in a diagram are empirically supported, we may obtain a clearer picture of findings by analysing the direct and indirect impacts of each construct on behavioural consequences with sufficient confidence. Thus, conclusions of the present study are supposed to be explained and practically applied with care. Meanwhile, this study lacks discussion on the linkages connecting share of consequences, relationship continuity, and word of mouth (cf. Kim and Cha, 2002). In order to further our insight into the relevant dynamics, additional studies that contrast competing models should be conducted.

Note

1. This study was supported partially by National Science Council, 93-2416-H-030-015.

References

Berry, L.L. (1983) 'Relationship Marketing', in L.L. Berry, L.K. Shostack and G.D. Upah (eds), *Emerging Perspectives on Services Marketing* (Chicago: American Marketing Association), pp. 25–8.

Choi, T.Y. and R. Chu (2001) 'Determinants of hotel guests' satisfaction and repeat patronage in the Hong Kong hotel industry,' *International Journal of Hospitality Management* 20(3), 67–82.

Crosby, L.A., K.R. Evans and D. Cowles (1990) 'Relationship quality in services selling: an interpersonal influence perspective' *Journal of Marketing* 54(July), 68–81.

Dwyer, F.R., P.H. Schurr and Sejo Oh (1987) 'Developing buyer-seller relationships', *Journal of Marketing* 51(April), 11–27.

Foster, B.D. and J.W. Cadogan (2000) 'Relationship selling and customer loyalty: an empirical investigation', *Marketing Intelligence & Planning* 18(4), 185–99.

Garbarino, E. and M.S. Johnson (1999) 'The different roles of satisfaction, trust, and commitment in customer relationships', *Journal of Marketing* 63(April), 70–87.

Hair, J.F., R.E. Anderson Jr, R.L. Tatham and W.C. Black (1998) *Multivariate Data Analysis* (5th edn, Upper Saddle River: Prentice Hall).

Hennig-Thurau, T., K.P. Gwinner and D.D. Gremler (2002) 'Understanding relationship marketing outcomes', *Journal of Service Research* 4(3), 230–47.

Hoelter, J.W. (1983) 'The analysis of covariance structures: goodness-of-fit indices', *Sociological Methods and Research* 11, 325–44.

Hrebiniak, L.G. (1974) 'Effects of job level and participation on employee attitudes and perceptions of influence', *Academy of Management Journal* 17, 649–62.

Iacobucci, D. and A. Ostrom (1996) 'Commercial and interpersonal relationships: using the structure of interpersonal relationships to understand individual-to-individual, individual-to-firm, and firm-to-firm relationships', *International Journal of Research in Marketing* 13(February), 53–72.

Jarvelin, A. and U. Lehtinen (1996) 'Relationship Quality in Business-to Business Service Context', in B.B. Edvardsson, S.W. Johnston and E.E. Scheuing (eds),

QUIS 5 Advancing Service Quality: A Global Perspective (Lethbridge: Warwick Printing Company), pp. 243–54.

Keller, K.L. (1998) *Strategic Brand Management: Building, Measuring and Managing Brand Equity* (Upper Saddle River, NJ: Prentice Hall).

Kim, W.G. and Y. Cha (2002) 'Antecedents and consequences of relationship quality in hotel industry', *Hospitality Management* 21, 321–38.

Kim, W.G., J.S. Han and E. Lee (2001) 'Effects of relationship marketing on repeat purchase and word of mouth', *Journal of Hospitality & Tourism Research* 25(3), 272–88.

Knutson, B. (1988) 'Frequent travelers: making them happy and bringing them back', *Cornell Hotel and Restaurant Administration Quarterly* 29(1), 83–7.

Moore, E.S., W.L. Wilkie and R.J. Lutz (2002) 'Passing the torch: intergenerational influences as a source of brand equity', *Journal of Marketing* 66(April), 17–37.

Moorman, C., G. Zaltman and R. Deshpande (1992) 'Relationships between providers and users of market research: the dynamics of trust within and between organizations', *Journal of Marketing Research* 29(3), 314–28.

Morgan, R.M. and S.D. Hunt (1994), 'The commitment-trust theory of relationship marketing', *Journal of Marketing* 58(July), 20–38.

Nunnally, J.C. (1978) *Psychometric Theory* (2nd edn, New York: McGraw-Hill).

Oh, H. (1999) 'Service quality, customer satisfaction, and customer value: a holistic perspective', *International Journal of Hospitality Management* 18(1), 67–82.

Smith, B. (1998) 'Buyer-seller relationships: bonds, relationship management, and sex-Type', *Canadian Journal of Administrative Sciences* 15(1), 79–92.

Sörbom, D. and K.G. Jöreskog (1982) 'The Use of Structural Equation Models in Evaluation Research', in C. Fornell (ed.), *A Second Generation of Multivariate Analysis* (New York: Praeger).

Venkatesh, R., A.K. Kohli and G. Zaltman (1995) 'Influence strategies in buying centers', *Journal of Marketing* 59(4), 71–82.

Wong, A. and A. Sohal (2002) 'An examination of the relationship between trust, commitment and relationship quality', *International Journal of Retail and Distribution Management* 30(1), 34–50.

Part II
The Conflict Perspective

9
The Moderating Effects of Situation Factors on the Relationship Between Chinese Cultural Values and Consumers' Complaint Behaviour in the Restaurant Setting

Simone C. L. Cheng and Oliver H. M. Yau

Introduction

Consumer dissatisfaction is a common phenomenon in the marketplace (Engel, Blackwell and Miniard, 1990). Empirical studies have found that one in every five consumers feels dissatisfied with the products or services that he/she purchases (Society of Consumer Affairs Professionals (SOCAP), 1996). The situation is even worse in the services industry. Tucci and Talaga (1997) reported that over 50 percent of restaurant patrons found few aspects of restaurant services satisfactory. A recent study conducted by Liu and McClure (2001) found that 35 percent of respondents were dissatisfied with their visits to restaurants. This phenomenon may be explained by the intangible and labour-intensive nature of restaurant service, which inevitably produces some levels of service failure and customer dissatisfaction (Auty, 1992; Chung and Hoffman, 1998). Even with conscientious quality controls in the service delivery process, most organizations cannot achieve 100 percent consumer satisfaction among all consumers at all times (Mack *et al.*, 2000).

Despite the high rate of consumer dissatisfaction, there is a common conception in both the literature and in folklore that Chinese consumers are reluctant to complain when they are dissatisfied with products or services (Le Claire, 1993). It is also widely believed that Chinese consumers are less likely to engage in complaint behaviour than are consumers from Western countries (Triandis, 1994; Bond, 1996). Huang, Huang and Wu (1996) attributed this behaviour to differences in the cultural orientations of people from different countries. Erdem, Oumlil and Tuncalp (1999) argued that actual behaviours resulting from concrete motivations in specific situations are partly determined by the actor's prior beliefs and values. This is evidenced in Liu and McClure's (2001) study that dissatisfied consumers from a collectivist culture (e.g., Korean consumers) are less likely to engage in complaint behaviour and are more likely to engage in private behaviour than are consumers from an individualist culture (e.g., US consumers). Several recent studies concur that Chinese, who are collectivists (Hofstede, 1980; Triandis, 1994), avoid complaint behaviour (e.g., Au, Hui and Leung; 2001; Huang, Huang, and Wu, 1996; Watkins and Liu; 1996).

Most of the studies about culture and consumer complaint behaviour have employed the cultural dimensions developed by Hofstede (1980) in explaining the complaint behaviour of Chinese. However, these cultural dimensions originate from Western countries and have been frequently criticized as insufficient to capture the values of Chinese (Chinese Cultural Connection, 1987; Yau, Chan and Lau, 1999). Yau *et al.* (1999) argued that there are more than four major values that can be used to interpret Chinese behaviour. They further claimed that the omission of some variables might make the classification meaningless and irrelevant to the Chinese culture. Hence, the employment of Hofstede's cultural dimensions in explaining the complaint behaviour of Chinese consumers is deemed to be insufficient.

Yang (1981) held a different view about the classification of cultural dimensions. He considered Chinese as socially oriented instead of collectivists. Yang (1981: 159–60) defined social orientation as a predisposition to 'act in accordance with external expectations or social norms, rather than internal wishes or personal integrity so that they would be able to protect their social self and function as an integral part of the social network'. He claimed that Chinese who have a social orientation have a tendency towards such behaviour patterns as social conformity; they tend to use non-offensive strategies; they tend to be submissive to social expectations; they tend to worry about external opinions, maintenance of harmony, impression management, face protection, and social acceptance; and they tend to avoid punishment, embarrassment, conflict, rejection, ridicule, and retaliation in social situations. Most likely, these predispositions would greatly influence the complaint behaviour of an individual. However, previous studies seem to have under examined these distinctive characteristics of the Chinese culture, as many past studies have employed only individualism and collectivism (e.g., Watkins and Liu 1996; Liu and McClure, 2001) in explaining consumer complaint behaviour.

This chapter proposes that distinctive Chinese cultural values influence the complaint behaviour of Chinese consumers. In addition, the chapter

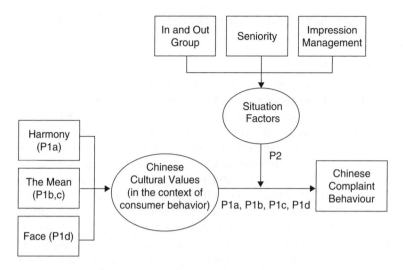

Figure 9.1: Conceptual model of Chinese cultural values and complaint behaviour

examines the relationship between Chinese cultural values, situation factors, and the complaint behaviour of Chinese consumers. The objectives of the chapter are twofold. First, it explores the impact of different Chinese cultural values on the complaint behaviour of Chinese. Second, it investigates whether situation factors have a moderating effect in the relationship between Chinese cultural values and the complaint behaviour of Chinese. The proposed conceptual model of Chinese cultural values and complaint behaviour is presented in Figure 9.1.

Chinese cultural values

The recorded history of China spans more than 4,000 years (Hookham, 1969). The culture of China has been largely influenced by various prevailing schools of thought in different eras. The most prestigious and influential schools of thought include Confucianism (儒家), Taoism (道家), Mohism (墨家), Legalism (法家), and Buddhism (佛家). Hwang (1990) argued that, among all schools of thought, Confucianism is the most influential and lasting philosophy that has shaped the social behaviours of Chinese. The philosophy of Confucianism has held a dominant position in China from the Han era onwards and has exerted substantial influence in shaping the ideologies that determine the behaviours of Chinese (Yao, 2001). This chapter discusses the impact of some culture values derived from Confucianism that relate to the complaint behaviour of Chinese consumers.

Cultural values

Culture can be defined as an evolving system of concepts, values, and symbols of interest in a society as well as a learned system of behaviour that organizes experience, determines an individual's position within social structures and guides actions in a multitude of situations, both known or unknown (Yau, Chan and Lau, 1999). Values are concepts or beliefs that guide selection or evaluation of behaviour and events (Chinese Cultural Connection, 1987; Schwartz, 1992; Feather, 1994). Some researchers view values as the outcomes of the culture and ethnicity of a society (e.g., Phinney, 1992). On the whole, cultural values represent implicitly or explicitly shared abstract ideas about what is good, right, and desirable in a society (Williams, 1970). Explicit and implicit values are imparted to societal members through everyday exposure to customs, laws, norms, scripts, and organizational practices (Markus and Kitayama, 1994). Therefore, cultural values (e.g., freedom, prosperity, security) are the bases for the specific norms that tell people what is appropriate in various situations (Schwartz, 1999).

Three influential values that derive from Confucian thought are harmony, 'the Mean', and face. Confucianism stresses intra-person harmony, harmony between people and the environment, and harmony in social relationships (Westwood, 1997). Harmony is a goal that Chinese strive to achieve (Chen, 2001, 2002). The adoption of 'the Mean' is also advocated in the 'The Four Books' of Confucianism. The Mean emphasizes the importance of maintaining a balanced state to keep harmony in hierarchical relationships. Another important feature in Chinese society is face (Chiu, Tsang and Yang, 1988). The meanings and the implications of these three Chinese cultural values are discussed below.

Harmony

The *Cambridge Advanced Learner's Dictionary* (Cambridge University Press, 2004) defines harmony as agreements and peaceful conditions among people. In Western ideology, harmony is a value orientation based upon notions of equality, egalitarianism and consensus (Westwood, 1997). Earley (1997) argued that harmony means more than just a balancing point or an equilibrium mode within a given social system. He defined harmony as the nature of interpersonal interactions and actions engaged in by social actors within a given organizational context and structure. According to the online dictionary of Lam Yu Tong, harmony represents peace and friendship. Yet, the Chinese term has a deeper meaning. In Chinese, the word *he* (和) appears as one of the most frequent characters in reference to the concept of 'harmony' (Leung, Koch and Lu, 2002). This Chinese character denotes 'on good terms with each other', 'gentle', 'mild', and 'peace' (Foreign Language Teaching and Research Press, 1988). Leung, Koch and Lu (2002) further explain it as 'unity','kindness', and 'amiableness'.

Harmony is the foundation of Chinese culture (Bond, 1996). It is deeply embedded as a social value that is emphasized in the dominant religious and philosophical traditions of Confucianism, Taoism and Buddhism (Westwood, 1997; Pitta, Fung and Isberg, 1999). The working imperative of these ideologies is to achieve harmony; all other goals are subordinate (Chen and Pan, 1993). Confucianism stresses the importance of harmony between people, between people and the natural environment, and of most significance, in social relationships (Westwood, 1997) to achieve the spirit of *Ren* (仁). Kong Ze (5,11–476 BC) made the issues, 以和爲貴' (i.e., harmony is precious) and 持中和諧' (i.e., maintaining the middle is harmony) as the handling strategy of conflict and disagreement.

The emphasis on social harmony can be explained by an underlying theme in Confucian philosophy that states that men are social beings and cannot live alone. Peace can only be maintained through harmonious relationships. Hence, interactions with others, or man-to-man relations are greatly emphasized in the Chinese society (Le Claire, 1993). It is not surprising to find numerous traditional Chinese sayings revolving around harmony, such as 以和爲貴' (harmony is valuable), 心平氣和' (tranquility in mind and peace in deposition), and 家和萬事興' (if the family lives in harmony, all affairs will prosper). The concept of harmony has permeated many aspects of Chinese interpersonal relationships (Westwood, 1997).

The implication of harmony on conflict avoidance   Chen and Chung (1994) pointed out that the importance of achieving harmony has lead to a negative view of conflict among Chinese. It is generally agreed that conflict avoidance is a common characteristic in Chinese culture (Kirkbride, Tang & Westwood, 1991). Chinese are inspired to live in harmony with family members, to be on good terms with neighbours, to achieve unity with the surrounding environment, and to make peace with other nations (Bond, 1996). Consequently, children in Chinese societies are trained to inhibit any form of physical aggression to promote interpersonal harmony in the society (Hwang, 1987). Empirical studies by Liao and Tsai (2002) reported that the desire for harmony has led to conflict avoidance behaviour by Chinese. Influenced by Confucian philosophy, Chinese repeatedly avoid confrontation and debates, while obedience and conformity are highly advocated in the Chinese culture (Leung, 1988). Westwood (1997) asserted that open conflict is not culturally acceptable in Chinese communities because it invites direct confrontation or dispute, which disrupts the harmonious fabric of personal relationships (Bond, 1991; Smith, 1991). Therefore, Chinese will avoid conflict at all costs (Bond, 1991). They adopt an indirect, avoiding style for handling conflicts (Morris, *et al.*, 1998). They use a non-confrontational communication style and resort to conflict avoidance tactics to maintain smooth interpersonal relationships (Leung, Koch and Lu, 2002).

   The concern for social harmony may deter Chinese from complaining even when they experience product or service dissatisfaction (Yau, 1988). Chiu, Tsang and Yang (1988) asserted that complaint behaviour is not a widely accepted behaviour in Chinese culture. Complaint behaviour requires the exposure of mistakes or criticizing others in public, which may provoke direct confrontation and endanger relationships with the business or its employees. Even when Chinese consumers are dissatisfied with restaurant services or products, they tend to avoid any conflicts at the restaurant. Yau (1988) explained that, in the Chinese context, the concern for harmony in human relations outweighs the importance of the quality of the products or services received and any associated dissatisfaction. Chinese have high propensity to forbear and suppress their personal goals in favour of maintaining harmonious relationships (Hwang, 1997). This is why it is not unusual to find Chinese showing reluctance to criticize others (Bond, 1996). An empirical study by Huang *et al.* (1996) supported this notion. They reported that hotel guests from a collectivist country, Japan, tend to avoid complaining to the hotel or a third party due to the undesirability of open conflict. The desire for harmony and conflict avoidance explains why Chinese consumers seldom complain to restaurant managers or a third party.

The Doctrine of the Mean
The Doctrine of the Mean (中庸) is advocated in the 'The Four Books' (四書). It refers to the state of equilibrium (Legge, 1960). Hwang (1983) described it as the middle way. Kong Ze put it '不偏之謂中,' 不易之謂庸' [being without inclination to either side is called *Zhong* (中); admitting to no change is called *Yong* (庸)]. Earley (1997) stated that the principle of 'the Mean' stresses a state of affairs in which there is a balance achieved among various potentially opposing forces. It

means that 'over the standard' or 'below the standard' is seen as inappropriate. Over or below the 'standard' is 'evil' (Miáo, 苗 1989). Hwang (1983) shared a similar view and asserted that the main idea of the Mean is to avoid going to the extreme ends. In short, the principle of *Zhong Yong* is to maintain a balanced state. In addition, *Zhong* signifies the correct course to be pursued by all under heaven; *Yong* describes the fixed principle regulating all under heaven (Legge, 1960). *Zhong* is defined as appropriate, while *Yong*, as Zong Ze puts it, '庸, 即用也, 常也, is 'common practice'. In other words, everything or every behaviour should act in accordance with the 'common practice' and should not incline in any direction or deviate from other people.

The Doctrine of the Mean has several implications on consumer behaviour. First, it discourages extreme behaviours. Second, it exerts great pressure to conform to social norms and to the expectations of the group members at the expense of personal wishes and goals. Third, the value of the Mean gives rise to the high degree of moral self control. The following sections discuss these three implications in detail.

The implication of the mean on extreme behaviour   Given the influence by the doctrine of the Mean, Chinese are cautious in showing extreme behaviour. Cavusgil and Kaynak (1982) claimed that complaint behaviour is seen to be unacceptable from a cultural perspective because Chinese consider complaints as an extreme behaviour. A number of researchers have asserted that Chinese consumers are less likely to undertake public action, such as making complaints to companies or to the Consumer Council when they are dissatisfied with products or services (Le Claire, 1993; Bond, 1996). Chinese regard public action as something very serious (Le Claire, 1993). Therefore, careful consideration has to be given to whether public action is an extreme way to solve the problem. Furthermore, Yau (1994) declared that legal action, which is also regarded as an extreme behaviour, is normally not considered by the Chinese. As a result, traditionally, Chinese consumers seldom complain even when services fail to meet expectations.

The implication of the mean on conformity and norm   According to the doctrine of the Mean, people should act in accordance with the 'common practice' in society. In Chinese society, social norms can be interpreted as the 'common practice'. The only way to avoid behaving extremely is to act according to the social norm or the expectations of the important others. This explains why Chinese have high motivation to comply with the group norms or conform to what is perceived to be 'right' by most of the members of reference group (Triandis, 1995). Hwang (1987) defined the national character of socially oriented Chinese as a complex of social conformity, inoffensive strategy, and submission to social expectations and authority. There is a demand for conformity to group pressure (Hwang, 1987). Chinese believe that conforming to others is the paramount way for maintaining harmonious social relations (Westwood, 1997). The concern for what others would say usually creates unbearable pressure on a Chinese, and the fear of being criticized and ridiculed by others has a controlling effect on their behaviour (Yu, 1990). If they find that complaining is not a social norm or a socially acceptable behaviour, they are under great pressure to inhibit the complaint behaviour and subordinate their own personal benefit in order to conform to the group norms. Richins (1983) claimed that the reluctance to complain is due to the fear of being criticized for undertaking socially unacceptable behaviour and forming negative impressions by others; people would not want to stand out in the crowd when dissatisfaction occurs. Yet, they tend to follow and act according to the norms prescribed for each instance of interpersonal relations.

The 'common practice' can also be interpreted as the social expectations of the group with which one is interacting. In order to avoid extreme behaving the Chinese tend to act according to the expectations of others instead of according to their own personal wishes or personal integrity (Ho, 1974). Yang (1981) maintained that Chinese, in deciding upon their behaviour, take into account the opinions of others (Yau, 1988) and attach a great weight to the anticipated reactions of others to their behaviour (Bond, 1993). A Chinese identifies with the goals and expectations of the collective to which he/she belongs and judges things from a perspective that he/she believes is shared by other members in the group. He/she upholds social norms and rules to avoid feelings of shame, guilt and anxiety, and to maintain the social order for its own sake (Westwood, 1997). Many decisions by Chinese are, therefore, made under the heavy influence of the group with which they are mostly interacting, such as family members, work groups, close friends, classmates, and leaders (Hofstede and Bond, 1988). Lam, Baum and Pine (2003) explained that the motivation to conform to others is due to the concern for other people's perceptions toward themselves. They may fear the sanctions imposed by others. Consequently, the concern for what others would say usually creates pressure on the behaviours of Chinese (Yau, 1994). In order not to perform deviant behaviour from others, Chinese tend to perform socially expected and the culturally approved behaviours. In other words, if complaining to a restaurant manager is not a socially desirable and approved behaviour in the society, the worry about external opinions makes Chinese silent about their dissatisfaction even though they think that a complaint would be righteous behaviour.

The implication of the mean on self control   Monitoring overt emotional expression is the basic rule for human interaction in Chinese society (Bond, 1996). Joy, love, anger, and sadness are regarded as forms of extreme behaviour. Any of these extreme ends may be against the doctrine of the Mean. A Chinese proverb puts it this way: '喜怒哀樂亥之未發，謂之中' (while there are no stirrings of pleasure, anger, sorrow, or joy, the mind may be said to be in the state of equilibrium). This proverb implies that the only way to achieve a state of equilibrium is by not openly expressing emotions. Bond (1993) pointed out that moderation in emotional expressions is considered as essential for achieving one's internal balance. Consequently, Chinese children are taught not to show their feelings of anger, disappointment, or vengeance (Smith, 1991). Chinese are socialized not to openly express their personal emotions, especially strong and negative ones (Bond, 1996). Yau (1988) suggested that it is the concern for the Mean that leads to a high degree of moral self control or self regulation in Chinese behaviour.

The moral self-control tends to make people appear shy in revealing ideas and thoughts in public places (Pitta, Fung and Isberg, 1999). Many people consider revealing their deep and private feelings as embarrassing (Le Claire, 1993). The empirical study by Le Claire found that it was the concern for avoiding embarrassment that led Chinese to deter from complaining. Hence, even when Chinese consumers receive dissatisfactory services, they avoid expressing their dissatisfaction and anger. Besides, by controlling their joy or anger, it is believed this may avoid imposing their feelings on others and thereby they will maintain harmony in interpersonal relationships (Bond, 1993; Bond and Hwang, 1986). As a consequence, emotional behaviour is highly restrained or suppressed in a Chinese society.

The value of the Mean also gives rise to indirect communication. Personal ideas, values, and feelings often are conveyed indirectly in the Chinese culture (Kleinman, 1980). Chinese try to avoid saying 'No' when asked to express an opinion. They believe that saying 'no' will embarrass or offend others. On the contrary, they realize that replying in an indirect way, making it impossible for others to have a definite and fixed understanding, is the best way to express disagreement and dis satisfaction. Therefore, even though Chinese consumers experience dis satisfactory services or products, they usually express their dissatisfaction in a subtle and indirect way or they wait for a favourable moment to air their complaints.

Face

Another distinctive feature of Chinese culture is the concept of face. Collectivist consumers are concerned with the concept of 'face', which indicates social status in society (Yau, 1988). 'Face' is the respect, pride, and dignity of an individual as a consequence of his/her social achievement (King, 1993; Lam and Wong, 1995). Face has two dimensions – *lien* (臉) and *mianzi* (面子) (Hu, 1944). *Lien* represents the confidence of society in the integrity of a person's moral character. *Lien* is the projection of the self-image and impression management. The goal of practising *lien* is to shape and instil a particular favourable image in the minds of others (Hwang, 1987). *Lien* is internalized in that everyone should be entitled by virtue. A person cannot maintain his/her relationships with others within a community if an individual loses *lien* because this person will feel guilty and it is impossible for him/her to function properly within the community (Yau, 1988;King, 1993). In other words, *lien* may be lost through misconduct, but cannot be gained back (King, 1993). *Mianzi* indicates an individual's social position or prestige. It is reputation achieved through successfully performing one or more specific social roles that are well recognized by others (Lam and Wong, 1995). An individual's *mianzi* is also a function of the perceived social position and prestige within one's social network (Hwang, 1987). Leung and Chan (2003) indicated that the possession of *mianzi* requires visible success in meeting the expectations of the relevant social hierarchy.

Face can be regarded as a package of social techniques that is used to protect one's *mianzi* and the *mianzi* of others in human interactions (King, 1993). The aim of practising face is to maintain the existing role relationships and preserve interpersonal harmony (Bond, 1996). Hence, the goal of 'face' is to shape and instil in the minds of others a particular favourable image (Schlenker, 1980). Chiu, Tsang and Yang (1988) claimed that Chinese attach great importance to face and that they are very face conscious in social interactions. Chinese not only make every attempt to avoid losing face but also to save the face of others (Hwang, 1990). Watkins and Liu (1996) agreed that saving face for others and avoiding losing face are essential to Chinese people. It is instilled in the culture of the Chinese not to put someone in an uncomfortable position (Pitta, Fung and Isberg, 1999). Hence, Bond (1988) suggested that the concern for face has significant consequences in many aspects of Chinese behaviour.

The implication of face on impression management   Impression management refers to the package of strategies or actions that aim at enhancing one's status and face (i.e., in the Chinese context) or minimizing the loss of face of others. The people in collectivist cultures are more concerned with the face of others than are those in individualist cultures (Ting-Toomey, 1988). Chinese people pay much attention to avoiding losing the face of others because the loss of face will cause Chinese to lose confidence in front of others and in personal interactions. Bond (1996) declared that it is the concern for protecting the face of others that leads Chinese to employ a non-confrontational style of conflict management, such as avoiding, obliging, compromising, and suppressing, to avoid face-threatening situations. To the Chinese, public disagreement is a face-losing act. Hu (1944) claimed that exposing a person's mistakes to social scrutiny is regarded as losing face for others. Any treatment that does not respect the humanness of others can also lead to a loss of face (Westwood, 1997). Therefore, the avoidance of criticizing the performance of someone helps to save face and to maintain good impressions for others (Hwang, 1987). In order to maintain the face or the good impression of others, Chinese are not encouraged to express disagreement or dissatisfaction in front of others. In other situations, some people may employ other strategies to save the face of others. This explains why Chinese consumers seldom criticize the performance of service providers or their staff.

However, complaint behaviour can be employed as a means to facilitate impression management. As *mianzi* is granted by others, if an individual's request or complaint is then made and accepted, it is said that the allocator 'gave him/her *mianzi*' and his/her face is thus increased. On the contrary, if an individual's request is rejected and the allocator does not give him *mianzi*, he may think that the refusal reflects badly on his *mianzi*. Le Claire (1993) said that face is lost when a satisfactory result is not obtained from the complaint. Hence, Chinese rarely express their dissatisfaction, such as through complaint behaviour, because they are not sure whether the allocator will give him/her *mianzi*. Earley (1997) asserted that many of the face-related actions are anticipatory of others' willingness or unwillingness to facilitate the display of face.

Consumer complaint behaviour

Consumer complaint behaviour refers to the actions undertaken by consumers who are dissatisfied, including the expression of dissatisfaction directly to the one who sells or manufactures consumer products (Hirschman, 1970). It is conceived as an active and constructive response in which consumers attempt to change rather than escape from an unsatisfactory situation and seek some form of remedy from management (Kostant, 1999).

The study of consumers' complaint behaviours has drawn considerable interest over the years from both academics and practitioners (e.g., Hirschman, 1970; Richins, 1983; Singh, 1990; Stephens and Gwinner, 1998). The primary reason for the increasing interest in the study of consumer complaints is the potential impact such behaviour has on brand and company loyalty, future repurchase intentions (Day, 1984), word-of-mouth communications (Richins, 1983), as well as strategies for handling business complaints (Fornell and Westbrook, 1984). Given the importance of consumer complaints to business practitioners, many studies have tried to understand the determinants that lead to different types of consumers' complaint behaviour. Consumer characteristics, such as culture, age, income, and education and situation factors, including the costs of making complaints, the attribution of blame, previous experiences with making complaints, and the price of the product, have been found to be the antecedents of consumer complaints (e.g., Andreasen and Manning, 1990; Blodgett, Wakefield and Barnes, 1995; Singh and Wilkes, 1996; Au, Hui and Leung, 2001; Liu and McClure, 2001; Su and Bowen, 2001).

Based on this literature review, several propositions emerge:

P_1. The greater the importance placed on Chinese cultural values (in terms of harmony, the Mean, and face), the less likely Chinese consumers will engage in complaint behaviour.

P_{1a}: The greater the concern for harmony and conflict avoidance, the more likely Chinese consumers will engage in conflict avoidance strategies and less likely they will undertake complaint behaviour.

P_{1b}: The greater the emphasis on the Mean, the more likely Chinese consumers will not undertake complaint behaviour when they are dissatisfied with the products or services received.

P_{1c}: The more desirable self control is, the more likely Chinese consumers will not undertake complaint behaviour when they are dissatisfied with the products or services provided.

P_{1d}: The greater the concern for saving one's own face and avoiding losing others' face, the more likely Chinese consumers will not undertake complaint behaviour when they are dissatisfied with the products or services provided.

Situation factors

Engel, Kollat and Blackwell (1968) proposed that situational factors should be considered in order to explain consumer choices. Ward and Robertson (1973) also asserted that situational factors may account for more variance than consumer characteristics in explaining consumer behaviour. Explicitly, situation factors may exert substantial influence on one's behaviour. For instance, even if an individual is strongly predisposed to make a complaint, the complaint situation may deter him/her from doing so when the channels for complaining are nonexistent (Chiu, Tsang and Yang, 1988). Belk (1974) shared a similar view and suggested that several dimensions of situations should be taken into account. He suggested five groups of situation characteristics that should be considered, including physical surroundings, social surroundings, temporal aspects, task features, and antecedent states.

Physical surroundings refer to the geographical and institutional location, decor, sounds, weather and other material surroundings of a consumer. Social surroundings are the dimensions of a situation in which there are interpersonal interactions occurring. Temporal aspects include the time description of a situation. The features of a task involve a situation including an intent or requirement to select, shop for, or obtain information about a general or specific purchase. Antecedent states refer to the momentary moods or monetary conditions stipulated to be immediately antecedent to the current situation.

Situation factors as a moderator

Hsu (1968) described the characteristics of the Chinese pattern of behaviour as situation-centred. Chinese consumers tend to act differently depending upon the situation. It is estimated that situation factors might moderate the relationship between cultural values and Chinese behaviours.

A moderator is an independent variable that affects the strength and/or direction of the association between another independent variable and an outcome variable (Bennett, 2000). That is, the moderator interacts with the independent variables' association with the outcome variable; the outcome variable is stronger or weaker with different levels of the moderator variable. More precisely, when the relationship between Chinese cultural values and complaint behaviour is weakened or strengthened by situation factors, it is believed that a moderating effect has occurred.

There are several different situations that might induce different strategies in dealing with unsatisfactory experiences in restaurants. The first is when the unsatisfactory experience occurs in front of different types of group members (i.e., in-group members versus out-group members). The second is when the dining occasion involves different dining companions (i.e., seniors versus peers). The third is when the situation requires the practice of face to facilitate impression management.

Dealing with different types of group members: In-group versus out-group members   Many researchers agree that Chinese are socially oriented and have a family focus. They behave differently toward others depending on whether or not the person with whom they are interacting is a member of their in-group or is an out-group member (Yang, 1981; Gire, 1997). Chinese make clear distinctions between in-group members and out-group members. People in collectivist cultures distinguish more sharply between behaviour directed at in-group versus out-group members than do people in individualist or autonomous cultures (Smith, Peterson and Schwartz, 2002). In-group members and out-group members are two important concepts in Chinese culture. Hwang (1987) divided relationships into three categories: expressive ties, including those with close family members; mixed ties, such as those with friends, and other kin; and instrumental ties, such as those with strangers and out-group members with whom there are no lasting relationships. Based on the typologies described by Hwang (1987), expressive ties and mixed ties are used with in-group members, while instrumental ties are used with out-group members. In-group members are so-called insiders (*zijiren*). They include members of the family and relatives; friends and others with whom one has established a special relationship are considered insiders in a social circle (Bond, 1996). In the work setting, work associates such as one's superior and subordinates are very likely to be seen as in-group members (Smith, Peterson and Schwartz, 2002). Other people who do not belong to the same relational circle or have not established close relationships (i.e., *guanxi*) with an individual are seen as out-group members, which are also called outsiders (*wairen*). This distinction between the two helps the Chinese position themselves in established hierarchical and role relationships.

Bond (1996) asserted that the social interaction expectations, norms, and behaviours differ in several ways. If service failures involve the in-group members, such as parents and children, a person might more likely stand out in the crowd to ask for compensation or service recovery. Triandis (1994) argued that the primary Chinese interest is to protect the benefits of one's kin. Therefore, regardless of the person's unfavourable attitudes towards complaint, the person might complain to the restaurant manager in the hope that the interests of the in-group members can be protected. However, if the situation involves dissatisfaction of the out-group members, such as peers or colleagues from other departments, one may be less likely to express dissatisfaction to the restaurant manager.

The Chinese are socially oriented. The needs, goals and beliefs of the in-group often take precedence over those of the individuals (Triandis, 1988). In other words, Chinese tend to subordinate their personal goals to in-group goals. They may exhibit different behaviours toward in-group versus out-group members (Gire, 1997). Triandis (1994) agreed that the behaviour of a collectivist is typically associative and may even involve self-sacrifice but only towards members of the in-group. If the unsatisfactory dining occasion occurs with family members, such as a spouse, a son and a daughter, the father will likely complain to the restaurant manager in order to protect the interests of his in-group members.

On another occasion, if an individual is a regular customer of a restaurant and has established a very good relationship (i.e., *guanxi*) with its manager, he/she may consider the restaurant manager as an in-group member and may express the dissatisfaction. There are two reasons for this possibility. First, the person may tend to express his/her dissatisfaction to help the restaurant because of the relationship with the restaurant and in the hope that the restaurant services/products can be improved in the future. Yau *et al.* (2000) stated that *guanxi* is a transferable relationship. That is, the *guanxi* between consumers and the employees of a company is transferable to the company. Therefore, the regular customer would like to see the restaurant improve. Second, the regular customer may feel certain that the restaurant manager may give him/her '*mianzi*' by accepting the complaint and by responding to the request because of their *guanxi*. One's face is a key component in the dynamics of *guanxi* (Luo, 1997). Under the unwritten rules of *guanxi*, each partner is obligated to help the other in an unlimited manner (Alston, 1989). Therefore, the restaurant or its staff is compelled to address the needs of his/her partners, otherwise their relationships will be ruined. In Chinese society, those who have an established relationship (*guanxi*) are considered as in-group members. With the desire to save the *mianzi* of the regular consumer, the restaurant manager may address the problem raised by the customer to maintain a harmonious in-group relationship within the social circle. Another reason is due to the value of relationships (*guanxi*). Hwang (1997) states that the Chinese, particularly in situations when relationships are very important, will not openly disagree. Instead, they will preserve the harmony of the relationship by agreeing with others in public while pursuing their goals in secret. Given the value of relationships with regular consumers and the desire to retain consumers, restaurant managers may answer consumers' complaints and fulfil their needs.

However, if the restaurant does not have an established relationship with an individual consumer, the reaction towards products or failures might be different. When the dissatisfaction is caused by an outsider to the social circle, that is, the out-group members, individual consumers are less likely to engage in complaint behaviour. By contrast, they may just stop patronizing the offending restaurant and switch to another service provider or engage in negative word-of-mouth communication to release their anger.

H_2: The involvement of different types of group members (in terms of in-group members versus out-group members) moderates the relationship between Chinese cultural values (in terms of the concept of harmony, the doctrine of the Mean, and the face) and consumers' complaint intentions.

Seniority versus peer group   The strength of the conformity force in the Chinese culture is obvious (Bond, 1996). In the Chinese societies, a good child is the one who shows listening-centredness (*tinghua* 聽話) not only in the family, but also in various situations beyond the family (Bond, 1996). Children are socialized to take in what their parents say. Children are to respect but not challenge their elders (Smith, 1991). When a child does not comply with the ideas of parents, deviant behaviour is exhibited and harmony in the family is disrupted. Salaff (1995) claimed that even when an individual is married, he/she still regards seeking approval from parents and elderly as mandatory and necessary. Further, the Chinese consider public disagreement as a face-losing act (Bond, 1996). Thus, when making decisions, an individual always takes into account the seniors in the family (Yau, 2001). This value also extends to other social settings. Students are expected to listen to their teachers the majority of the time. In the working environment, a good employee is one who practises *tinghua*, does what he or she is told. Chinese are always under a strong constraint to meet the expectations of superiors (Yau, 1994).

The concept of conformity has several implications in the situation in which the dining companions are the senior of the actor. First, if the seniors of the host, including parents, elders, leaders or bosses, expect the host to express their dissatisfaction to the restaurant, the host would do so. By contrast, if complaint behaviour is not culturally accepted or approved by parents or authorities, the host would not be offended by not complaining in front of his/her seniors even if he/she possesses a positive attitude towards complaint behaviour. Otherwise, the face of the seniors may be lost because the actor does not meet the expectations of the group members and the seniors (Jacobs, Guopei and Herbig, 1995). If the host disagrees with their parents or superiors and acts in opposition, this may lead to the loss of face of the parents or superiors, which is a serious mistake in Chinese society. Yet, if the dining companions are people in the same generation, such as colleagues and friends, the pressure to conform to their opinions is less momentous. In short, the types of dining companions and their opinions may exert influence on the complaint behaviour of Chinese consumers. Cheng (2003) found that the expectations and opinions of the important others was more critical than personal attitudes in the Chinese context when consumers make complaints.

The concern for not to being looked at undesirably and differently leads to high conformity to the social norm and what is perceived to be right by the members in the social circle (Triandis, 1995). It is common that Chinese conform with the expectations of others and the social norm (Bond, 1996). That is, if complaint behaviour is socially and culturally accepted, consumers may have high propensity to undertake complaint behaviour. On the contrary, if complaint behaviour is seen as a negative behaviour in the social circle, people may hesitate to engage in complaint behaviour. Kowalski (1996) asserted that many Chinese consumers perceived that the action of complaining may lead to others forming negative impressions towards the actor and they therefore feel reluctant to express their dissatisfaction. Consequently, the complaint intention/behaviour of Chinese consumers is heavily affected by the acceptance of complaint behavior and the social norm towards dissatisfactory experiences.

H_3: The opinions of different dining companions (in terms of seniority versus people in the same generation) moderate the relationship between Chinese cultural values (in terms of the concept of harmony, the doctrine of the Mean, and the face) and consumers' complaint intention.

The need for face   Chinese consumers may see complaint behaviour as an interpersonal action that facilitates impression management (Bond, 1996). That is, complaint behaviour can be employed as means to practice face, including maintaining one's *lien*, gaining one's *mianzi* and saving the *lien* of others. Having *mianzi* enhanced and saving the *mianzi* of others are the primary objectives in Chinese society (Hwang, 1987). There are many Chinese consumers who intensively arrange the settings of interactions with others to flaunt the symbols of power that signal their social status. Consumer complaints can be used as a means to enhance one's *mianzi*. In an incident, an individual consumer complains to a restaurant manager to show his/her *mianzi* when his/her requests are entertained, particularly, when an exclusive arrangement is made in response to the complainer. However, when dining with someone special, such as the boss or leaders, the host may feel a loss of face when the restaurant services are poor. Goffman (1967) asserted that the 'loss of face' may involve a shameful or humiliating experience of being dishonoured before others. Therefore, the host might complain to the restaurant management in the hope of regaining *mianzi* from the restaurant through proper recovery of services and apologies in front of others. This might indicate one's status and power and regain *mianzi*.

In another scenario, in the situation in which Chinese consumers maintain a very good relationship with the restaurant or its staff, the practice of face is essential to maintain existing role relationships. To maintain the relationship with the restaurants or its staff, consumers may protect the face of the restaurant or its staff by not to arguing or complaining overtly with the staff. The exercise of caution to prevent hurting other's face is regarded as a social skill (Bond, 1996). In short, the need to practice face largely depends on the situation. That is, if the situation requires the facilitation of face, including the gaining of one's face and protecting the others' face, to complain or not to complain becomes the means of impression management.

H_{4a}: The need to practice face moderates the relationship between the cultural value of harmony and consumers' complaint intention.

H_{4b}: The need to practice face moderates the relationship between the cultural values of the Mean and consumers' complaint intention.

Conclusion

This chapter represents a first attempt to explain consumers' complaint behaviour based on the distinctive characteristics of Chinese cultural values. The chapter discusses the unique values of Chinese, such as the desire for harmony and conflict avoidance, the rule of the Mean, and face, and examines their effect on the complaint behaviour of Chinese in the restaurant setting. This chapter proposes a conceptual model, associating the relationship between Chinese cultural values, complaint behaviour, and situation factors. A moderating relationship is also proposed between cultural values and complaint behaviour through situation factors.

Research and managerial implications

The chapter makes several contributions. First, so far there were only efforts explaining the complaint behaviour of Chinese on the basis of collectivist and individualist dimensions. Yet, the uniqueness of Chinese values is not limited to the collectivist orientation. Several other Chinese values, such as the concept of harmony, the doctrine of the Mean, and face, also exert influence on the behaviour of the Chinese.

Clearly, there is a lack of understanding of the complaint behaviours of the Chinese. This study is the first attempt to explain Chinese' consumer complaint behaviour based on traditional Chinese values other than collectivism. This study advances the current knowledge on the complaint behaviour of the Chinese.

Second, despite a general conception that Chinese consumers are reluctant to complain even when they are dissatisfied with products and services, no previous study proposed the importance of situation factors in moderating the relationship between cultural values and complaint behaviour in the Chinese setting. This chapter asserted that the complaint intention of Chinese consumers is largely moderated by situations. Although the complaint intention of Chinese consumers is low in many situations, they may complain in order facilitate impression management. This chapter takes a step further by proposing the moderating effect of situation factors.

From the managerial perspective, the paper has important strategic implications for restaurant practitioners. Although many studies reported that Chinese seldom complain even when they are dissatisfied, the propositions associated with the moderating role of situation factors highlight the importance of situation factors in enhancing complaint intentions of Chinese consumers. For instance, when an individual consumer wants to show his/her status and power in front of other diners, if the person realizes that consumer complaint can enhance one's *mianzi* when his/her requests are entertained, he/she may have higher motivation to engage in complaint behaviour. This reflects that one way for business management to encourage consumer complaints is to 'reward' the complainers through engaging in face-giving actions, such as apologizing to the complainer in front of the other diners or offering free wine to the dining companions of the complainer.

Future research

Cultural studies of consumer complaint behaviour are not new. Many researchers have examined the effect of cultural values on consumer complaints. However, most of the studies employed cultural dimensions developed by Hofstede (1980), which are frequently criticized as culturally bound and are not adaptable to eastern cultures, such as Chinese cultures (Yau *et al.*, 1999). Explicitly, the culture of the Chinese is different from the culture of other nations. The unique cultural values of Chinese are not limited to the doctrine of the Mean, the concern for harmony, and the sensitivity to face. There are a number of other Chinese values that may affect the complaint behaviour of Chinese consumers. This study only suggested the effect based on a few values. Thus, future studies may explore the effects of other cultural values, such as *Jen* (仁), *li* (禮), *Hao* (孝), and *Yuarn* (緣), on consumer complaint behaviours.

References

Alston, J.P. (1989) 'Wa, guanxi, and inhwa: managerial principles in Japan, China, and Korea', *Business* Horizons 3(4), 26–31.

Andreasen, A.R. and J. Manning (1990) 'The dissatisfaction and complaining behaviour of vulnerable consumers', *Journal of Customer Satisfaction, Dissatisfaction and Complaining Behaviour* 3(1), 12–20.

Au, K., M. K. Hui and K. Leung (2001) 'Who should be responsible? effects of voice and compensation on responsibility attribution, perceived justice, and post-complaint behaviours across cultures', *International Journal of Conflict Management* 2(4), 350–64.

Auty, S. (1992) 'Consumer choice and segmentation in the restaurant industry', *Service Industries Journal* 12(3), 324–39.

Belk, W.R. (1974) 'An exploratory assessment of situational effect in buying behavior', *Journal of Marketing Research* 11(5), 156–63.

Bennett, J.A. (2000) 'Mediator and moderator variables in nursing research: conceptual and statistical difference', *Research in Nursing & Health*, 415–20.

Blodgett, J.G., K. Wakefield and J. Barnes (1995) 'The effects of customer service on consumer complaining behaviour', *Journal of Services Marketing* 9(4), 31–42.

Bond, M.H. (1988) 'Finding universal dimensions of individual variation in multi-cultural studies of values: The Rokeach and Chinese value surveys', *Journal of Personality and Social Psychology* 55, 1009–15.

Bond, M.H. (1991) *Beyond the Chinese Face: Insights from Psychology* (Hong Kong: Oxford University Press).

Bond, M.H. (1993) 'Emotions and their expression in Chinese culture', *Journal of Nonverbal Inquiry* 5, 114–17.

Bond, M.H. (1996) *The Handbook of Chinese Psychology* (New York: Oxford University Press).

Bond, M.H. and K.K. Hwang (1986) 'The Social Psychology of Chinese People', in M.H. Bond (ed.), *The Psychology of Chinese People* (Hong Kong: Oxford University Press), pp. 213–66.

Cambridge University Press (2004) *Cambridge Advanced Learner's Dictionary* (London: Cambridge University Press).

Cavusgil, S.T. and E. Kaynak (1982) 'A Framework for Cross-cultural Measurement of Consumer Satisfaction', in R.L. Day and H.K. Hunt (eds), *New Findings on Consumer Satisfaction and Complaining* (Bloomington: Indiana University Press), pp. 81–4.

Chen, G.M. (2001) 'Towards Transcultural Understanding: A Harmony Theory of Chinese Communication', in V.H. Milhouse, M.K. Asante and P.O. Nwosu (eds), *Transculture: Interdisciplinary Perspectives on Cross-Cultural Relations* (Thousand Oaks, CA: Sage), pp. 55–70.

Chen, G.M. (2002) 'The Impact of Harmony on Chinese conflict management', in G.M. Chen and R. Ma (eds), *Chinese Conflict Management and Resolution* (Westport, CT: Ablex), pp. 3–17.

Chen, G.M. and J. Chung (1994) 'The impact of confucianism on organizational communication', *Communication Quarterly* 42, 93–105.

Chen, M. and W. Pan (1993) *Understanding the Process of Doing Business in China, Taiwan and Hong Kong* (Lewistown, NY: Edward Mellen Press).

Cheng, S. (2003) *Measuring Consumer Complaining Intention: Using Theory of Planned Behavior'* (unpublished thesis).

Chinese Cultural Connection (1987) 'Chinese cultural values and the search for culture-free dimensions of culture', *Journal of Cross-cultural Psychology* 18, 143–64.

Chiu, C.Y., S.C. Tsang and C. F. Yang (1988) 'The role of face situation and attitudinal antecedents in Chinese consumer complaint behavior', *Journal of Social Psychology* 128(2), 173–80.

Chung, B. and K.D. Hoffman (1998) 'Critical incidents: service failures that matter most', *Cornell Hotel and Restaurant Administration Quarterly* 38(6), 66–71.

Day, R.L. (1984) 'Modelling Choices among Alternative Responses to Dissatisfaction', in T. Kinnear (ed.), *Advances in Consumer Research* (Ann Arbor, MI: Association for Consumer Research) pp. 496–9.

Earley, P.C. (1997) *Face, Harmony, and Social Structure: An Analysis of Organizational Behaviour across Cultures* (New York Oxford University Press).

Engel, J., R. Blackwell and P. Miniard, (1990) *Consumer Behaviour* (6th edn, Hinsdale, IL: Dryden Press).

Engel, J.F., D.T. Kollat and R.D. Blackwell (1968) *Consumer Behaviour* (New York: Holt, Rinehart & Winston).

Erdem, O., A.A. Oumlil A.A. and S. Tuncalp (1999) 'Consumer values and the importance of store attributes', *International Journal of Retail & Distribution Management* 27(4), 137–44.

Feather, N.T. (1994) 'Values and national identification: Australian evidence', *Australian Journal of Psychology* 46(1), 35–40.

Foreign Language Teaching and Research Press (eds) (1988) *A Modern Chinese-English Dictionary* (Beijing: Foreign Language Teaching and Research Press).

Fornell, C. and R. A. Westbrook (1984) 'The vicious circle of consumer complaints', *Journal of Marketing* 48(3), 68–78.

Gire, J.T. (1997) 'The varying effect of individualism-collectivism on preference for methods of conflict resolution', *Canadian Journal of Behavioural Science* 29(1): 38–43.

Goffman, E. (1967) *Interaction Ritual: Essays on Face-to-Face Behaviour* (New York: Aldine).

Hirschman, A.O. (1970) *Exit, Voice, and Loyalty: Responses to Decline in Firms, Organizations and States* (Cambridge, MA: Harvard University Press).

Ho, D.Y.F. (1974) 'Early socialization in contemporary China', in *Proceedings of the Twentieth International Congress of Psychology*, (Tokyo: University of Tokyo Press), p. 442.

Hofstede, G. (1980) *Culture's Consequences: National Differences in Thinking and Organizing* (Beverly Hills, CA: Sage).

Hofstede, G. and M. H. Bond (1988) 'The Confucius connection: from cultural roots to economic growth', *Organizational Dynamics* 16(4), 4–21.

Hookham, H. (1969) *A Short History of China* (New York: New American Library).

Hsu, F.L.K. (1968) *Psychological anthropology: an essential defect and its remedy*, paper presented at the 1968 annual meeting of the American Anthropologist Association, Seattle, WA.

Hu, H.C. (1944) 'The Chinese concept of face', *American Anthropologist* 46, 45–64.

Hwang, K.K. (1983) 'Business organizational patterns and employee's working morale in Taiwan' (in Chinese), Bulletin of the Institute of Ethnology, *Academic Sinica* 56, 145–93.

Hwang, K.K. (1987), 'Face and favor: the Chinese power game', *American Journal of Sociology* 92(4), 944–74.

Hwang, K.K. (1990) 'Modernization of the Chinese family business', *International Journal of Psychology* 25, 593–618.

Hwang, K.K. (1997) 'Guanxi and Mientze: conflict resolution in Chinese society', *Intercultural Communication Studies* VII(1), 17–42.

Jacobs, L., G. Guopei and P. Herbig (1995) 'Confucian roots in China: a force for today's business', *Management Decision* 33(10), 29–34.

King, K.K. (1993) *Chinese Society and Culture* (Hong Kong: Oxford University Press, in Chinese).

Kirkbride, P.S., S.F.Y. Tang and R.I. Westwood (1991) 'Chinese conflict preferences and negotiating behavior: cultural and psychological influences', *Organization Studies* 12(3), 365–86.

Kleinman, A. (1980) *Patients and Healers in the Context of Culture* (Berkeley: University of California Press).

Kostant, P. (1999) 'Exit, voice and loyalty in the course of corporate governance and counsel's changing role', *Journal of Socio-Economics* 28(3), 203–46.

Kowalski, R.M. (1996) 'Complaints and complaining: functions, antecedents, and consequence', *Psychological Bulletin* 119(2), 179–96.

Lam, K.Y. and Y.L. Wong (1995) *Chinese Culture* (Hong Kong: Hong Kong Educational Books, in Chinese).

Lam, T., T. Baum and R. Pine (2003) 'Moderating effect on new employee's job satisfaction and turnover intentions: the role of subjective norm', *Annals of Tourism Research* 30(1), 160–77.

Lam, Y.T. (online dictionary) at <http://huamnum.arts.cuhk.edu.hk/Lexis/Lindict/>.

Le Claire, K.A. (1993) 'Chinese complaints behaviour', *Journal of International Consumer Marketing* 5(4), 73–92.

Legge, J. (1960) *The Chinese Classics* (Hong Kong: Hong Kong University Press).

Leung, K. (1988) 'Some determinants of conflict avoidance', *Journal of Cross-Cultural Psychology* 19, 125–36.

Leung, T.K.P. and R.Y.K. Chan (2003) 'Face, favor, and positioning: a Chinese power game', *European Journal of Marketing* 37(11/12), 1575–98.

Leung, K., P.T. Koch and L. Lu (2002) 'A dualistic model of harmony and its implications for conflict management in Asia', *Asia Pacific Journal of Management* 19, 201–20.

Liao, D.C. and T.C. Tsai (2002) 'The democratic concepts held by local elites on both sides of the Taiwan strait: the perception of political participation, economic equality, and conflict reconciliation', *Journal of Contemporary China* 11(31), 319–60.

Liu, R. and P. McClure (2001) 'Recognizing cross-cultural differences in consumer complaint behaviour and intentions: an empirical examination', *Journal of Consumer Marketing* 18(1), 54–74.

Luo, Y. (1997) 'Guanxi and performance of foreign-invested enterprises in China: an empirical inquiry', *Management International Review* 37(1), 51–70.

Mack, R., R. Mueller, J. Crotts, and A. Broderick (2000) 'Perceptions, corrections and defections: implications for service recovery in the restaurant industry', *Managing Service Quality* 10(6), 339–46.

Markus, H.R. and S. Kitayama (1994) 'A collective fear of the collective: implications for selves and theories of selves', *Personality and Social Psychology Bulletin* 20(5), 568–85.

Miáo, L.T. (1989) *The Psychology of Greece* (China: Press of China Renmin University, in Chinese).

Morris, M.W., K.Y. Williams and K. Leung *et al.* (1998) 'Conflict management style: accounting for cross-national differences', *Journal of International Business Studies* 29(4), 729–48.

Phinney, J.S. (1992) 'The multi-group ethnic identity measure: a new scale for use with diverse group', *Journal of Adolescent Research* 7(4), 156–76.

Pitta, D.A., H.G. Fung and S. Isberg (1999) 'Ethical issues across cultures: managing the differing perspectives of China and the USA', *Journal of Consumer Marketing* 16(3), 240–56.

Richins, M.L. (1983) 'Negative word-of-mouth by dissatisfied consumers: a pilot study', *Journal of Marketing* 47(1), 68–78.

Salaff, J.W. (1995) *Working Daughters of Hong Kong: Filial Piety or Power in the Family?* (New York: Columbia University Press).

Schlenker, B.R. (1980) *Impression Management: The Self-Concept, Social Identity, and Interpersonal Relations* (Monterey, CA: Brooks/Cole).

Schwartz, S.H. (1992) 'Universals in the Content and Structure of Values: Theoretical Advances and Empirical Tests in 20 Countries', in M.P. Zanna (ed.), *Advances in Experience SocialPsychology* (New York, Academic Press).

Schwartz, S. (1999) 'A theory of cultural values and some implications for work', *Applied Psychology: An International Review* 48(1), 23–47.

Singh, J. (1990) 'Voice, exit, and negative word of mouth behaviours: an investigation across three service categories', *Journal of the Academy of Marketing Science* 18(1), 1–15.

Singh, J. and P.E. Wilkes, (1996) 'When consumers complain: a path analysis of the key antecedents of consumer complaint response estimates', *Journal of the Academy of Marketing Science* 24(4), 350–65.

Smith, D.C. (1991) 'Children of China: an inquiry into the relationship between Chinese family life and academic achievement in modern Taiwan', *Asian Culture Quarterly* 14, 1–29.

Smith, P.B., M.F.Peterson and S.H.Schwartz (2002) 'Cultural values, sources of guidance, and their relevance to managerial behaviour: a 47-nation study', *Journal of Cross-Cultural Psychology* 33(2), 188–208.

Society of Consumer Affairs Professionals (SOCAP) (1996) *Consumer Loyalty Study* (Alexandria, VA: Society of Consumer Affairs Professionals).

Stephens, N. and K. Gwinner (1998) 'Why don't people complain? a cognitive-emotive process model of consumer complaint behaviour', *Journal of the Academy of Marketing Science* 26(3), 172–89.

Su, W.Y. and J. Bowen (2001) 'Restaurant customer complaint behaviour', *Journal of Restaurant & Foodservice Marketing* 4(2), 35–63.

Ting-Toomey, S. (1988) 'Intercultural Conflict Styles: A Face-negotiation theory', in Y.Y. Kim and Y. Gudykunst (eds), *Theories in Intercultural Communication* (Beverly Hills, CA: Sage), pp. 213–35.

Triandis, H.C. (1988) 'Cross-cultural Contributions to Theory in Social Psychology', in M.H. Bond (ed.), *The Cross-Cultural Challenge to Social Psycholgoy* (Newbury Park, CA: Sage), pp. 122–40.

Triandis, H.C. (1994) *Culture and Social Behaviour* (New York: Praeger).

Triandis, H.C. (1995) *Individualism and Collectivism* (Boulder, CO: Westview Press).

Tucci, L.A. and J. Talaga (1997) 'Service guarantees and consumers' evaluation of service', *Journal of Services Marketing* 11(1), 10–18.

Ward, S. and T.S. Robertson (1973) *Consumer Behaviour: Theoretical Sources* (Englewood Cliffs, NJ: Prentice Hall).

Watkins, H.S. and R.R. Liu (1996) 'Collectivism, individualism and in-group membership: implications for consumer complaining behaviours in multicultural contexts', *Journal of International Consumer Marketing* 8(3/4), 69–96.

Westwood, R. (1997) 'Harmony and patriarchy: The cultural basis for paternalistic headship among the overseas Chinese', *Organization Studies* 18(3), 445–80.

Williams Jr, R.M. (1970) *American Society: A Sociological Interpretation* (3rd edn, New York: Knopf).

Yang, K.S. (1981) 'Social orientation and individual modernity among Chinese students in Taiwan', *Journal of Social Psychology* 113(2),159–70.

Yao, X. (2001) 'Who is a Confucian today? a critical reflection on the issues concerning Confucian identity in modern times', *Journal of Contemporary Religious* 16(33), 313–28.

Yau, H.M. (1988) 'Chinese cultural values: their dimensions and marketing implications', *European Journal of Marketing* 22(5), 44–57.

Yau, O.H.M. (1994) *Consumer Behaviour in China: Customer Satisfaction and Cultural Value* (London: Routledge).

Yau, O.H.M. (2001) 'Chinese cultural values: Their dimensions and marketing implications', *European Journal of Marketing* 22(5), 44–57.

Yau, O.H.M. and L.Y.M. Sin (2001) 'Female role orientation and consumption values: some evidence from Mainland China,' *Journal of International Consumer Marketing* 13(2), 49–75.

Yau, O.H.M., T.S. Chan and K.F. Lau (1999) 'Influence of Chinese cultural values on consumer behaviour: a proposed model of gift-purchasing behaviour in Hong Kong', *Journal of International Consumer Marketing* 11(1), 97–116.

Yau, O.H.M., J.S.Y. Lee and R.P.M. Chow *et al.* (2000) 'Relationship marketing the Chinese way', *Business Horizons* (January/February), 16–24.

Yu, A.B. (1990) *The Construct Validity of Social-Oriented and Individual-Oriented Achievement Motivation* (unpublished doctoral dissertation, Department of Psychology, National Taiwan University).

10
Buyers of Pirated VCD/DVDs in Hong Kong: Their Profile and Perceptions

Wah-leung Cheung and Gerard Prendergast

Introduction

The international trade in counterfeit goods is, from all accounts, enormous. The United States estimates that counterfeiting volumes represent 9 percent of world trade and that it loses about $100 billion annually from counterfeiting (Chugani, 2001). On nearly a weekly basis, popular media such as CNN report another haul of pirated products manufactured in Mainland China or Hong Kong, and such reports are often accompanied by statistics pointing to a serious pirate problem. Such reports and statistics, however, need to be questioned since they are seldom, if ever, supported by primary research. What is certain, however, is that a wide variety of products are now pirated. Although the piracy of branded goods originated in the counterfeiting of elite consumer products such as branded clothing and accessories, such activity is now affecting a wide range of industries, including recorded music, VCDs/DVDs, fertilizers, pharmaceuticals, aircraft parts and food products such as coffee beans and Chinese herbs (Bush *et al.*, 1989). Of these, brand name products that carry a marketable and prestigious logo (such as VCDs/DVDs) are especially prone to product piracy. The focus of this chapter is on buyers of *pirated* products (as opposed to counterfeit, grey area or imitation products). In other words, the focus is on the purchase of fake products that are sold at a fraction of the original price, and the consumer knows they are fake. These are sometimes known as 'non-deceptive fakes' (Bamossy and Scammon, 1985; McDonald and Roberts, 1994; Wee *et al.*, 1995; Lai and Zaichkowsky, 1998).

This chapter, in contrast to previous studies, profiles heavy and light buyers of pirated VCDs/DVDs: their demographics, buying behaviour, and perceptions of pirated VCDs/DVDs *vis-à-vis* their original equivalents. Such information will provide a blueprint for creating better counter-strategies to eradicate the 'demand' for pirated VCDs/DVDs. Indeed, by distinguishing between heavy and light buyers, the results of this study can direct actions to counteract the buying of pirated products on those who buy them most often rather than focusing on those who may buy them only once or infrequently.

The Hong Kong context

Although piracy is a worldwide problem, Asia is notoriously considered as the world's worst violator of intellectual property rights (IPR). Hong Kong, in particular, has been identified as the main centre for the pirating of audio and video compact discs and for the supply of pirated branded consumer wear (Phau and Prendergast, 1998; A.J. Park & Son, 1999). Hong Kong is a highly developed economy that has a large trade in pirated products. In 2001, the Hong Kong government seized about 8.95 million pirated CDs/VCDs/DVDs with a total value of approximately US$23 million (Customs and Excise Department, 2002). A 2003 report by the Office of the US Trade Representative (USTR) states that, 'Hong Kong continues to make good progress in IPR protection' (Office of the US Trade Representative, 2003). The US government believes that Hong Kong's enforcement efforts, in particular, have become more effective in recent years. Nevertheless, the US government has not relaxed its monitoring efforts, and notes with concern that, 'the retail sale of pirated optical discs remains a problem'.

The preceding discussion suggests that counterfeiting is a serious problem in Hong Kong. While the literature focuses abundantly on the supply side of the problem, such as regulatory actions and studies of illegitimate distributors, empirical work on the demand for pirated products is still deficient. Previous studies tend to be based on consumer perceptions of pirated products, regardless of whether or not they are buyers of pirated products, and no studies have profiled heavy versus light buyers.

Previous studies

Many prior studies on product piracy emphasize the supply side of counterfeiting activities by considering various anti-pirating strategies that the firm can use to combat pirates (Bamossy and Scammon, 1985; Bush *et al.*, 1989; Olsen and Granzin, 1992; Chaudhry and Walsh, 1996). There are, however, a small number of studies on the demand for pirated products. For instance, Cordell *et al.* (1996) found three motivators for pirated good consumption, namely, the status symbol of the brand, the retailer's channel of distribution and the price of the pirated product. Research in Singapore by Swee *et al.* (2001) focused on pirated music CDs, and found that males and lower income groups had more favourable attitudes towards pirated products. More recently, Kwong *et al.* (2003) discovered that gender and age help explain consumer intentions to purchase pirated CDs in Hong Kong. Despite these studies, however, there are still some unanswered questions and contradictory findings regarding the purchasing of pirated goods, especially in relation to perceptions of pirated products *vis-à-vis* their original equivalents.

Objective

Previous studies have usually been based on consumer perceptions of pirated products, regardless of whether or not they are buyers of pirated products, and with no comparison of light versus heavy buyers. The objective of this chapter, in contrast, is to compare light and heavy buyers of pirated products in Hong Kong according to their demographics and buying behaviour. In addition, the research seeks the buyers' perceptions of pirated products vis-à-vis their original equivalents.

Hypotheses

Previous research (Prendergast *et al.*, 2002; Kwong *et al.*, 2003) has suggested that, contrary to what one might think, buyers of pirated products are not necessarily from lower socio-economic groups. This contradicts the findings in Singapore of Swee *et al.* (2001). They found that when it comes to purchasing pirated CDs, members of lower income groups had more favourable attitudes towards pirated products. This contradiction in the literature may arise because pirated goods buying behaviour is product-specific. For products which are consumed privately, especially in a household family setting, one could assert that family income is more relevant than personal income, and higher income households will spend more. This leads to H1:

> H1: Higher income households are more likely to be heavy buyers of pirated VCDs/DVDs than lower income households.

VCDs/DVDs are a relatively high tech product. Swee *et al.* (2001) and Kwong *et al.* (2003) found that, at least towards pirated music CDs, males had more favourable attitudes and purchase intentions than females. Such findings are consistent with other studies comparing male and female attitudes towards technology and technology-related products in general (Kantrowitz, 1999). This leads to H2:

> H2: Males are more likely to be heavy buyers of pirated VCDs/DVDs than females.

There has been no research reported comparing pirated product buyers' perceptions of pirated products with their perceptions of the equivalent original products. The theory of reasoned action (Fishbein and Azjen, 1975) would suggest that consumers make conscious choices based on two factors: how strongly they perceive the benefits to lead to a positive outcome, and the social norms, risks, and rewards they associate with that choice. Relating this to pirated VCDs/DVDs, one would assume that buyers perceive the benefits from these products to be greater than the illegal, unethical, or socially unacceptable aspects of these products. Cordell *et al.* (1996) found three motivators for using pirated goods: the status symbolized by the brand, the retailer's channel of distribution and the price of the pirated product. However, they did not directly compare the performance of pirated products with their original equivalents. Therefore, a research question is posed:

RQ1: How are pirated products perceived relative to their original equivalents?

Methodology

Focus group interviews were conducted in Hong Kong to generate more information about pirated goods buying behaviour. All the participants in the focus groups had recently purchased pirated VCDs/DVDs. Responses elicited from the focus groups included information on perceptions of pirated products and original products (later to be used in factor analysis), and definitions of heavy and light buyers of pirated products.

Sample

In order to investigate how different people view pirated products, and to test the hypotheses, the quota sampling method was used. Within this method, the bases were sex and age. Equal numbers of male and female respondents, and different age groups, were interviewed. Mall intercepts were used to find the target interviewees. These mall intercept interviews were conducted by a team of trained field workers. Interviewees who had knowingly purchased pirated VCDs/DVDs within the past six months were chosen. Roughly half of those people approached met this criteria, although the response varied according to whether or not the interviews were taking place in a 'fake district' or not.

Instrument

The questionnaire was divided into two parts. The first part investigated people's pirate VCD/DVD purchasing behaviour: how often did they buy, how did they buy, and, using 7-point Likert scales, their perceptions of the pirated products vis-à-vis their original equivalents. In the second part, demographic questions were asked. The questionnaire was originally written in English, translated into Chinese, and then back-translated to check for translation accuracy. Interviews were conducted in Chinese.

Purchase of pirated products

In order to get a true measure of the quantity of pirated products consumers are buying, both purchase frequency and purchase quantity must be taken into account. Interviewees were asked how often (in a four-month period) they normally purchased pirated VCDs/DVDs, and in what quantity. The purchase quantity weighting (Q) was then multiplied by the purchase frequency (F) weighting, to arrive at a sum figure. The responses were ranked based on these sums and the sample was split into two groups, which were labelled *light* and *heavy* buyers:

Light buyer: $Q \times F = 1$–5 (57 percent of the sample)
Heavy buyer: $Q \times F = 6$–15 (43 percent of sample)

Findings

Sample demographics can be viewed in Appendix 1. The sample demographics equate with the quota criteria in terms of roughly equal distributions across gender and age groups.

Demographics and purchasing behaviour of buyers of pirated products

Heavy and light buyers were compared according to their demographics. Looking, first, at family monthly income, there were no significant differences across family income groups. H1 is therefore rejected. Looking at gender: $\chi^2 = 3.34$, df = 1, p = 0.044, with males more likely to be heavy buyers of pirated VCDs/DVDs. This supports H2.

For the remaining demographic groups (personal monthly Income, occupation, education, age, marital status) there were no demographic differences in the profile of heavy and light buyers of pirated VCDs/DVDs. These findings therefore suggest that VCDs/DVDs are being especially purchased by males.

How do buyers identify pirated products?

Interviewees were asked to indicate how they identify pirated VCDs/DVDs. The results are shown in Table 10.1.

Table 10.1:   Methods for identifying pirated VCDs/DVDs

Method	(n = 283)
Lower price	82.3%
Buying location	64%
Poor package	70.7%
Poor printing on VCD/DVD	53.4%
Without original logo	26.1%
Friends or family members' opinions	7.4%
Available before launch of original VCD/DVD	16.3%

Note: Multiple response.

Table 10.2:   For whom they buy pirated VCDs/DVDs

	(n = 283)
For own self	92.5%
For family members	42.4%
As gift to others	.7%
Other	0%

Note: Multiple response.

A high percentage of respondents said that they identify pirated VCDs/DVDs by their low prices, the location of the purchase and poor packaging.

For whom are pirated products bought?

When respondents were asked for what purpose pirated VCDs/DVDs would be used, most interviewees reported that the VCDs/DVDs were for their private entertainment. This is consistent with the argument that VCDs/DVDs are consumed privately. Less than one half reported that they buy them for family entertainment, while very few buy them for gifts. Table 10.2 shows the results.

Perceptions of pirated VCDs/DVDs

To address the research question posed in this chapter, the interviewees were asked to indicate how they perceived pirated VCDs/DVDs in terms of 12 attributes (generated from focus groups and literature). With the aim of developing a deeper understanding of buyer perceptions of pirated VCDs/DVDs, the 12 items were subjected to principal components analysis (PCA). The PCA revealed the presence of four components with

Table 10.3: Rotated component matrix: pirated VCD/DVD perceptions

	Component	
	1	*2*
The purchase is ethical	0.854	
The purchase is legal	0.801	
VCD/DVD quality is reasonable	0.658	
VCD/DVD after sale service is reasonable	0.513	
VCD/DVD supported by VCD/DVD machines	0.593	
VCD/DVD supply is adequate		0.771
VCD/DVD variety is adequate		0.768
VCD/DVD popular with friends		0.516
VCD/DVD is published quickly		0.519
VCD/DVD is accepted by family		0.475

Notes: Extraction method: principal component analysis; Rotation method: varimax with Kaiser normalization; Rotation converged in three iterations.

eigenvalues exceeding 1, and factor loadings of 0.4 and above. An inspection of the screeplot revealed a clear break after the second component. After consideration of the conceptual validity and reliability of the extracted factors and the ability of the results to lead future research, a two factor solution was determined to provide the most valid and parsimonious solution. To aid in the interpretation of these two factors, the varimax rotational method was used. The rotated solution revealed the presence of simple structures, with the two components showing a number of strong loadings, as shown in Table 10.3. The items 'price is reasonable', as well as 'VCD/DVD can be viewed many times', did not adequately load onto any of the factors, and they were dropped from further analysis.

The two-factor solution explained a total of 48.81 percent of the variance. The two factors (with alpha scores) measuring pirated VCD/DVD perceptions are labelled as:

(1)   Confidence in pirated VCDs/DVDs 0.75
(2)   Convenience of pirated VCDs/DVDs 0.67

There is no standard cut-off point for the alpha coefficient, but the generally agreed upon lower limit for Cronbach's alpha is 0.70, although it may fall to 0.60 (Hair *et al.*, 1998) or even 0.50 in exploratory research. The reliabilities reported here clearly are not exceptional, but for the purposes of this research they were deemed to be reasonable.

Table 10.4:   Perceptions of pirated VCDs/DVDs versus expectations of VCDs/DVDs in general

	Perf	*Expect*	*t*	*Sig*
Component 1				
The purchase is ethical	4.53	2.05	20.42	0.000*
The purchase is legal	4.99	1.95	22.53	0.000*
VCD/DVD quality is reasonable	3.64	1.53	19.46	0.000*
After-sales service (e.g., liberal return policy) is reasonable	4.98	1.99	23.03	0.000*
They are supported by VCD/DVD machines	3.72	1.55	19.43	0.000*
Component 2				
VCD/DVD supply is adequate	2.80	1.76	11.48	0.000*
VCD/DVD variety is adequate	2.84	1.73	11.81	0.000*
They are popular with my friends	2.76	2.44	3.17	0.002*
They are published quickly after the public screening of the movie	2.17	2.33	−1.34	0.181
VCD/DVD accepted by family	2.82	2.24	5.23	0.000*

Notes: *sig at 0.001; **sig at 0.05; 1 = strongly agree and 7 = strongly disagree; Perf = performance of pirated VCD/DVDs; Expect = expectation from VCDs/DVDs in general.

Perceptions of pirated VCDs/DVDs and expectations of VCDs/DVDs in general

Interviewees were asked to identify their perceptions of pirated VCDs/DVDs, and, on the same scale and using the same items, to identify their expectations of VCDs/DVDs in general. Paired sample t-tests were then run to identify how pirated VCDs/DVDs perform relative to what consumers expect from this product in general. The results are shown in Table 10.4.

Pirated VCDs/DVDs tended to perform most poorly in terms of their after sales service, and ethical and legal aspects. However, buyers gave high ratings to pirated VCD/DVD's speed of publishing, supply, variety and acceptability from friends and family. Compared to expectations from original VCDs/DVDs, pirated VCDs/DVDs performed significantly below expectations on most dimensions. The largest gaps where pirated VCDs/DVDs are underperforming relative to expectations of VCDs/DVDs in general appear to be in the areas of variety, quality, ethical and legal aspects, and after sales service.

Discussion

Heavy buyers of pirated VCDs/DVDs were typically males. This is consistent with the findings of Kwong *et al.* (2003), although they found that not only were buyers of pirated CDs male, but they were also younger. Overall, however, perhaps the most curious demographic finding is that essentially pirated VCDs/DVDs are purchased by a broad spectrum of consumers, with (apart from more males buying VCDs/DVDs) no particular demographic group appearing dominant. Pirated VCDs/DVDs in Hong Kong, therefore, are purchased by the mass market. As Kwong *et al.* (2003) have said, there is often a misconception that customers buying pirated goods tend to have a low income and a low education. The pirated market in Hong Kong is big, and the trade is only partially concealed. Despite the Chinese being a proud people who treasure face (Graham and Lam, 2003) there is a strange dichotomy between this attitude and the seemingly shameless trading in pirated products. For the local people, pirated purchases may not be as dishonourable as one might think. Indeed the practice is so rampant that one would have to assume that it is perceived as being quite normal and acceptable. Perhaps, as suggested by Swinyard *et al.* (1990), for traditional Chinese society the reproduction of others' works is an acceptable way of promoting, learning, and admiring their talents.

Pirated VCDs/DVDs, which buyers purchased primarily for themselves or their family, were identified mainly through their price and buying location. Regarding location, it is well known that within Hong Kong there are 'fakes districts', which sometimes only come to life after nightfall and may involve many mobile hawkers as well as more permanent retailers.

An inconsistency surfaced when the results of this study are compared with prior studies. The general belief that pirated products are used as gifts is challenged here. Only a small number of respondents said that they buy pirated brands of VCDs/DVDs as gifts. This may be a cultural reflection of Chinese consumers. Chinese are believed to be more concerned about how they project themselves socially (Phau and Prendergast, 1998). If receivers know that gifts given to them are pirated, the giving of such a gift may result in the loss of *lien* (face) for the giver. This embarrassment may have a detrimental effect on the reputation of the presenter, a phenomenon documented by Yau (1988).

The research question in this study was aimed at identifying how pirated VCDs/DVDs are perceived relative to their original equivalents. Results showed that pirated VCDs/DVDs were perceived as being in adequate supply and having adequate variety, and to be up to date. Comparing consumer perceptions of pirated VCDs/DVDs with their expectations from original equivalents, pirated VCDs/DVDs were felt to under perform in all respects, but most strongly in the areas of variety, quality, their ethical and legal aspects, and after sales service. Coming back to the theory of reasoned action, one can logically deduce from these finding that buyers presumably feel that, in sum, the benefits of pirated VCDs/DVDs outweigh the drawbacks relating to the ethical and legal aspects, and after sales service.

Recommendations for reducing pirated buying

There are two basic strategies for reducing pirated product buying: one is to eradicate supply through stronger law enforcement, and the other is through changing consumer attitudes towards pirated products. It is unlikely that government measures alone will protect multinational organizations from being victimized by counterfeiters and pirated product producers. Perhaps, as an alternative strategy, multinationals might target the *demand* for pirated products rather than the supply. The preceding findings have several implications for policy makers and legitimate manufacturers in their fight against the demand for pirated products. The government needs to implement large-scale campaigns to educate the public about the economic and social consequences of consumption of counterfeit goods. Publicity campaigns to highlight the repercussions of piracy such as those sponsored by Louis Vuitton and Ralph Lauren (Wada, 1996) should be encouraged. When consumers realize that they can also become direct victims, they will be more hesitant to buy pirated products.

Buying location is a key way to identify pirated VCDs/DVDs, and Hong Kong is known to have 'pirated districts'. Legitimate manufacturers should publish and distribute a list of genuine distributors and retailers to inform consumers where they can buy genuine brands. Also, manufacturers should advise the distributors and retailers to exhibit 'a genuine logo' explicitly in their shops. Moreover, manufacturers should not distribute their genuine brands in 'pirated districts'. As a result, consumers can easily differentiate between genuine brands and pirated products.

Since pirated VCDs/DVDs tend to perform most poorly (relative to original products) in terms of after sales service, and the legal and ethical aspects of the purchase, these are the aspects that original brand manufacturers would do well to emphasize in their promotion. Also, in order to convince counterfeit buyers not to buy pirated VCDs/DVDs, there is a need to promote the ways in which it is not in their self-interest to do so (Tom *et al.*, 1998). Giving warranties and after-sales service are some ways in which original goods manufacturers might effectively differentiate their products from pirated copies according to the results of this study.

Conclusions and future research

Despite the importance of the findings, this research has several limitations. First, only buyers in Hong Kong were surveyed. However, it is not intended that Hong Kong be representative of Mainland China. Second, other categories of pirated products may elicit different responses from the subjects, bearing in mind that the criteria for choice of pirated products differ by product category as suggested by Greenberg *et al.* (1983).

Limitations aside, this chapter has shed light on buyers of pirated products in Hong Kong. In particular, more is now known about the demographics of heavy and light pirated buyers in Hong Kong, and their buying behaviour and perceptions. The challenge now is to deter both heavy and light buyers from buying pirated products while taking into consideration their different demographic backgrounds, and buying behaviour and perceptions.

Future research should be extended to products with varying degrees of involvement and also other product categories. Extending the study to the purchase of pirated products on the Internet may be another worthwhile direction. As this study highlighted a number of inconsistencies when compared to prior studies, the cultural climate of the consumers may be a factor. Replicating this study in other Asian countries with high incidences of piracy is therefore recommended. This is especially important since the literature seems to suggest that the proliferation of counterfeiting activities is rampant in many Asian countries and not just in Hong Kong. In addition, this study has reduced the information about many perception variables into a set of weighted factors. These factors need to be further validated in future research and incorporated into models of pirated product buying.

Future studies could also look at the influence of materialism, conformity, and ethical considerations among pirated product buyers. All these constructs have established scales in the literature which could be adapted to the Chinese context. Since Hong Kong is a modern economy, does materialism play a part in the purchase of pirated products? In terms of conformity, Chinese consumers, it is believed, have a high motivation and propensity to conform in their consumption choices, and the profound influence of Confucius' teachings on Chinese consumers' consumption choices is manifested in their high motivation to comply (Gong, 2003). Does conformity play a role in the purchase of pirated products? Finally, pirated products did not score highly in terms of their legal and ethical aspects. An ethics scale could be used to identify how ethical considerations influence the behaviour of pirated product buyers and, for that matter, non-buyers.

Note

Part of this chapter has been published in *Marketing Intelligence and Planning*, 24(5) (2006), pp. 446–62, and the Journal of International Consumer Marketing, 18(3) (2006), pp. 7–31.

References

A.J. Park & Son (1999) Consultant's Report on 'Theft of Intellectual Property – Piracy and Counterfeiting', Ministry of Commerce, New Zealand, available at <http://www.moc.govt.nz/gbl/int_prop/theft/index.html>.

Bamossy, G. and D. Scammon, D. (1985) 'Product Counterfeiting: Consumers and Manufacturing Beware', in E.C. Hirshman and M.B. Holbrook (eds.), *Advances in Consumer Research*, Vol 12 (Provo, UT: Association for Consumer Research), pp. 334–9.

Bush, R.F., H.P. Bloch and S. Dawson (1989) 'Remedies for product counterfeiting', *Business Horizons* January/February, 56–66.

Chaudhry, P.E. and M. Walsh, (1996) 'An assessment of the impact of counterfeiting in international markets: the piracy paradox persists', *Columbia Journal of World Business* Fall, 35–48.

Chugani, M. (2001) 'US seizes $280 m in pirated watches', *South China Morning Post*, 24 June p. 1.

Cordell, V., N. Wongtada and R. Kieschnick (1996) 'Counterfeit purchase intentions: role of lawfulness attitudes and product traits as determinants', *Journal of Business Research* 35, 41–53.

Customs and Excise Department (2002) *Annual Review 2001* (Hong Kong: HKSAR).

Fishbein, M. and I. Azjen (1975) *Belief, Attitude, Intention and Behavior: An Introduction to Theory and Research* (Reading, MA: Addison-Wesley).

Gong, W. (2003) 'Chinese consumer behavior: A cultural framework and implications' *Journal of American Academy of Business* 3(1/2), 373.

Graham, J.L and N.M. Lam (2003) 'The Chinese negotiation,' *Harvard Business Review* 81(10) October.

Greenberg, C.J., E. Sherman and L.G. Schiffman (1983) 'The Measurement of Fashion Image as a Determinant of Store Patronage', in W.R. Darden and R.F. Lusch (eds), *Patronage Behavior and Retail Management* (New York: North Holland), pp. 151–63.

Hair, J.F., R.E. Anderson, R.L Tatham and W.C Black, (1998) *Multivariate Data Analysis* (Englewood Cliffs, NJ: Prentice Hall).

Kantrowitz, B. (1999) *Men, Women, and Computers. CyberReader* (2nd edn, Boston, MA Allyn and Bacon)

Kwong, K.K, O.H.M. Yau, J.S.Y. Lee, *et al.* (2003) 'The effects of attitudinal and demographic factors on intention to buy pirated CDs: the case of Chinese consumers', *Journal of Business Ethics* 47(3), 223–35.

Lai, K. and J.L Zaichkowsky (1999) 'Brand Imitation: Do the Chinese have Different Views?', *Asia Pacific Journal of Management*, 16(2), 179–92.

MacDonald, G. and C. Roberts (1994) 'Product Piracy: The Problem that will not go Away', *Journal of Product and Brand Management*, 3, 55–65.

Office of the United States Trade Representative 2003 Inventory of trade barriers. At http://www.mindfully.org/WTO/2003/USTR-Trade-Barriers1apr03.htm

Olsen, J.E and K.L. Granzin (1992) 'Gaining retailers' assistance in fighting counterfeiting: conceptualisation and empirical test of a helping model', *Journal of Retailing* 68(1), 90–112.

Phau, I. and G. Prendergast (1998) 'Counterfeit products – riding the waves in the new millennium', Business and Economics Society International Conference, Rome, July.

Porteous, S.D. (2001) 'China's trade advantage undermined by counterfeiting menace', *World Trade* November, 28–9.

Prendergast, G., H.C. Leung and I. Phau (2002) 'Understanding consumer demand for non-deceptive pirated brands', *Marketing Intelligence and Planning* 7(20), 405–16.

Swee, H.A., S.C. Peng, E. Lim and S.K. Tambyah (2001), 'Spot the difference: consumer responses towards counterfeits', *Journal of Consumer Marketing* 18(3), 219–35.

Swinyard, W.R., R. Heikki and A.K. Kau (1990) 'The morality of software piracy', *Journal of Business Ethics* 9, 655–64.

Wada, T. (1996) 'Brand Name Demand Brings More Fakes', *The Nikkei Weekly* 32(1), 742.

Wee, C.H., S.J Tan and K.H. Cheek (1995) 'Non-price determinants of intention to purchase counterfeit goods – an exploratory study', *International Marketing Review* 12(6), 1–20.

Yau, O.H.M. (1988) 'Chinese cultural values: their dimensions and marketing implications', *European Journal of Marketing* 22(5), 44–57.

Appendix 1:   Sample demographics

		Frequency	Percent
Gender			
Male		189	50.0
Female		189	50.0
	Total	378	100.0
Marital status			
Single		158	41.9
Married		202	53.6
Divorced		9	2.4
Others		8	2.1
Missing		1	–
	Total	378	100.0
Age			
19 or below		18	4.8
20–24		42	11.1
25–29		50	13.2
30–34		40	10.6
35–39		49	13.0
40–44		41	10.8
45–49		48	12.6
50–54		74	19.6
55–59		12	3.2
60 or above		4	1.1
	Total	378	100.0
Education level			
Primary school		28	7.4
Junior middle school		81	21.4
Senior middle school		137	36.2
Technical secondary school		29	7.7
Associate degree		48	12.7
University		52	13.8
Post-graduate or above		3	0.8
	Total	378	100.0
Occupation			
Entrepreneur		35	9.3
Professional		50	13.2
Associate professional		19	5.0
Manager/section head		17	4.5
Technical worker		22	5.8
Business/service personnel		60	15.9
General clerical personnel		55	14.6
General production worker		23	6.1
Elementary occupation		10	2.6
Housewife		49	13.0
Student		17	4.5

(*Continued*)

Appendix 1: (*Continued*)

		Frequency	Percent
Retired		14	3.7
Unemployed		7	1.9
	Total	378	100.0
Personal income (monthly)			
No income		55	14.6
HK$1–HK$1 k		8	2.1
HK$1.1–3.9 k		8	2.1
HK$4–5.9 k		19	5.0
HK$6–7.9 k		33	8.7
HK$8–9.9 k		64	16.9
HK$10–14.9 k		97	25.7
HK$15–19.9 k		43	11.4
HK$20–24.9 k		20	5.3
HK$25–39.9 k		23	6.1
HK$40–59.9 k		6	1.6
HK$60 k or above		2	0.5
	Total	378	100.0
Family income (monthly)			
No income		2	0.5
HK$1–HK$1 k		1	0.3
HK$1.1–3.9 k		1	0.3
HK$4–5.9 k		2	0.5
HK$6–7.9 k		5	1.3
HK$8–9.9 k		13	3.4
HK$10–14.9 k		43	11.4
HK$15–19.9 k		76	20.1
HK$20–24.9 k		85	22.5
HK$25–39.9 k		87	23.0
HK$40–59.9 k		43	11.4
HK$60 k or above		20	5.3
	Total	378	100.0

11
The Competitive Potential of Asian Business Groups: A Comparative Analysis of *Kigyo Shudan* and *Chaebol*

Martin Hemmert

Introduction

Large, diversified business groups from Asian countries have attracted the interest of researchers and practitioners for many years. Until the 1990s, they were mostly regarded as one of the key factors for the long-term economic success of the East Asian region (Tselichtchev, 1999). Following Japan's economic stagnation throughout the past decade and the serious trouble that most East Asian countries experienced during and after the 1997 financial crisis, however, the Asian business groups have been assessed with more critical eyes recently. They are now often seen as an obstacle to the structural reform of the economic system of Asian countries (Jwa and Lee, 2000).

Notably, business groups are not a phenomenon that are limited to East Asian countries. Rather they can be found in many emerging countries all over the world (Khanna and Palepu, 1997). However, their organizational structures and functions appear to vary considerably between countries. As a result of this structural heterogeneity, their very definition is a non-trivial task (Khanna, 2000). Whereas economists tend to focus on the cross-ownership patterns of their member firms, sociologists, political scientists and historians are emphasizing the formal and informal relationships between these firms. According to Granovetter (1995), they are characterized by an 'intermediate' level of binding between short-term alliances on the one hand and legally consolidated firms on the other hand. For the discussion in this chapter, they are understood as clearly identifiable, horizontally diversified groups of legally independent firms that are linked together by governance structures that at least partially go beyond the formal managerial control mechanisms based on equity ownership in conglomerate firms of Western countries.

Given the fact that business groups thus can be defined by their difference from Western-style conglomerate firms, it is not surprising that Western observers often find it difficult to understand their internal structure and to assess their competitive potential. Managers of Western firms that are competing with member firms of Asian business groups tend to suspect that they are effectively competing not only with these single member firms, but with whole business groups which back them through invisible links. Another frequent assumption of Western observers is that business groups from different Asian countries are fundamentally similar due to the cultural and structural economic commonalities of the countries in which they reside. The validity of this assumption has not been frequently discussed since Asian business groups have been mainly analysed on a country-specific base hitherto, in most cases with a focus either on Japan (e.g., Gerlach, 1992; Shimotani, 1993) or on Korea (e.g., Cho, 1991; Chang, 2003). Relatively few attempts (Orru *et al.*, 1997; Shin and Kwon, 1999) have been made to analyse Asian business groups from an international comparative perspective.

Given the varying and partially contradicting structural and economic assessments of Asian business groups that can be found in the academic as well as the popular literature and the mostly country-specific nature of the research on them, two questions are evolving. First, how strong is the business groups' competitive potential? Are they dynamic competitive giants that are threatening domestic and international rivals? Or are they fading organizations that are representing the past, dinosaurs in the competitive landscape of the 21st century? Second, how similar or dissimilar are Asian business groups in different countries? Do they share common governance structures or are they fundamentally different?

This chapter contributes to the literature by addressing those two research questions. First, in order to analyse the competitive potential of business groups from a strategic management perspective, a new conceptual framework is developed. Thereafter, based on this framework, a comparative assessment of the competitive potential of Japanese and Korean business groups is conducted through an analysis of a variety of recent data sources and publications. Whereas business groups can also been observed in many other Asian countries such as India (Khanna and Palepu, 2000), China (Lee and Hahn, 2003), Thailand (Polsiri and Wiwattanakantang, 2003) or Taiwan (Hamilton, 1997), the focus on these two countries has been guided by the notion that Japanese and Korean business groups are perceived as the most important in the context of international competition.

Conceptual framework

Business groups, by definition, consist of multiple firms. Therefore, they are approached in the literature from the viewpoint of inter-organizational networks (Imai, 1992). However, they are also frequently perceived by other firms as direct competitors. Following this perspective, an analysis of business groups from the viewpoint of strategic management appears helpful.

One basic approach in the strategic management literature is the market-based view. According to this view, which is strongly founded on industrial economics, the competitive strength of firms is derived from their ability to create and sustain cost or quality advantages over their competitors, and to build up a favourable position towards other market forces such as customers, suppliers, or producers of substitution goods (Porter, 1980, 1985). Thus, the market-related competitive position of a firm can be assessed by its market share and relative market position in an industry as well as by its relative bargaining position towards other market forces, such as suppliers and customers.

The other approach to strategic management frequently adopted is the resourced-based view, which stresses the internal resources of a firm instead of its position towards external market forces (Penrose, 1959; Wernerfelt, 1984). Resources are understood as any internal assets that could constitute a strength or weakness of a firm, such as brand names, in-house knowledge of technology, employment of skilled personnel, trade contacts, machinery, efficient procedures, capital, etc. (Wernerfelt, 1984). Specifically, the ability of firms to create resource position barriers through the acquisition of unique or sustainable resources is emphasized by this approach. The resource-based competitive strength of a firm can be measured by the quantity and quality of their resources, for example, the number and the skills of their personnel, when compared with their competitors.

Thus, by applying the market-based view and the resource-based view to business groups, their competitive potential may be evaluated by analysing the combined market-based and resource-based competitive potential of the member firms. However, both views have been originally developed to analyse single firms, not business groups. The concepts are built on the assumption that a firm can effectively be controlled by its management in order to build up a favourable market- or resource-based competitive position. This assumption of managerial control cannot be taken for granted in the case of business groups. Therefore, when analysing the competitive potential of a business group, it also has to be analysed to what extent managerial control can be exerted over it. Only a business group case which is managerially controlled like a single firm can utilize

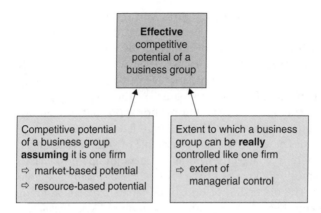

Figure 11.1: Conceptual framework

its market or resource potential to the same extent as a single firm. The less such control can be exerted, the more is a group's ability paralysed to take advantage of its market- or resource-based competitive potential. The amount to which a business group can be managerially controlled can be assessed by analysing the existence and strength of group-level managerial boards, by the strength of the ties between its member firms and by the extent to which these ties are hierarchical.

In sum, the amount of a business group's effective competitive potential is determined by (1) its (a) market-based and (b) resource-based competitive potential, and (2) the degree to which it can be managerially controlled (Figure 11.1). Japanese and Korean business groups are analysed from these three viewpoints.

Empirical analysis

Overview: Japanese *Kigyo Shudan*

Japanese business groups became prominent in the course of the country's industrialization since the end of the 19th century under the term *zaibatsu* (literally: financial cliques). They were family-owned, very diversified and played a prominent role in Japan's economic development in the first half of the 20th century when the country's resources were strongly concentrated on them (Morikawa, 1992).

After the Second World War, the *zaibatsu* were expropriated from their owner families and dissolved into single-business member firms (Biggart and Hamilton, 1997). Following Japan's regained political independence in the 1950s, however, the horizontal business groups rebuilt themselves.

Three of the newly created groups, Mitsui, Mitsubishi and Sumitomo, strongly resembled prewar *zaibatsu* with regard to the composition of their member firms. An important difference between these business groups and their prewar predecessors, however, was the fact that the former owner families were no more involved in the postwar groups, which rather constituted themselves based on the voluntary membership of firms. Furthermore, three additional horizontal business groups, namely Fuyo, Sanwa, and Dai-Ichi Kangyo, founded themselves during the post-war decades based on the same principle of voluntary membership.[1]

Therefore, six large horizontal business groups now exist in Japan. These groups are known as the *roku dai kigyo shudan* (six large business groups). The discussion of horizontal Japanese business groups will be focused on these six groups under the term of *kigyo shudan*.[2]

Overview: Korean *Chaebol*

Diversified business groups play an important role in South Korea since the 1960s when the country started its rapid industrialization and economic development. These business groups became generally known as *chaebol*. The term *chaebol* is based on the same Chinese characters as the prewar Japanese *zaibatsu*. Furthermore, *chaebol* are, like the former *zaibatsu* and in contrast to the contemporary *kigyo shudan* in Japan, linked to owner families.

Until the 1970s, there were frequent changes in the ranks of the leading *chaebol*, which reflected the extremely fast and disruptive development of Korea's economy. Thereafter, the ranks of the *chaebol* became more stable. In particular, five *chaebol* established themselves as the leading Korean business groups during the 1980s and the 1990s: Hyundai, Samsung, LG, Daewoo and SK. These five groups clearly dominated all other *chaebol* in terms of economic size (Chang, 2003).

The Asian financial crisis of 1997, however, resulted in another shake-out among the Korean business groups (Kim *et al.*, 2004). About half of the 30 largest *chaebol* underwent bankruptcy or bank-sponsored restructuring. The most prominent victim was the Daewoo group, which was one of the five leading *chaebol*. Daewoo became bankrupt in 1999 and ceased to exist as a business group. Another recent development was the voluntary breakup of Hyundai, the formerly largest *chaebol*: Hyundai Motor, which is centred on the automobile business, was separated from the Hyundai group. The new Hyundai Motor group ranks now among the top four *chaebol* together with Samsung, LG and SK. Accordingly, the subsequent analysis of the present situation of Korean business groups will be focused on these four *chaebol*.

The market-based competitive potential

Tables 11.1 and 11.2 provide an overview of the member firms of the six large *kigyo shudan* in Japan and of the four leading *chaebol* in Korea by industries. The data show that the business groups in both countries are highly diversified in general as they embrace one or several member firms in many industries.

Since the industry level is the main level of analysis from the market-based perspective, however, the position of the business groups in each industry appears to be more relevant than their overall size in order to evaluate their market-based competitive potential. From this viewpoint, the picture is quite different. The Japanese business groups often have only one firm in one industry, indicating that they do not possess a stronger market-related competitive potential in these industries than single-firm competitors. In other fields such as the banking and insurance industry or the chemical and pharmaceutical industry, most of *kigyo shudan* possess several firms. A closer look at these firms reveals, however, that they are mostly specialized on separate market segments. As a result, whereas most of the business groups embrace one firm that is focused on each market segment within these industries, they do not possess a particular strong market position *within* any of these market segments. Therefore, from this viewpoint, there is little evidence that any of the Japanese business groups possess a particularly strong market-based competitive potential in specific industries on the domestic Japanese market, not to speak of the international market.

The Korean business groups are also highly diversified in general. However, the overall picture is somewhat different from the Japanese case. It seems that the *chaebol* have concentrated their resources to a certain extent on specific industries. For instance, the LG and SK groups possess a considerable number of member firms in the oil, gas and energy business, suggesting that their competitive potential in the domestic market is quite significant in these industries. Nevertheless, most of the four leading *chaebol* have one or a few member firms in most industries, resulting in a limitation of the market potential of each group in each industry.

There is, however, one clear exception among the leading Korean business groups as regards the industry-level concentration of its activities: the Hyundai Motor group. This group holds a dominant market position in the automobile industry on the domestic market since it embraces both Hyundai Motor, which is now by far the largest Korean automobile firm, and Kia Motors. Moreover, it also holds a strong position in the steel industry, which is one of the main supplier industries of the automobile industry. Notably, the wish to create a leaner business

Table 11.1: Member firms of the six Japanese *Kigyo Shudan* by industry (2000)

	Mitsui (n = 25)	Mitsubishi (n = 28)	Sumitomo (n = 20)	Fuyo (n = 27)	Sanwa (n = 44)	Daiichi-Kangyo (n = 48)
Banking and Insurance	Sakura Bank, Chuo Mitsui Trust and Banking, Mitsui Life Insurance, Mitsui Marine & Fire Insurance	Bank of Tokyo-Mitsub., Mitsubishi Trust and Banking, Meiji Life Insurance, Tokyo Marine & Fire Insurance	Sumitomo Bank, Sumitomo Trust and Banking, Sumitomo Life Insurance, Sumitomo Fire & Marine Insurance	Fuji Bank, Yasuda Trust and Banking, Yasuda Life Insurance, Yasuda Fire & Marine Insurance	Sanwa Bank, Toyo Trust and Banking, Nissay	Daiichi-Kangyo Bank, Asahi Life Insurance, Fukoku Life Insurance, Nissan Fire & Marine Insurance, Taisei Fire & Marine Ins.
Trade and Retailing	Mitsui & Co., Mitsukoshi	Mitsubishi Corp.	Sumitomo Corp.	Marubeni	Nichimen, Nissho Iwai, Iwatani International, Takashimaya	Itochu, Nissho Iwai, Kanematsu (inactive), Kawasaki Trading, Seibu Department Stores
Forestry and Mining	Mitsui Mining		Sumitomo Forestry, Sumitomo Coal Mining			
Construction	Mitsui Construction, Sanki	Mitsubishi Construction	Sumitomo Construction	Taisei	Obayashi, Toyo Construction, Zenitaka, Sekisui House	Shimizu
Food	Nippon Flour Mills	Kirin Beer		Nisshin Seifun, Sapporo Beer, Nichirei	Itoham, Suntory	

Textiles				Nisshinbo, Toho Rayon	Unitika	
Paper	Oji Paper, Nippon Paper	Mitsubishi Paper Mills		Nippon Paper		Oji Paper
Chemicals, Pharmaceuticals & Homecare	Mitsui Chemicals, Toray, Denka	Mitsubishi Chemicals, Mitsubishi Gas Chemical, Mitsubishi Yushi, Mitsubishi Rayon	Sumitomo Chemicals, Sumitomo Bakelite	Showa Denko, Kureha Chemical Industry, NOF	Teijin, Tokuyama, Sekisui Chemical, Ube Industries, Hitachi Chemical, Tanabe Seiyaku, Fujisawa Pharmaceutical, Kansai Paint	Denka, Kyowa, Zeon, Asahi Denka, Sankyo, Shiseido, Lion, Asahi Kasei
Oil & other Raw Materials	Taiheiyo Cement	Nippon Mitsubishi Oil, Asahi Glass	Nippon Sheet Glass, Sumitomo Osaka Cement	Taiheiyo Cement	Cosmo Oil, Toyo Rubber, Osaka Gas	Showa Shell Sekiyu, Yokohama, Rubber; Taiheiyo Cement
Steel	Japan Steel Works	Mitsubishi Steel Manufacturing	Sumitomo Metals	NKK	Kobe Steel, Nisshin Steel, Nakayama Steel Works, Hitachi Metals	Kobe Steel, Kawasaki Steel, Japan Metals and Chemicals
Non-ferrous Metals	Mitsui Kinzoku	Mitsubishi Material, Mitsubishi Aluminum, Mitsubishi Cable Industries, Mitsubishi Shindoh	Sumitomo Metal Mining, Sumitomo Light Metal Industries, Sumitomo Electric Industries		Hitachi Cable	NLM, Furukawa Co, Furukawa Electric

(Continued)

Table 11.1: (Continued)

	Mitsui (n = 25)	Mitsubishi (n = 28)	Sumitomo (n = 20)	Fuyo (n = 27)	Sanwa (n = 44)	Daiichi-Kangyo (n = 48)
Machinery		Mitsubishi Kakoki	Sumitomo Heavy Industries	Kubota, NSK	NTN	Niigata Engineering, Iseki, Ebara
Electronics	Toshiba	Mitsubishi Electric, Nikon	NEC	Hitachi, Ltd., Oki, Yokogawa Electric, Canon	Hitachi, Ltd., Iwasaki Electric, Sharp, Nitto Denko, Kyocera, Hoya	Hitachi, Ltd., Fuji Electric, Yaskawa Electric, Fujitsu, Nippon Columbia, Asahi Optical
Transportation Equipment	Toyota Motor (observer), Mitsui Engineering & Shipbuilding, IHI	Mitsubishi Heavy Industries, Mitsubishi Motors		Nissan Motor	Hitachi Zosen, ShinMaywa Industries, Daihatsu Motor	Kawasaki, IHI, Isuzu Motors
Real Estate	Mitsui Fudosan	Mitsubishi Estate	Sumitomo Realty & Development	Tokyo Tatemono		
Transportation and Logistics	Mitsui O.S.K. Lines, Mitsui Soko	NYK Line, Mitsubishi Logistics	Sumitomo Warehouse	Tobu Railway, Keihin Electric Express Railway	Hankyu Corp., Nippon Express, Mitsui O.S.K. Lines	Nippon Express, Kawasaki Kisen, Shibusawa Corp.
Others		Mitsubishi Research Institute				Orient Corp., Tokyo Dome

Source: KTI (2001); author's composition.

Table 11.2: Member firms of the four largest Korean *chaebol* by industry (2003)

	Samsung (n = 63)	Hyundai Motor (n = 25)	LG (n = 46)	SK (n = 58)
Banking, Insurance & Finance	Samsung Life Insurance, Samsung Fire & Marine Insurance, Samsung Fire & Marine Insurance Claim Adjustment Service, Samsung Securities, Samsung Card, Samsung Venture Investment, Samsung Futures, Samsung Allat, FnGuide, Insvalley, SamsungFund	Hyundai Capital, Hyundai Card	LG Investment &, Securities, LG Funds, LG Futures, Bumin Bank	SK Life Insurance, SK Securities, SK Loan, SK Funds, Paxnet, Global Credit & Information
Trade and Retailing (inc. e-business)	Samsung Corporation, Living Plaza, imarketkorea		LG Corporation, LG Inter-national, LG Mart, LG Home Shopping, LG MMA, Hiplaza	SK Corporation, SK Networks, SK DtoD, MRO Korea
Forestry				SK Forest
Construction	Samsung Engineering	Amco	LG Engineering & Construction	SK Engineering & Construction
Textiles	Cheil Industries			Segye Corporation
Chemicals, Pharmaceuticals & Homecare	Samsung Atofina, Samsung Fine Chemicals, Samsung General Chemicals, Samsung Petrochemial, Handuk Chemistry, Carecamp, 365Homecare		Hyundai Petrochemical, LG Chemistry, LG Petrochemial, LG Life Science, Ceti	SK Chemicals, SKC, Dongshin, SK Pharma, SK UCB

(*Continued*)

Table 11.2: (Continued)

	Samsung (n = 63)	Hyundai Motor (n = 25)	LG (n = 46)	SK (n = 58)
Oil, Gas & Energy			LG Energy, LG Power, Haeyang City Gas, Seorabol City Gas, LG-Caltex, Oil Chain	SK-Enron, SK Gas, Daehan City Gas, Dopco, Pusan City Gas, Kumi City Gas, Chongju City Gas, Chungnam City Gas, Pohang City Gas, Kangwon City Gas, Chonnam City Gas, Iksan City Gas, SK NJC, Iksan Energy, K Power, Pusan City Gas Development, Oil Chain
Steel		INI Steel, Hyundai Hysco, BNG Steel, AJM		
Machinery	Samsung Heavy Industries, Samsung Electro-Mechanics, Samsung Techwin, Novita	Wia Corporation, Eco Energy		Deahan City Gas Engineering
Electronics and IT	Samsung Electronics, Samsung SDI, Samsung Corning, Samsung	Autoeversystems, e-hd.com	LG Electronics, LG Philips LCD, LG Telecom,	SK Telecom, SK Teletech, SK&C, SK

	Corning Precision Glass, Samsung Gwangju Electronics, Samsung SDS, Samsung Thales, SNMD, Bluetek, Samsung Networks, Seoul Commtech, Samsungsvc, Steco, Korea DNS, SECUI.com, Secron, e Samsung, OpenTide Korea, CVnet, MPON, Global Component	VENS	power comm., DACOM, Siltron, LG Micron, LG Innotech, LG CNS, Korea Internet Data Center, LG-IBM PC, LG-DOW Polycarbonate, LG Nsys, Dacom Crossing, CIC Korea, Dacom Multimedia Internet	Communications, TU Media, SK Tellink, Wider Than, SK Telesys, The Contents Company, Innoace, Infosec, Iwingz
Transportation Equipment		Hyundai Motor Company, Kia Motors Corporation, Hyundai Mobis, Hyundai Powertech, Dymos, Kefico, DHTC, Bontec, Yisco, NGV		
Real Estate	Saengbo Real Estate Trust			Jungjiwon
Transportation and Logistics	Samsung Electronics Logitech, HTH	Rotem, Gloves	High Business Logistics	SK Shipping, Stela Shipping
Others	Cheil Communications, Samsung Everland, Hotel Shilla, S1 Corp., Seri, Samsung Electronics Service, Credu, eMFORCE, Anycarland, International Cyber Marketing, SamsungLions, Gaccinet	Haevichi, Kia Tigers	Hanmu Development, LG Care, LG MRO, Konjiam, LG Sports, LG Management Development	Walkerhill, Entro, E&M, Encar Network, AirCross, SK Wyverns, Benex International, Smartic

Source: Kim (2004); author's composition.

group that is more focused on a specific sector was the very motive for the breakup of the former Hyundai group and the constitution of new Hyundai Motor group (Kim *et al.*, 2004). Altogether, Hyundai Motor's overall business portfolio looks more similar to some large conglomerate firms from Western countries than to the Japanese or the other large Korean business groups.

The market-based competitive assessment is not limited to the analysis of the actual market share of a firm as compared with its competitors, however. As was mentioned before, the position of a firm towards other competitive forces is also considered as relevant. Specifically, the potential to build up exclusive relations with supplier or customer firms may constitute a competitive advantage. As a consequence, competitors could be locked out from access to important supply sources or customers (Porter, 1980).

The group membership data in Tables 11.1 and 11.2 show that for many member firms of the Japanese and Korean business groups, some potential for such preferred or exclusive access to suppliers or customers may exist due to their highly diversified structure. For instance, all of the Japanese business groups embrace at least one steel firm and several chemical firms which may serve as suppliers for (and may find their customers in) other membership firms in assembly industries like automobiles or electronics. However, as discussed above, with the exception of the Hyundai Motor group in the automobile industry, none of business groups holds a dominant position in any industry on the domestic market.[3] Therefore, the preferred or exclusive access to suppliers or customers that member firms may possess is regularly limited to suppliers or customers with a small or moderate market share only. As a result, the competitive advantage, which member firms may potentially derive from these vertical ties, appears to be very limited.

Additionally, the fact that each of the Japanese and Korean business groups (with the exception of the Hyundai Motor group) embraces at least one general trading firm may be considered. These general trading firms specialize on the export and import of a wide range of industrial and consumer goods and are quite important in some Asian countries. For instance, they account for almost half of the total international trade in Japan's case (Heger-Wesselowsky, 1996). Thereby, through close or exclusive business relations with general trading companies that are members of the same business group, incumbent firms may potentially possess advantages over their competitors with regard to access to imported input supplies or overseas exports of finished goods. However, the same limitation to this kind of potential competitive advantage applies as to the previously discussed issue of access to group-internal suppliers and customers: since none of the groups holds a particularly strong or dominant position in general trading, other firms cannot be effectively locked out from access to general trading firms. At most, it could be argued that because all large general trading companies in Japan and Korea are members of one of the business groups, firms that are not a member in *any* of the business groups may potentially suffer from a disadvantage when compared with member firms as regards access to general trading firms.

A final aspect which may be considered is the potential of incumbent firms of business groups to exert informal pressure on their employees and their families to buy products of the group's member firms. Since the overall size of the business groups within Japan's and Korea's economy is quite significant, the potential competitive advantage that may be derived through this kind of mechanism is not negligible. Such an advantage would be limited again, however, to help securing a certain minimum market share for some consumer products rather than to develop a dominant market position over competitors. Moreover, whereas the very informal nature of this phenomenon impedes a quantitative assessment, the general impression is that such practices by member firms of business groups now have become much less common than in previous decades.

In sum, the discussion of Japanese and Korean business groups' market potential has shown that their ability to create market-related competitive advantage generally appears to be very limited. With the exception of the Hyundai Motor group in the automobile industry, none of the groups appears to have the potential to build up a dominant competitive position on the industry level.

The resource-based competitive potential

For a resource-based competitive assessment of Asian business groups, their overall size may be taken into consideration first. According to the most recent available data in Japan, the six *kigyo shudan* accounted for 13.15 percent of the total equity, 11.21 percent of the total assets and 10.82 percent of the total sales of Japanese enterprises in 1999. These shares were steadily declining since 1989, when they peaked with 17.24 percent, 13.54 percent and 16.23 percent, respectively (KTI, 1992; KTI, 2001). With regard to the weight of *chaebol* in the Korean economy, Chang (2003) reports that the five largest *chaebol* accounted for approximately 8 percent and the largest 30 *chaebol* for 10 percent of Korea's GNP in 2000, down from 10 percent and 16 percent in 1995, respectively.

Whereas the weight of the business groups has thus declined recently in both economies, these percentages still suggest that they embrace an enormous amount of resources. This view is further confirmed by employment statistics. Each of the six Japanese *kigyo shudan* employed between 230,000 and 410,000 people in the mid-1990s (Heger-Wesselowsky, 1996). This gives the Japanese business groups a size similar to the world's largest firms.[4] The leading *chaebol* are somewhat smaller than the *kigyo shudan*, but still of a size comparable to that of very large Western firms: the Hyundai group gave work to 161,000 employees in 1996 and the total employment of the LG group stood at 100,000 in 1994 (Ungson *et al.*, 1997).

Moreover, there is reason to believe that the above statistics still underestimate the amount of resources that the Asian business groups embrace both in quantitative and qualitative terms. From a quantitative viewpoint, it has to be taken into consideration that the statistics cover only the business groups' member firms, but not their affiliates which they also control. Estimations by the Japanese Fair Trade Commission, which include these affiliates, suggest that in 1989, more than 29 percent of the equity, 22 percent of the assets and 18 percent of the sales of all Japanese firms fell to the six large business groups (KTI, 1992). In Korea's case, the share of the largest 30 *chaebol* of the country's shipments has even been estimated at 35 percent in 1990 (Ungson *et al.*, 1997).

Furthermore, qualitative considerations also give reason to evaluate the Asian business groups' resources even more highly. Both in Japan and in Korea, the most valuable economic resources have been highly concentrated on the largest firms throughout the past decades. The leading firms could regularly hire from the best universities the graduates who had a strong preference to work for them, giving them highly educated and qualified workforces. Moreover, due to the large firms' long-term employment practices and seniority-based pay schemes, the employees were given strong incentives to work hard for their present employers instead of looking for alternative jobs (Itoh, 1994). As a result, the workforces of the large firms in the two countries were not only highly skilled, but also highly motivated.

The favourable position of the large firms in Japan and Korea with regard to resource access was not limited to human resources. Banks and other financial institutions provided preferential supply of capital to them at low interest rates. Moreover, the Japanese and Korean governments further supported the leading firms in their countries considerably with a variety of direct and indirect measures, because they believed that the nurturing of competitive large firms was a key factor for their countries' economic development (Hemmert, 1992).

Altogether, the analysis shows that in contrast to their market-based competitive potential, the resource-based competitive potential of the Japanese and Korean business groups has to be evaluated as very high. During the past decades, the groups embraced an amount of resources that put them at even or even beyond that of leading firms from the Western countries.

The extent of managerial control

Measurement of managerial control in business groups

The degree to which the market- or resource-based competitive potential of a business group can be utilized depends on the extent of coherent managerial control that can be exerted over the group as a whole. The management of a business group, insofar as it exists, needs an organizational framework of structures and processes through which such control can be applied.

In general, the strength of the internal ties between the member firms of a business group may serve as an indicator of their managerial coherence. According to Adler and Kwon (2002), three categories of internal ties between group members can be distinguished in general: market-based, hierarchical, and social ties.

Firms are basically regarded as organizations that are primarily based on hierarchies rather than market mechanisms or social relations (Williamson, 1975). Therefore, hierarchical ties, such as majority shareholdings, appear to be of predominant importance for an assessment of the extent of managerial control within business groups. Market-based or social ties may also play an important role to support group-internal coherence, but cannot substitute for hierarchical ties.

Managerial control of Kigyo Shudan

In the case of the Japanese *kigyo shudan*, the membership of a firm in a business group is constituted by its participation in the regular presidents' meetings of the member firms. These meetings are held monthly in five of the *kigyo shudan* and quarterly in the Daiichi-Kangyo group (KTI, 1992). Notably, there is no legal entity such as a parent or holding company which can be associated with the managerial core of any of the six business groups. Still, there remains the possibility that the presidents' meetings effectively function as a managerial board of the business groups, even in the absence of any legal entity that accommodates it. In order to enable the presidents' meetings to fulfil this function, however, there need to be strong ties between the member firms.

Table 11.3 shows some data regarding the amount of cross-shareholding relationships and other types of links between the member firms of the six *kigyo shudan*. On the average, more than half of the member firms of a business group hold shares of each group firm. Moreover, about one-fifth of all shares of the group firms are held group-internal. This indicates that

Table 11.3:   Business ties within the six Japanese *Kigyo Shudan*

Type of link	Type of business group					
	Former zaibatsu business groups (*Mitsui, Mitsubishi, Sumitomo*)		*New business groups (Fuyo, Sanwa, Daiichi-Kangyo)*		*Total average of all six business groups*	
	1989	*1999*	*1989*	*1999*	*1989*	*1999*
Share-holding						
Average proportion of group firms which hold shares of each group firm (%)	75.29	75.85	33.96	33.22	54.63	54.53
Proportion of total group internal shareholding (%)	27.46	24.95	15.82	15.16	21.64	20.05
Group-internal trade:						
Purchases from all group firms among all purchases (%)	11.11	8.09	4.86	4.93	7.28	6.44
Purchases from group-internal general trading companies among all purchases (%)	7.46	6.28	2.78	2.74	4.59	4.43
Exchange of management personnel						
Firms with directors sent by other group firms (%)	62.74	42.67	61.78	31.67	62.26	37.17
Proportion of directors sent by other group firms (%)	7.91	4.67	4.78	3.67	6.34	4.17

Source: KTI (1992); KTI (2001).

whereas there is a significant amount of cross-shareholding among the firms of each business group, there appears to be, at least on the average, no ownership control among the group firms which would require majority ownership. Furthermore, the shareholding relationships within the group are not hierarchical, with certain firms controlling other firms, but reciprocal cross-shareholdings. This suggests that the Japanese business groups function more like networks than like hierarchical, firm-like organizations.

However, there still remains the possibility that even without majority ownership, a strong effective group-internal control might be exerted through a combination of minority shareholding and other forms of human or financial ties. The data in Table 11.3 indicate that such ties between the group firms do exist with regard to both internal trade and the exchange of management personnel. They do not support the notion that a strong group-internal managerial control may be exerted, however. Only a relatively small fraction of the overall purchasing volume of the member firms falls to transactions with other group firms, with the general trading companies accounting for the majority of this internal transaction volume. Recently, less than 40 percent of all group firms had a director who was sent by another member firm of the group. Moreover, less than one out of 20 directors of the group firms came from other group firms. The overall impression is that the links within the Japanese *kigyo shudan* are rather weak and non-hierarchical. Moreover, they have been losing importance as compared with 10 years ago, particularly with regard to the exchange of management personnel. This applies to the former *zaibatsu* groups, which have comparatively stronger internal ties, as well as to the other three business groups.

Further insights into the governance structure of the Japanese business groups can be gained from survey results regarding the functions of the presidents' meetings. A survey among the member firms of the *kigyo shudan* revealed that more than 80 percent of the group firms perceived these meetings as a medium for information exchange. The only other function observed by a majority of the member firms of the three former *zaibatsu* business groups was the strengthening of the group brand (KTI, 2001). Furthermore, 30.9 percent of the member firms of the three former *zaibatsu* groups and 11.8 percent of the member firms of three new groups reported that they received requests by other group firms on concrete business matters. Most of these requests were related to financial or managerial help when group firms encountered serious difficulties in their business situation or financial trouble.

This function of mutual assistance may be also related to role of the so-called 'main banks' within the Japanese business groups. In each group, there is one such main bank which is commonly regarded as one of its cornerstone firms. In fact, the main banks appear to have played a relatively influential role within the *kigyo shudan* throughout the last decades (Hoshi, 1994). However, recent survey data show that only about 20 percent of all directors sent to other firms within the business groups come from these banks (KTI, 2001). This clearly indicates that whereas the main banks may be relatively influential within the business groups, they lack by far the potential to exert managerial control like a parent firm of a conglomerate.

Altogether, the data analysis suggests that the links between the member firms of the six Japanese *kigyo shudan* are far too weak and non-hierarchical to allow managerial control of the groups through the presidents' meetings or the main banks. The main functions of the *kigyo shudan* appear to lie in the exchange of information, in the strengthening of brands and in reciprocal assistance in case of financial difficulties.

The relative weakness of the links within the Japanese business groups has been further proven by a series of recent horizontal mergers between member firms of different groups. Among these mergers, the fusion of Sakura Bank and Sumitomo Bank into Sumitomo Mitsui Banking Corp. in 2001 is particularly remarkable because two main banks of former *zaibatsu* business groups merged into one, suggesting a blurring of the boundaries of the groups, even in their core areas.

Managerial control of chaebol

Likewise in Japan, the Fair Trade Commission in Korea also regularly reports on the largest business groups in the country. A list of the 30 largest *chaebol* is published annually by the government. According to the 'Monopoly Regulation and Fair Trade Act', *chaebol* affiliates are identified either through a group-internal ownership of 30 percent or more or through a substantial influence on management, such as appointing officers (Chang, 2003). The second criteria was included since sometimes a strong influence on the management of a firm can be exerted even with a shareholding of less than 30 percent when the remaining ownership is widely dispersed.

Thus, it seems that managerial control can be exerted over *chaebol* group firms by their very definition. It still appears necessary, however, to have a closer look on the internal structure of the Korean business groups to evaluate the degree to which such managerial control may be effectively exercised on the group level.

In Table 11.4, some recent data on the internal shareholding of the four largest *chaebol* are summarized. As can be seen, the average group-internal

Table 11. 4:   Ownership of member firms within the four largest *chaebol* (%)

Indicator	Group				
	Samsung	*Hyundai Motor*	*LG*	*SK*	*Average*
Group-internal ownership (1997)	32.41	45.64*	37.52	32.84	37.42
Group-internal ownership (2003)	32.25	39.80	45.23	36.68	36.99
Group firms majority owned within the group (2003)	60.32	76.00	54.35	72.41	64.58

Source: Kim (2004); author's calculations.
Note: * former Hyundai group.

shareholding ratio is below 50 percent in all four groups, but much higher than in the Japanese *kigyo shudan*. The internal ownership has been largely stable throughout the last years, providing no evidence that the Asian financial crisis has had a noticeable impact on the ownership structure of the Korean business groups in the years after 1997. Moreover, more than half of the group firms are majority owned by the other group firms in all of the four largest *chaebol*. Therefore, the ownership data suggest the existence of strong hierarchical links within the groups.

Chang (2003) also gives data on group-internal trade and on the frequency of the exchange of management personnel between group firms. The intra-group trade accounted on the average for 21.2 percent of the total transaction volume of the largest 30 *chaebol* in 1997. In the five largest groups, the according ratio was even higher. Moreover, many of the presidents of group firms were initially hired or held a previous executive position at other group firms of the leading *chaebol*.

All of these data strongly suggest that in stark contrast to the Japanese *kigyo shudan*, the internal links of the member firms of the *chaebol* should be strong enough to allow an effective managerial control of a group as a whole. Another question is, however, whether there exists a hierarchical governance structure within the *chaebol* that allows specific individuals or groups of individuals to exert such central control over the business group.

As in the Japanese business groups, there are regular meetings of the presidents of the *chaebol's* member firms. Unlike the case of the *kigyo shudan*, however, these meetings are not perceived as the most important institution of the Korean business groups. Rather, the owner family is commonly perceived as the core of a *chaebol*. Since the *chaebol* were founded by individuals during the postwar decades, these founders typically still own a high amount of the shares of a business group's core firms, which in turn hold a stock majority of most other group firms (Chang, 2003). Therefore, it may be expected that the owner families of the *chaebol* have sufficient leverage to exert a significant influence on the business groups' managerial strategies.

Notably, there were no legal entities such as holding companies at the core of the Korean business groups throughout the past decades. The group level business planning of the *chaebol* was supported by staff organizations that were working 'privately' for the *chaebol* owners, who gave directions to the managers of the core companies about the business strategies at the group level (Shin and Kwon, 1999). Only in recent years, the central staff organizations were formally transferred to the core firms of the business groups under pressure from the Korean government. However, there appears to be little change with regard to the actual governance structure of the *chaebol* because the staff organizations are still reporting to the owner families rather than to the management of the firms which they are formally working for (Chang, 2003).

In sum, the review of the governance structure of the Korean business groups suggests that the owner families function as the central institution within the *chaebol* and do have the leverage to exert a strong and permanent control over a group's business strategy. In fact, it seems that their managerial control over the business groups is effectively even stronger than the influence which the chairmen and CEOs of Western conglomerate firms can exert (Shin and Kwon, 1999; Chang, 2003). The *chaebol* owners can, in contrast to managers of Western firms, not be held legally accountable for the results of their actions and decisions because they do not hold any formal managerial position in any of the group firms.

After having seen that the *chaebol*, in contrast to the *kigyo shudan*, have strong, hierarchical internal links that allow the enactment of managerial control at the group level and that the governance structure of the *chaebol* gives the founder and owner families as their core institution the leverage to exert such control, the remaining question is whether and to what extent this managerial control over the Korean business groups was *really* exerted throughout past years and decades. Empirical observations strongly indicate that there was a high amount of such managerial control over the *chaebol* that frequently resulted in aggressive product diversification strategies (Chang, 2003; Kim *et al.*, 2004). The above-mentioned lack of accountability of the founders and owners who formulated and implemented these strategies contributes to explain why the Korean business groups were moving and growing so dynamically throughout the past decades. As mentioned above, a highly favourable institutional environment also supported the dynamic expansion and apparent long-term success of the Korean business groups.

Another crucial factor for the fast growth of the *chaebol* was their ability to share and reallocate internal resources, however (Chang, 2003). Human resources, capital, technologies and brands were shared by all group firms who could utilize them. Moreover, these resources were concentrated in certain periods on specific group firms or business lines whenever the overall group strategy gave priority to them.

This ability to share internal resources shows that the Korean business groups could utilize the enormous resource-based competitive potential which was identified before. Moreover, referring to the wide definition of resources in the resource-based view and the importance of their uniqueness (Wernerfelt, 1984), the *chaebols'* internal resource-sharing ability may be identified as an important resource that helped them gain a competitive edge over domestic as well as foreign competitors. This ability was particularly important during the postwar decades because the external markets for such resources were highly underdeveloped in Korea (Kim *et al.*, 2004).

Discussion and overall evaluation

The findings of the previous evaluation of the competitive potential of Asian business groups are summarized in Table 11.5. The analysis has shown that both the Japanese *kigyo shudan* and the Korean *chaebol* have a much higher resource-based than market-based competitive potential. Whereas their market position in specific industries is in most cases not particularly strong, both the amount and the quality of their resources is on a level similar to the largest conglomerate multinational firms from Western countries.

The striking difference between the Japanese and the Korean business groups, however, lies in the extent to which managerial control can be exerted over them. The Japanese *kigyo shudan* are loose, network-type organizations without a strong core institution. The links between their member firms are non-hierarchical, relatively weak and have been weakening further in recent years. The functions of the *kigyo shudan* appear to be limited to a mutual insurance against hostile takeovers and bankruptcy, to a rather general exchange of information and, in the case of the three former *zaibatsu* business groups, to the protection and strengthening of group brands.

The Korean *chaebol*, in contrast, generally have much stronger ties between member firms. Moreover, they have a hierarchical structure that gives their owner families the leverage to formulate and implement group-level strategies. Since the founders and owners formally do not work as managers of the *chaebol* firms and therefore also cannot be held legally accountable for their decisions, the amount of managerial control they can exert over the business groups appears to be even stronger than that of chairmen and CEOs of Western conglomerate firms.

Table 11.5: Evaluation of the competitive potential of Japanese and Korean business groups

	Kigyo Shudan	*Chaebol*
Market-based Competitive Potential	Low to moderate	Moderate (exception: Hyundai Motor group)
Resource-based Competitive Potential	Very high	High
Extent of Managerial Control	Very low	Very high

In sum, the analysis suggests that whereas both Japanese and Korean business groups have a very significant resource-based competitive potential, only in the case of Korean groups sufficient managerial control can be exerted to utilize it. The remaining question is whether and to what extent this *competitive potential* could by transferred by the *chaebol* into an actual *competitive advantage*.

Chang and Choi (1988) compared the profitability of *chaebol*-affiliated and independent Korean firms for the period from 1975 to 1984 and found that the *chaebol* firms were significantly more profitable. In a further study which covered the period from 1985 to 1996, Chang and Hong (2000, 2002) observed that *chaebol* firms were still generating higher profits than independent Korean firms during this period, but that this difference was diminishing over time. Furthermore, their analysis indicates that whereas during the 1980s, the sheer size, that is, the amount of resources of a business group, was strongly contributing to their economic performance, the effective utilization of these resources through group-internal resource sharing became more important for profitability during the 1990s.

Recent observations, however, cast shadows on the economic performance of Korean business groups. Following the Asian financial crisis of 1997, about half of the 30 largest *chaebol* either became bankrupt or underwent large-scale restructuring (Chang, 2003; Kim *et al.*, 2004). Moreover, the economic soundness of some of the *chaebols'* diversification strategies was already questioned prior to the 1997 crisis. A prominent example was the expansion of the Samsung group into the automobile business in 1994 at a time when this industry faced global consolidation. In fact, the aggressive diversification strategies of many *chaebol* that were increasingly debt-financed during the 1990s appear as the main reason for their failures during and after the crisis (Lee, 2000; Chang, 2003).

Altogether, empirical work suggests that, first, Korean business groups enjoyed a considerable competitive advantage at least over other Korean firms during the recent decades. Second, this advantage can be largely attributed to their high resource-based competitive potential and its effective utilization through internal resource sharing. Third, the managerial control over the *chaebol* was also used by their owners to conduct aggressive product diversification strategies that often appeared economically unsound and contributed to the bankruptcies of several business groups since 1997. In other words, whereas the high resource potential of Korean business groups was utilized through effective managerial control and internal resource sharing to create competitive advantages, these advantages were increasingly outweighed in recent years by the negative consequences of unsound diversification strategies.

Conclusions and implications

The analysis in this chapter is mainly based on overall structural data and information regarding the largest business groups in Japan and Korea. Due to this approach, the competitive potential of each group could not be analysed in detail. However, two main findings have become very clear. First, Japanese and Korean business groups have some considerable similarities such as their relatively limited market-based competitive potential and their high resource-based competitive potential. Second, there is also one very fundamental difference between them. The Japanese business groups are loose horizontal networks with weak internal links and no group-level managerial control. As a consequence, they have a very limited competitive potential. The Korean business groups, in contrast, are hierarchically organized and centrally managed, giving them a high competitive potential.

Managers of firms that are competing with member firms of the *chaebol* should be aware of this potential when developing their competitive strategies. For instance, a member firm of a *chaebol* may enter a foreign market very quickly and on a large scale when the management of the business group gives a high priority to the international expansion of this firm and provides it with a large amount of human and financial resources. However, not all kinds of competitive advantages can be achieved with the same speed and ease through such group-internal resource sharing and transfer. For example, whereas a *chaebol* may have the capability to build up considerable research and development (R&D) activities in a certain field within a relatively short period of time, this does not mean that it will also rapidly accomplish technological superiority over its competitors. Certain competitive advantages, such as the acquisition of technological leadership, can be achieved only in the long term and with much difficulty and uncertainty. Therefore, managers should try to acquire such advantages that are relatively sustainable if they want to protect their business from strong competition with *chaebol* member firms.

Overall, it becomes clear that a differentiated approach is required when analyzing Asian business groups. The strong differences between the Japanese and Korean business groups show that the assumption that business groups from different Asian countries are fundamentally similar is highly invalid and misleading. Instead, researchers as well as practitioners should approach them on a differentiated, country-specific basis. Moreover, whereas the attention on business groups has been highly concentrated on Japan and Korea hitherto, more international comparative research on business groups, which also includes other countries, is desirable to improve the understanding of their structure and competitive potential.

On the conceptual level, the proposed framework that considers the extent of managerial control within a business group in addition to their market-based and resource-based competitive potential, proved to be useful to gain a broad, comprehensive understanding of the competitive potential of business groups. Therefore, this three-tiered approach may also be helpful when analysing business groups from other countries.

Notes

1. The Fuyo group, notwithstanding its common classification as 'new' business group, also has some strong roots in the prewar Yasuda *zaibatsu* (Dolles, 1997).
2. Japanese business groups are also frequently referred to as *keiretsu*. However, the concept of *keiretsu* is very fuzzy and also refers to vertical supplier networks (*seisan keiretsu*) and vertical distribution networks (*ryutsu keiretsu*), which are totally different from horizontal business groups (Hemmert, 1997). Therefore, to avoid confusion, the term *keiretsu* is not used in this chapter, which is focused on horizontal business groups only.
3. The seemingly dominant position of the Hyundai Motor group in the steel business is qualified by the fact that Posco, the largest Korean steel firm by far, is not a member of any of the four leading business groups.
4. According to the Fortune Global 500 list, there were only nine firms in the world with more than 400,000 employees in 2003 (*Fortune*, 2004).

References

Adler, P.S. and S.-W. Kwon (2002) 'Social capital: prospects for a new concept', *Academy of Management Review* 27, 17–40.
Biggart, N.W. and G.G. Hamilton (1997) 'Explaining Asian Business Success: Theory No. 4', in M. Orru, N.M. Biggart and G.G. Hamilton (eds), *The Economic Organization of East Asian Capitalism* (Thousand Oaks, CA: Sage), pp. 97–110.
Chang, S.-J. (2003) *Financial Crisis and Transformation of Korean Business Groups: The Rise and Fall of Chaebols* (Cambridge: Cambridge University Press).
Chang, S.J. and U. Choi (1988) 'Strategy, structure and performance of Korean business groups: a transactions cost approach', *Journal of Industrial Economics* 37, 141–58.
Chang, S.J. and J. Hong (2000) 'Economic performance of group-affiliated companies in Korea: intragroup resource sharing and internal business transactions', *Academy of Management Journal* 43, 429–48.
Chang, S.J. and J. Hong (2002) 'How much does the business group matter in Korea', *Strategic Management Journal* 23, 265–74.
Cho, D.-S. (1991) *Hanguk chaebol yongu* (Research on Korean chaebol) (Seoul: Maeil Kyongjae Sinmunsa).

Dolles, H. (1997) *Keiretsu: Emergenz, Struktur, Wettbewerbsstärke und Dynamik japanischer Verbundgruppen* (Frankfurt a.M.: Peter Lang).

Fortune (2004) 'The Fortune Global 500' (Special Edition), *Fortune*, 26 July.

Gerlach, M. (1992) *Alliance Capitalism* (Berkeley, CA: University of California Press).

Granovetter, M. (1995) 'Coase revisited: business groups in the modern economy', *Industrial and Corporate Change* 4, 93–130.

Hamilton, G.G. (1997) 'Organization and Market Processes in Taiwan's Capitalist Economy', in M. Orru, N.M., Biggart and G.G., Hamilton (eds), *The Economic Organization of East Asian Capitalism* (Thousand Oaks, CA: Sage), pp. 237–93.

Heger-Wesselowsky, C. (1996) *Genese, Evolution and Wesen industrieller Unternehmensallianzen in Japan: Eine sozio-systemische Betrachtung* (Munich: Akademischer Verlag München).

Hemmert, M. (1992) 'Konflikte zwischen Klein- und Großunternehmen: Ist die Struktur der japanischen Industrie dualistisch?', *Japanstudien* 3, 195–219.

Hemmert, M. (1997) 'Japanische keiretsu: Legenden und Wirklichkeit', in W. Schaumann (ed.), *Japanologie und Wirtschaft – Wirtschaft und Japanologie* (Munich: Iudicium), pp. 55–79.

Hoshi, T. (1994) 'The Economic Role of Corporate Grouping and the Main Bank System', in M. Aoki and R. Dore (eds), *The Japanese Firm: The Sources of Competitive Strength* (Oxford: Oxford University Press), pp. 285–309.

Imai, K. (1992) 'Japan's corporate networks', in S. Kumon and H. Rosovsky (eds), *The Political Economy of Japan, Vol. 3: Cultural and Social Dynamics* (Stanford: Stanford University Press), pp. 198–230.

Itoh, H. (1994) 'Japanese Human Resource Management from the Viewpoint of Incentive Theory', in M. Aoki and R. Dore (eds), *The Japanese Firm: The Sources of Competitive Strength* (Oxford: Oxford University Press), pp. 233–64.

Jwa, S.-H. and I.K. Lee (2000) 'Introduction', in Korea Economic Research Institute (ed.) *Korean Chaebol in Transition: Road Ahead and Agenda* (Seoul: Korea Economic Research Institute), pp. 17–34.

Khanna, T. (2000) 'Business groups and social welfare in emerging markets: existing evidence and unanswered questions', *European Economic Review* 44, 748–61.

Khanna, T. and K.G. Palepu (1997) 'Why focused strategies may be wrong for emerging markets', *Harvard Business Review* 75(4), 41–51.

Khanna, T. and K.G. Palepu (2000) 'Is group membership profitable in emerging markets? an analysis of diversified Indian Business groups', *Journal of Finance* 55, 867–91.

Kim, C.B. (2004) 'Hanguk chaebol ui soyu kujo: 1997-2003' (The ownership structure of Korean chaebol: 1997–2003), in Chamyo Sahoe Yonguso (ed.), *Hanguk ui chaebol: kicho jaryo sujip, bunsok mit byongga* (Korean chaebol: basic data collection, analysis and evaluation) (Seoul: Chamy o Sahoe Yonguso), pp. 1–182.

Kim, H., R.E. Hoskisson, L. Tihanyi and J. Hong (2004) 'The evolution of diversified business groups in emerging markets: the lessons from Chaebols in Korea', *Asia Pacific Journal of Management* 21, 25–48.

KTI – Kōosei Torihiki Iinkai (1992) *Nihon no roku dai kigyo shudan: sono soshiki to kodo* (The six large business groups in Japan: Their organization and behaviour) (Tokyo: Toyo Keizai Shinposha).

KTI – Kōsei Torihiki Iinkai (2001) *Kigyo shudan no jittai ni tsuite, dai 7-ji chosa hokokusho* (About the situation of the business groups, 7th survey report) (Tokyo: Kosei Torihiki Iinkai Jimu Sokyoku).

Lee, J.-W. (2000) 'Chaebol Restructuring Revisited: A Coasian Perspective', in Korea Economic Research Institute (ed.), *Korean Chaebol in Transition: Road Ahead and Agenda* (Seoul: Korea Economic Research Institute), pp. 151–221.

Lee, K. and D. Hahn (2003) 'Why and what kinds of the business groups in China: market competition, plan constraints, and the hybrid business groups', *Proceedings of the International Symposium on Business Groups in East Asia*, 26 September 2003, Seoul, pp. 275–314.

Morikawa, H. (1992) *Zaibatsu: The Rise and Fall of Family Enterprises in Japan* (Tokyo: University of Tokyo Press).

Orru, M., N.W. Biggart and G.G. Hamilton (1997) 'Organizational Isomorphism in East Asia', in M. Orru, N.M. Biggart and G.G. Hamilton (eds), *The Economic Organization of East Asian Capitalism* (Thousand Oaks, CA: Sage), pp. 151–87.

Penrose, E. (1959) *The Theory of the Growth of the Firm* (London: Basil Blackwell).

Polsiri, P. and Y. Wiwattanakantang (2003) 'Business groups in Thailand: before and after the east Asian Financial Crisis', *Proceedings of the International Symposium on Business Groups in East Asia*, 26 September 2003, Seoul, pp. 151–85.

Porter, M.E. (1980) *Competitive Strategy, Techniques for Analyzing Industries and Competitors* (New York: Free Press).

Porter, M.E. (1985) *Competitive Advantage, Creating and Sustaining Superior Performance* (New York: Free Press).

Shimotani, M. (1993) *Nihon no keiretsu to kigyo gurupu* (Japanese keiretsu and business groups) (Tokyo: Yuhikaku).

Shin, D. and K.-H. Kwon (1999) 'Demystifying Asian Business Networks: The Hierarchical Core of Interfirm Relations in Korean Chaebols', in F.-J. Richter (ed.) *Business Networks in Asia: Premises, Doubts, and Perspectives* (Westport, CT: Quorum), pp. 113–46.

Tselichtchev, I.S. (1999) 'Japanese-Style Intercompany Networks: New Dimensions in the Asian Context', in F.-J. Richter (ed.) *Business Networks in Asia: Premises, Doubts, and Perspectives* (Westport, CT: Quorum), pp. 91–111.

Ungson, G.R., R.M. Steers and S. Park (1997) *Korean Enterprise: The Quest for Globalization* (Boston: Harvard Business School Press).

Wernerfelt, B. (1984) 'A resource-based view of the frm', *Strategic Management Journal* 5, 171–80.

Williamson, O.E. (1975) *Markets and Hierarchies* (New York: Free Press).

12
SARS Versus the Asian Financial Crisis

Oliver H.M. Yau, W.F. Leung, Fanny S.L. Cheung
and Cheris W.C. Chow

Introduction

The experience in Asia during the past few years has provided new perspectives on the effects of crises. Following the collapse of the Thailand stock market on 2 July 1997, most Asian economies have faced economic downturn. The slow recovery resulted in many companies having hard times, and struggling to even survive. Another crisis occurred in Asia following the outbreak of severe acute respiratory syndrome (SARS) in southern China during late 2002 and early 2003. The SARS crisis spread to many other Asian economies and even Canada, where the previously unknown disease killed a number of people. During the outbreak of SARS, the economic perspective was very pessimistic and many industries, especially tourism and retail, were hurt seriously. However, SARS was under control in May 2003, and since then the recovery of the economies has been very strong, even beyond the expectations of most economists and marketers.

Although it may still be too early to claim that Asian economies have already recovered from the recession that started in 1997, the SARS crisis seemed to have save economies, although only through the cost of thousands of lives. The phenomenon seems to contradict with most past studies on the crises, which predict a cuts in income and consumption. This chapter tries to point out the different natures between an economic crisis and a health crisis: the former lowers consumers' expected income and thus consumption is lowered accordingly, whereas the latter lowers consumers' expected life but the consumption is pushed up.

Past studies have investigated mainly why an economic crisis occurs and how an economic crisis affects consumption and employment. Recently, the studies have focused on the Asian financial crisis, and investigations of marketing impacts have been relatively ignored. The impacts of health crises began to receive research attention mainly due to the outbreak of SARS. The studies are mainly related to the medical aspect of the health crisis (e.g., Kang and Hong, 2004), and the marketing impacts of a health crisis have not been addressed, at least to our knowledge. This chapter aims to address the different impacts of economic crises (or financial crises) and health crises on marketing activities, which are critical for a firm's business development and even a firms' survival.

This chapter is based on a simple model of life-cycle hypothesis to analyse the different impacts on the consumption between a health crisis and an economic crisis. Under an economic crisis, the consumption was cut due to lower income expectation; however, under a health crisis, the consumption was pushed up due to lower life expectation. SARS is an example of a health crisis, while the Asian financial crisis is an example of an economic crisis. The lessons to the business sector are that clear understanding of the characteristics of a crisis is important for survival or even an opportunity to achieve success. The 4Ps framework is applied as suggestions for the business sector.

The objectives of this study are twofold. First, the current study aims to examine the different impacts on consumption between an economic crisis and a health crisis. Life-cycle hypothesis is applied as the framework for the analysis. Hong Kong cases during the Asian financial crisis and SARS are used for illustration. Second, marketing implications are provided for practitioners in developing marketing strategies during a crisis. The precision of the judgement is critical to the success of the marketing strategy.

Literature review

Although crises have been discussed widely in the literature, there have been no discussions directly related to this chapter. Most of the literature is related to the explanation of crises. Even though the literature is very indirect, it is important for marketing activities and thus, we also briefly discuss the selected literature. Some other literature is related to marketing for consumers under business crises. For health crises such as SARS, the literature is basically related to medical analysis and thus we only include limited literature here.

Since the recent economic crises are mainly financial crises, we also focus in this direction. Models have been developed on explaining the business cycle phenomena and many models have been based on the exchange rate crisis. Krugman (1979) assumes that an economy adopts pegged exchange rate, while the government is running out of reserves to support the pegged rate. When speculators are provoked to attack the exchange rate when the foreign exchange reserves fall below the critical level, investors struggle to avoid capital losses and then financial crisis occurs. The other models follow similar assumptions but self-fulfilling crises are generated (Cole and Kehoe, 2000). Other type of models such as Obstfeld (1986) instead explains crises from the inconsistency between a fixed exchange rate and the government's intention of expansionary monetary policy. When investors believe that the government may choose not to maintain the fixed exchange rate, the pressure on interest rates can push the government into a difficult position and then a crisis occurs.

The two types of models have a problem in explaining the Asian financial crisis beginning in 1997. Various models try to address the crisis, including the issues of (1) contagion, (2) transfer problems and (3) balance sheet problems. The contagion is important under globalization. A financial crisis in small economies such as Thailand, led to crises in economies thousand of kilometres away, even though direct trade or financial links are very limited. The dramatic reversal of the current account of an economy has been observed. For example, the capital flow of Thailand changed from a deficit of 10 percent of the gross domestic product (GDP) in 1996 to a surplus of 8 percent of the GDP in 1998. The transfer problem has to be addressed in this case. The deterioration of firms' balance sheets under sharp domestic currency depreciation was a key role in the crisis itself. A significant example is the disastrous effects of the depreciation of rupiah on those Indonesian firms with huge US dollar debts. Bernanke and Gertler (1989) and Kiyotaki and Moore (1997) are the pioneers for the literature on balance sheet, effects while Aghion *et al.* (2000) focus on contagion. Krugman (1999) includes all the three issues in the model.

Another type of model is balance sheet effects. Many countries experienced boom-bust episodes over the past two decades that were related to balance-of-payments crises. From a typical episode, a country started with a lending boom and the exchange rate was appreciating. A sudden crisis came unexpectedly to the financial markets and resulted in an end to the lending boom – the currency depreciated and this coincided with domestic private sector defaults on unhedged foreign-currency-denominated debt. After the crisis, foreign lenders were usually bailed out but domestic credit fell rapidly and recovered much more slowly than output. Schneider and Tornell (2004) apply a two-sector model by incorporating the bail-out guarantees: lenders will be bailed out if the quantity of borrower defaults reaches a critical value. Not only exogenous shocks are causes of crisis – a self-fulfilling crisis is also possible.

There are various discussions on the effects of economic crises on consumers. Shama (1981) divided consumers into two types and concentrated on the 'voluntary simplicity consumers' (VS consumers). One main characteristic of VS consumers is that they prefer smaller, fewer, simple and quality products. Marketing strategies and mix were suggested under the 4Ps framework. Ang *et al.* (2000) analyse the reaction of consumers in face of the Asian financial crisis and also suggest the marketing strategies under the 4Ps framework.

For the literature on the marketing effects of SARS, Dombey (2003) was among the earliest to report on it. Dombey focused on the effects of SARS on China and he suggested that the effects on the Chinese economy were minimal, while the social habits of the Chinese and political handling on the health issues should be improved. Henderson (2003) described the effects on the Singaporean tourism industry during the outbreak of SARS and suggested a few measures on how the administrators could handle similar crises.

The life-cycle model

The underlying assumption of the life-cycle hypothesis (Modigliani and Brumberg, 1954) is that people try to maintain an optimal and smooth consumption path. The main building block of the model is the saving decision, that is, how to divide income into consumption and saving. The saving decision is determined by the expected income and life expectancy.

Simple model

This is based on the life-cycle model on the analysis of the effects of a crisis. It is assumed that a typical consumer spends all of his/her income on either consumption or savings and no surplus is left. All consumers are also assumed to have income from period 0, that is, the per-working periods are ignored.

Let $E(I_t)$ be expected income, $E(C_t)$ be expected consumption, $E(S_t)$ be expected savings at period t, t = 0, ..., $E(L)$, β be time preference, $0 < \beta < 1$, and α be interest rate, $\alpha > 1$, while $\gamma = \alpha\beta$. No inflation is considered in this model. For a typical consumer's expected life period $E(L)$, we have the following life-cycle income equation from period 0 to period $E(L)$:

$$\sum_{t=0}^{E(L)} \beta^t E(I_t) = \sum_{t=0}^{E(L)} \beta^t E(C_t) + \sum_{t=0}^{R} \gamma^t E(S_t) + \sum_{t=R}^{E(L)} \gamma^t E(-S_t)$$

where R is the retirement period. As there is no surplus,

$$\sum_{t=0}^{R} \gamma^t E(S_t) = \sum_{t=R}^{E(L)} \gamma^t E(-S_t)$$

and thus,

$$\sum_{t=0}^{E(L)} \beta^t E(I_t) = \sum_{t=0}^{E(L)} \beta^t E(C_t)$$

Economic crisis

Let F be the extent of financial problems (as a representative of economic problems). When there is a financial crisis at time T, F becomes larger and it is assumed that the expected income will be lowered.

(i) If $0 \leqslant T < R$:

$$\sum_{i=T}^{E(L)} \beta^t \frac{\partial E(I_t)}{\partial F} = \sum_{i=T}^{R} \beta^t \frac{\partial E(I_t)}{\partial F} < 0$$

the expected income equation at T is:

$$\sum_{t=0}^{T} \gamma^t S_t + \sum_{t=T}^{E(L)} \beta^t E'(I_t) = \sum_{t=T}^{E(L)} \beta^t E'(C_t)$$

where $E'(I_t)$ and $E'(C_t)$ are the expected income and expected consumption after the financial crisis. As F has no effects on S_t, the financial crisis has a negative effect on expected consumption:

$$\sum_{i=T}^{E(L)} \beta^t \frac{\partial E(I_t)}{\partial F} = \sum_{i=T}^{E(L)} \beta^t \frac{\partial E(C_t)}{\partial F} < 0$$

(ii) If $R \leqslant T < E(L)$, as there is no income after retirement, no effects on expected income are observed:

$$\sum_{t=0}^{R} \gamma^t S_t - \sum_{t=R}^{T} \beta^t C_t = \sum_{t=T}^{E(L)} \beta^t E(C_t)$$

and no effects are on the consumption.

From the above analysis, we can see that financial crisis lowers the consumption of the working people but has no effects on the retired people. For the society as a whole, the total consumption will decrease.

Health crisis

Suppose there be another type of crisis, health crisis. Let H be the extent of health problems; a large H will decrease the expected life, E(L):

$$\frac{\partial E(L)}{\partial H} < 0$$

Let E'(L) be the shorter expected life after the health crisis.

(i) If $0 \leqslant T < R$ and $E'(L) > R$,

$$\sum_{t=0}^{T} \gamma^t S_t + \sum_{t=T}^{R} \beta^t E(I_t) = \sum_{t=T}^{E'(L)} \beta^t E'(C_t) = \sum_{t=T}^{E(L)} \beta^t E(C_t)$$

As $E'(L) < E(L)$,

$$\sum_{t=T}^{E'(L)} \beta^t E'(C_t) = \sum_{t=T}^{E'(L)} \beta^t E(C_t) + \sum_{t=E'(L)}^{E(L)} \beta^t E(C_t)$$

and thus,

$$\sum_{t=T}^{E'(L)} \beta^t E'(C_t) > \sum_{t=T}^{E'(L)} \beta^t E(C_t)$$

the aggregate $E'(C_t)$ is larger than $E(C_t)$. If smooth consumption is achieved, as assumption under the life cycle hypothesis, the expected consumption in each period after the health crisis will be larger the original expected consumption.

(ii) If $0 \leqslant T < R$ and $E'(L) \leqslant R$ after the health crisis,

$$\sum_{t=0}^{T} \gamma^t S_t + \sum_{t=T}^{E'(L)} \beta^t E(I_t) = \sum_{t=T}^{E'(L)} \beta^t E'(C_t)$$

from the income equation before the health crisis,

$$\sum_{t=T}^{E'(L)} \beta^t E(I_t) + \sum_{t=E'(L)}^{R} \beta^t E(I_t) = \sum_{t=T}^{E'(L)} \beta^t E(C_t) + \sum_{t=E'(L)}^{R} \beta^t E(C_t)$$
$$+ \sum_{t=T}^{E'(L)} \gamma^t E(S_t) + \sum_{t=E'(L)}^{R} \gamma^t E(S_t)$$

while

$$\sum_{t=T}^{E'(L)} \beta^t E(I_t) = \sum_{t=T}^{E'(L)} \beta^t E(C_t) + \sum_{t=T}^{E'(L)} \gamma^t E'(S_t)$$

If life expectancy is shorter than the retirement age, no savings are necessary from time T onwards and the existing savings will be used for the consumption immediately. Thus,

$$\sum_{t=T}^{E'(L)} \beta^t E'(C_t) = \sum_{t=T}^{E'(L)} \beta^t E(C_t) + \sum_{t=T}^{E'(L)} \gamma^t E(S_t) + \sum_{t=0}^{T} \gamma^t S_t$$

Apparently, the expected consumption will be larger after the health crisis:

$$\sum_{t=T}^{E'(L)} \beta^t E'(C_t) > \sum_{t=T}^{E'(L)} \beta^t E(C_t)$$

Similarly, the expected consumption in each period after the health crisis will be larger than the original expected consumption under smooth consumption.

(iii) If $R \leqslant T < E(L)$, no expected income is available and all consumption will be supported by savings:

$$\sum_{t=0}^{R} \gamma^t S_t - \sum_{t=R}^{T} \beta^t C_t = \sum_{t=T}^{E'(L)} \beta^t E'(C_t) = \sum_{t=T}^{E(L)} \beta^t E(C_t)$$

as $E'(L) < E(L)$,

$$\sum_{t=T}^{E'(L)} \beta^t E'(C_t) = \sum_{t=T}^{E'(L)} \beta^t E(C_t) + \sum_{t=E'(L)}^{E(L)} \beta^t E(C_t)$$

and thus,

$$\sum_{t=T}^{E'(L)} \beta^t E'(C_t) > \sum_{t=T}^{E'(L)} \beta^t E(C_t)$$

We can see that for consumers at any age, no matter whether working or retired, expected consumption will be larger.

Disaster

A disaster means that a person may have lower values in both expected life term and expected income.

(i) If $0 < T < R \leqslant E'(L) < E(L)$,
before the disaster, the expected income plus savings at time T is as below:

$$\sum_{t=0}^{T} \gamma^t S_t + \sum_{t=T}^{R} \beta^t E(I_t) = \sum_{t=T}^{R} \beta^t E(C_t) + \sum_{t=R}^{E(L)} \beta^t E(C_t)$$

After the disaster,

$$\sum_{t=0}^{T} \gamma^t S_t + \sum_{t=T}^{R} \beta^t E(I_t) = \sum_{t=T}^{R} \beta^t E'(C_t) + \sum_{t=R}^{E'(L)} \beta^t E'(C_t)$$

as

$$\sum_{t=T}^{R} \beta^t E(I_t) > \sum_{t=T}^{R} \beta^t E'(I_t)$$

thus,

$$\sum_{t=T}^{E(L)} \beta^t E(C_t) > \sum_{t=T}^{E'(L)} \beta^t E'(C_t)$$

From the fact that $E(L) > E'(L)$, $E'(C_t)$ may be smaller, larger or even equal to $E(C_t)$.

(ii) If $0 < T < E'(L) \leqslant R < E(L)$, after the disaster,

$$\sum_{t=0}^{T} \gamma^t S_t + \sum_{t=T}^{E'(L)} \beta^t E'(I_t) = \sum_{t=R}^{E'(L)} \beta^t E'(C_t)$$

we have the similar result:

$$\sum_{t=T}^{E(L)} \beta^t E(C_t) > \sum_{t=T}^{E'(L)} \beta^t E'(C_t)$$

$E'(C_t)$ may be smaller, larger or even equal to $E(C_t)$

(iii) If $0 < R \leqslant T < E'(L) < E(L)$,
There are no effects on income:

$$\sum_{t=0}^{R} \gamma^t S_t - \sum_{t=R}^{T} \beta^t C_t = \sum_{t=T}^{E'(L)} \beta^t E'(C_t) = \sum_{t=T}^{E(L)} \beta^t E(C_t)$$

As $E'(L) < E(L)$,

$$\sum_{t=T}^{E'(L)} \beta^t E'(C_t) = \sum_{t=T}^{E'(L)} \beta^t E(C_t) + \sum_{t=E'(L)}^{E(L)} \beta^t E(C_t)$$

and thus,

$$\sum_{t=T}^{E'(L)} \beta^t E'(C_t) > \sum_{t=T}^{E'(L)} \beta^t E(C_t)$$

The consumption becomes larger for retired people after a disaster.

The effects are not certain for working people, although the effects on consumption are positive.

Based on the life-cycle model, we can see that the effects of an economic crisis (or financial crisis) and a health crisis on consumption are different: an economic crisis will lower consumption while a health crisis will raise it. The effect of a disaster (such as a war) is not so clear-cut, depending on which of expected income or expected life is larger. The following discussions on the Asian financial crisis and SARS show the different impacts of the two types of crises on consumption.

Case 1: The Asian financial crisis

The Asian financial crisis started in Thailand in July 1997, and then spread to other southeast Asian countries. The crisis had caused severe economic turbulence in the economies of southeast Asia, including Hong Kong, Singapore, Malaysia, Taiwan, Korea, the Philippines and Indonesia. It led to sharp declines in currencies, stock markets, and other asset values of several Asian countries.

The crisis was initiated by the depreciation of the Thai baht that began in early summer 1997, followed by the precipitous drop of the Malaysian ringgit, Philippines peso, and Indonesian rupiah. The second phase of the crisis was caused by Taiwan's decision to float its currency in October 1997. As the currencies stabilized at lower levels, downward pressure of other currencies was triggered, leading to the devaluation of the Korean won, Singaporean dollar, and the Hong Kong dollar. Interest rates rose significantly as a result of the currency devaluation and thus the number of bankruptcies increased. This led to instability of the entire international financial system.

The unhealthy economy was also reflected in sharp falls in the stock markets. Due to the lack of confidence in the Hong Kong dollar and extraordinary high interest rates, the stock markets in Hong Kong became more and more volatile. The Hang Seng index (HSI, Hong Kong's stock market) dropped from its peak at over 16,000 in early August to around 9,000 in a three-month period. Furthermore, it dropped by 20 percent in three days from 20 October to 23 October 1997. Therefore, Hong Kong's economy staged a sharp challenge after the Asian financial crisis. This economic crisis plunged Hong Kong into deep recessions that brought rising unemployment, devaluation and social disorder. Some companies could not survive during this hard time and eventually closed. Due to sluggish retails sales, many Japanese department stores were about to close. Most have gone through all the economic cycles in Hong Kong. Daimaru and Yaohan, two giant department stores with a Japanese corporate parent, declared bankruptcy after the crisis. More than 3,000 staff were laid off. Moreover, one of the city's biggest bakery chains, Maria's, closed its doors and 400 people lost their jobs. The unemployment rate jumped to multi-decade highs with 5.9 percent in the last quarter of 1998 and 6.3 percent in the first quarter of 1999. Lay-offs were increased, especially in the restaurant, construction and hotel industries. Over 6,000 lost their jobs in one year due to the crisis (*Hong Kong Standard*, 1998). Most of the victims were from Cathay Pacific Airways, Maria's, Hutchison Telecommunications, and Yaohan department store.

Furthermore, salaries declined drastically for those who remained in their jobs. Most of the companies announced wage freezes or even reductions. Business and consumer confidence evaporated in this situation. Consumers suffered job insecurity and lost the confidence in making purchases. The run on the chain of Maria's cake shops reflected the anxieties of a community under strain. Apart from this, a 50 percent drop in property prices was recorded after the crisis, showing that consumers did not want to engage in any long-term commitment at that time. The collapse in property prices caused negative equity, making peoples' lives even harder. Bankruptcy petitions increased from 829 cases in 1997 to 1,362 and 3,876 cases in 1998 and 1999 respectively (Official Receiver's Office, 2005). On the whole, the Asian financial crisis was one of the biggest economic crises in the past few decades as far as Hong Kong was concerned.

The economic turmoil affected the consumption pattern of the people. As noted by Ang *et al.* (2000), the prospects of greater unemployment and slower growth led to adverse effects on consume spending. Moreover, income uncertainty played a critical role in predicting consumption. People were threatened in the financial perspective under the economy crisis as they are expected to earn less after the disaster. Under the life-cycle model, the expected life period remains unchanged, and thus people need to lower their consumption so as to maintain savings throughout the lifetime. Nevertheless, the gap will narrow down over time. That means, the impact of financial crisis on consumption will decrease over time. This proposition was supported by the real gross domestic product (GDP) and private consumption expenditure in Hong Kong (as shown in Table 12.1 and Table 12.2).

In 1998, GDP went down to −5.1 percent and −6.7percent in the second and third quarter respectively. Meanwhile, private consumption expenditure slipped down to −10.2 percent in the third quarter. The agreements for sale and purchase of building units peaked at 25,572 in April 1997 but slumped to an average of 6,000 in the third quarter of 1998. Since then, the Hong Kong economy has started to recover and thus consumer purchasing has been revived. The GDP resumed to −5.3 percent in the fourth quarter of 1998, −2.7 percent in the first quarter of 1999 and a sharp rebound followed since the second quarter of 1999. Besides, private consumption expenditure returned to −5.0 percent and even climbed up to 1.5 percent in the first and second quarters of 1999 respectively. These data indicate that people have been reluctant to make important commitments immediately after the financial crisis. However, the situation showed improvement after a certain period.

Table 12.1:   Real GDP in Hong Kong before and after the 1997 financial crisis

	Real GDP (HK$ million)	Real GDP (Year-on-year % change)
1997 Q1	282,657	5.6
1997 Q2	291,955	6.5
1997 Q3	309,483	5.8
1997 Q4	305,988	2.6
1998 Q1	275,427	−2.6
1998 Q2	277,078	−5.1
1998 Q3	288,716	−6.7
1998 Q4	289,882	−5.3
1999 Q1	268,077	−2.7
1999 Q2	282,230	1.9

Source: Census and Statistic Department, HKSAR, available at
<http://www.info.gov.hk/censtatd/eng/hkstat/index.html>.

Table 12.2:   Private consumption expenditure in Hong Kong before and after the 1997 financial crisis

	Private Consumption Expenditure* (HK$ million)	Private Consumption Expenditure Year-on-year % change)
1997 Q1	192,884	4.2
1997 Q2	203,553	8.3
1997 Q3	210,468	9.2
1997 Q4	218,225	2.8
1998 Q1	193,304	−2.6
1998 Q2	198,104	−5.0
1998 Q3	194,983	−10.2
1998 Q4	200,652	−9.1
1999 Q1	180,958	−5.0
1999 Q2	191,528	1.5

Note: in current prices
Source: Census and Statistic Department, HKSAR, available at
<http://www.info.gov.hk/censtatd/eng/hkstat/index.html>.

Case 2: Severe acute respiratory syndrome (SARS)

The atypical pneumonia, known as severe acute respiratory syndrome (SARS), became publicly recognized at the end of February 2003. It first appeared in the Chinese province of Guangdong in November 2002 and spread to Hong Kong during late February. As of 2 June 2003, SARS had infected around 8,398 people around 32 economies and caused around 800 deaths.

In economic terms, SARS represents a crisis of confidence. It severely affected the economies of many Asian countries. The Asian Development Bank (ADB) cut its economic growth forecast for developing Asia in 2003 by 0.3 percent to 5.3 percent, mainly due to SARS.

The ADB indicated that Asian economies severely affected by the SARS crisis include the People's Republic of China, Hong Kong, Singapore, and Vietnam. A study of the Treasury of the Australian Government (2003) reported that the country most affected by SARS was Hong Kong, with the largest number of infections and deaths relative to its population. With services, business travel and tourism comprising a very high proportion of economic activity (around 80 percent of GDP), the negative impact on growth would be significant.

It could not have occurred at a worse time. SARS comes at a time when Hong Kong was facing high unemployment and economic downturn. When a health crisis meets economic downturn, the effect could be disastrous. The spread of SARS since mid-March 2003 hit the Hong Kong

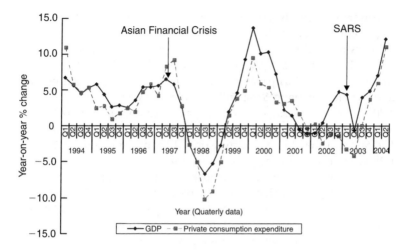

Figure 12.1: Changes in Hong Kong GDP and private consumption

economy hard. According to the *Half-yearly Economic Report* by the Government of the Hong Kong Special Administrative Region (2003), SARS caused GDP in the second quarter of 2003 to slacken to a 0.5 percent decline in real terms compared with the figures for a year earlier, from a solid growth of 4.5 percent in the first quarter. On a seasonally adjusted quarter-to-quarter comparison, GDP fell visibly, by 3.7 percent in real terms in the second quarter of 2003, following a 0.3 percent decline in the first quarter (Figure 12.1)

The Hong Kong Purchasing Manager's Index, which measures business output, employment, and other economic indicators, fell 21.3 percent from March to April 2003 (International Insights, 2003).

According to the special report prepared by the World Trade & Tourism Council (WTTC, 2003), there was a rapid downturn in arrivals followed the first outbreak of SARS in Hong Kong from mid-March onwards. Hong Kong received 1.3 million visitors in March 2003. Compared to the same month in 2002, arrivals dropped from +19.1 percent growth in the first 15 days of the month to −9.9 percent 'growth' in the last 16 days.

According to the Hong Kong Hotel Association, occupancy rates at Hong Kong's five-star hotels during the SARS crisis plunged to between 8 percent and 10 percent.

According to a mid-April 2003 Australian Tourist Commission report, Cathay Pacific Airlines cut 42 percent of its flights in the light of falling passenger traffic and Hong Kong International Airport reported that over

30 percent of flights had been cancelled and passenger traffic declined by 60 percent by mid-April.

Shares of tourism-related stocks had been affected by SARS as well. Cathay Pacific fell 15.4 percent from HK$11.7 on 21 March to close at HK$9.9 on 1 April as passengers cancelled flights in and out of Hong Kong while the Hang Seng index lost 5.2 percent from 9,179.19 to 8,706.19 within the same period. According to stock indices, the impact of the outbreak proved more serious in Hong Kong than in Singapore. The Straits Times Index slumped only 1.98 percent from 1,326.15 to 1,299.77 within the same period (*Asia Times*, 2003).

SARS also created a big demand shock. In order to avoid being affected by SARS, the majority of Hong Kong people reduced the level of travelling, eating out, face-to-face contact, and engaging in activities in public areas. As a result, the consumer expenditure, especially those in the tourism and travel-related service sector including restaurants, retail stores, hotels, airlines and entertainment business, dropped sharply.

This was reflected by retail sales figures. April retail sales fell 15.2 percent from a year earlier to HK$12.7 billion. The 44.3 percent fall in sales of jewellery, watches and clocks reflected a marked decline in inbound tourism after the SARs outbreak, while the 29.6 percent drop in sales of clothing and the 23.8 percent slide in sales of motor vehicles and parts reflected dampened consumer confidence (*Business Day*, 2003).

According to the managing director of Hong Tai Travel Agency, his company experienced a near 90 percent drop in business during the SARS period because Hong Kong people were not willing to travel at that time even when special package tours were offered (*Wei Wen Wei*, 2004).

The situation worsened further with the significant impact of SARS on the labour market. Hong Kong's unemployment rate rose to 8.2 percent in the three months from March to May 2003 as SARS wiped out jobs in tourism, hotels and catering services. The increase compared with the jobless rate of 7.8 percent and 7.5 percent in the February to April period and the January to March period respectively (Hong Kong Census and Statistic Department, website; BBC News online, 20 May 2003). Companies cut employee wages or offered unpaid leave after the outbreak of SARS in varying degrees. All of these factors reduced consumer spending power further. For the second quarter of 2003 as a whole, private consumer expenditure fell by 4.1 percent in real terms when compared with the level of over a year earlier.

For instance, South China Morning Post cut the wages of 241 employees by up to 10 percent following a warning that its profits would be hit by SARS.

Post-SARS

The recovery process for the city's economy started after the World Health Organization (WHO) removed Hong Kong from the list of areas affected by SARS on 23 June 2003. This could be seen by the fact that private consumer expenditure rose from −4.1 percent in the second quarter to +0.1 percent in the third quarter and even to +3.7 percent in the fourth quarter of 2003. Private consumer expenditure even surged by 11.0 percent in real terms in the second quarter of 2004 over a year earlier, and further rocketed from the 6.0 percent growth in the first quarter of 2004.

This is reflected from the fact that the real GDP of Hong Kong immediately rose after SARS. In the second half of 2003, GDP rose from −0.6 percent to +4 percent in the third quarter and to +4.9 percent in the fourth quarter. In the second quarter of 2004, GDP increased by 12.1 percent in real terms over the same period in 2003, at a faster pace than the 7.0 percent growth in the first quarter of 2004.

The recovery was particularly noticeable in tourism and related sectors. With the lifting of the WHO SARS-affected status, the trickle of visitors back into Hong Kong grew in momentum. Hong Kong welcomed 1.3 million visitors in July 2003 – up 78 percent from June. Tourist arrival figures further went up to 1.68 million in August; a further 30 percent up from July. Passenger traffic numbers at Hong Kong's Chek Lap Kok Airport reached an all-time high of 3.45 million in July (*Airwise News*, 27 August 2004).

Hotel bookings moved back up to 80 to 90 percent compared to the single-digit occupancy rates during the SARS outbreak (according to <www.info.gov.hk/gia/general/200309>). The Hotel Miramar, one of the main business visitor hotels in Hong Kong, reported occupancy of 100 percent just one week after the all-clear. In June 2003 alone, occupancy levels in Accor's three Hong Kong hotels improved by more than 13 percent (according to <www.Caterer.com>).

Regarding retail sales, the decline in retail sales volume narrowed further in June 2003, in line with the inbound tourism and return of customer confidence. Retail sales in June fell 6.4 percent from a year earlier after a fall of 11.1 percent in May. Hong Kong retail sales in August returned to positive for the first time since the SARS outbreak, boosted by a rebound in visitor arrivals, especially from China. August retail sales rose 1.2 percent from a year earlier after a fall of 2.5 percent in July. In volume terms, retail sales were up 3.0 percent in August, compared with a fall of 0.3 percent in July. After netting out the effect of price change, the overall volume of retail sales increased by 15.5 percent in May 2004 from a year earlier (Business Report, 7 October 2003, at <www.info.gov.hk>).

For the real estate market, property sales rose to 140 percent in the fourth quarter of 2003 compared to sales figures in the SARS period. Prices of some estates and luxury properties rose 30 percent. Asking prices of some new deluxe properties reached HK$15,000 per square foot (<bwww.atimes.com>, 26 May 2004).

The upsurge after the SARS outbreak was due not only to enhanced consumer confidence, but also the impacts of the health crisis on consumers' life expectancy. Consumers will spend more as a result of the bad experience that had arisen from the disease. Explained by the life-cycle hypothesis, in view of the severe threat on their health, a shortern life/span will be expected and the overall savings will be much more than expected. The additional savings will be used immediately and hence their expected spending will be greater.

This was precisely what happened to Hong Kong people after the SARS incident. Spokesmen of leading travel agencies reported that there was a 40 percent increase in the number of people travel abroad during Christmas 2003 compared to a year earlier (*Sun Pao*, 17 December 2003).

The travelling pattern and mentality of Hong Kong people has also changed after the SARS crisis. Ever since 1997, price is the most important criteria for customers to determine their travel plan and people usually join short-distance tours to southeast Asian countries as the price of those tours are much less. However, since the SARS incident, people have paid more attention to the destination and luxury levels of tours. They prefer to travel to areas they have never visited before or areas that will offer them new experiences, even if the price is higher. Moreover, people are willing to pay much more for a luxury package. It was recorded that customers were willing to pay 36 percent more for holidays Thailand or three times more for holidays in Japan in that enable them to live in five star hotels and travel in business class (*Wei Wen Pao*, (2003); *Ming Pao Daily News* (2003a); *Hong Kong Commercial Daily News*, 2004).

Besides, there was a sharp increase by 70 percent in numbers on long-distant tours compared to the figures for 2002. Tours to Europe, the Mediterranean Sea and even the 10-day HK$13,000 luxury tour to South Africa were fully booked within a very short period and this was very rare in previous year (*Hong Kong Commercial Daily News*, 2004).

Beside travelling, nowadays people are willing to spend huge amounts of money on dining in high-class restaurants and hotels, entertaining themselves, buying luxury items such as automobiles, jewellery, leather goods, watches, designer-brand clothing and expensive Chinese medicines.

According to the hotel and catering industries, the booking situations of buffet meals on Christmas and New Year time were much better than expected even though there was an average of 8–10 percent increase in the price level compared to the previous year. The most popular buffets were the most luxurious and expensive, such as the premium 'bird-nest lobster' buffet offered by Miramar Hotel or the luxury 'red wine fountain' buffet offered by Royal Plaza Hotel (*Ming Pao Daily News*, 2003b).

Just within three days at the beginning of the Chinese New Year in 2004, Fu Lam Restaurant, which was claimed to be the 'canteen for rich men in Hong Kong' sold out 200 expensive abalones and generated sales volume of half a million Hong Kong Dollars. According to the owner of the restaurant, all tables were fully booked most of the time, average spending was higher and many new faces turned up after the SARS incident (*Apple Daily News*, 2004c).

According to the *Hong Kong Economic Times* (2004), there was a 25 percent increase in sales volume of Chinese New Year gift sets sold by the Tung Fong Hung Chinese medicine retailer compared to a year earlier. The expensive wild ginseng was the most popular gift item among Hong Kong people. Spokesman of Ann Kee Seafood told the reporter that people nowadays buy expensive Chinese medicine and seafood for their own consumption, while they only purchased for the elderly in the past. Moreover, it was recorded that a retailer had sold out 50 automobiles alone on the first day of the Chinese New Year.

Marketing Implications

An interesting phenomenon was found in our preliminary study. If there is a financial crisis, the total purchases of people will be lowered. In contrast, if there is a health crisis, the total will rise immediately once the crisis is controlled. In sum, different consumer patterns were found in relation to financial crises and health crises. Marketers should therefore identify the nature of a crisis before developing marketing strategies.

According to Ang *et al.* (2000), the general reaction of an economic crisis is lower consumption and wastefulness. Consumers will adjust their buying behaviour in view of the expected lay-offs and salary cuts. They will delay the purchase of expensive items and search for the cheapest alternatives of necessities. In response to consumers' unwillingness to spend, marketers should stimulate their buying intention by reducing their uncertainty in making purchases. A lower price can reduce the perceived risk and hence boost consumer confidence. Given the increased price consciousness after the financial crisis, cash incentives and discounts can be offered to drive sales. The successes of the two biggest supermarkets in Hong Kong, Park'N Shop and Wellcome, are largely attributed to their wise use of pricing strategies. External reference prices can also be showed up by merchants to demonstrate the reasonableness of current prices, and thus enhance the perceived value of products. However, products could be augmented with warranties to lower consumers' perceived risk. One of the largest electricity retail chains in Hong Kong, Fortress, grants its customers the 'Pay-the-Difference Guarantee' in purchasing the goods. Such strategies could increase consumer confidence in product buying, especially in times of economic downtown. Furthermore, due to deteriorating consumption, marketers should minimize stocks and avoid introducing new products in periods of economic hardship. Companies could move the distribution channel from retail stores to the virtual store (e.g., the Internet) so as to increase the accessibility and reduce the cost. However, advertising should be maintained for minimal brand presence as advertising budgets should not be viewed as a cost; on the contrary, it is an investment in the long run. Sales promotion and public relations activities could be kicked off to react to lower consumption.

Nonetheless, the situation will be entirely different after health crisis. Marketers should modify their strategies in adapting to enlarged consumption. At such times, the spending appetite of Hong Kong people would get stronger and 'bigger'. As consumers had already got high propensity to spend, more should be invested in advertising budgets to make the brand more appealing. Besides, promotions such as thematic campaigns should be organized to stay in tune with heightened purchase intentions.

Apart from surging consumption, people tended to buy luxury goods after the SARS crisis. Many premium packages were launched to attract consumers and the responses were quite encouraging. For example, luxury travel packages with special themes have been introduced by various travel agents and the tours became fully booked within a short time. In order to seize the marketing opportunity after the health crisis, some marketing implications are recommended on the basis of the 4Ps framework.

Product

As the expected lifespan seems to be shorter and thus consumers are more willing to spend after the health crisis, luxury products or premium packages should be launched to grasp the opportunity. Gimmicks can be used to make the products perceived as more up-market in the eyes of consumers. For example, the 'speaking rose' (with words printed on the flower) cost five times more than the 'ordinary rose' (*Ming Pao Daily News*, 30 Jan 2004). Luxury tours with special themes, such as an Olympic tour and photography tours, were subject to surcharge in most travel agents (*Apple Daily News*, 2004a). These additional payments were still welcomed by consumers.

Promotion

Effective promotions are necessary to make brands more tempting after the health crisis. For example, one of the largest international hotel groups, the Peninsula Hotel, successfully recruited copious number of customers compared with its competitors. This may be largely due to good timing in launching various campaigns with special themes, such as 'Peninsula 75th Anniversary' (*Sing Tao Daily*, 2003). Such activities could attract consumers' attention and offset industry competition.

Price

Unlike the financial crisis, price is not the biggest concern for health-crisis-hit consumers. They have encountered a shorter expected lifespan and thus resulted in a higher spending desire. For example, the occupancy rate for fireworks displays for most hotels, Marriott and Grand Hyatt, was very satisfactory even though they charged a premium (*Apple Daily News*, 2004b). Charging a higher price can definitely increase the profit margin if consumers are willing to pay for it. As a result, instead of offering a price promotion, businesses can raise the quality of the product and add values on it.

Distribution

Being threatened by the health crisis, consumers may perceive a shorter life and look for immediate happiness through purchasing. They want to own the products or enjoy the services without delay. In view of this, companies should ensure adequate stocks and a smooth operation in order to deal with consumers' increased consumption. Moreover, in response to consumers' tough demands, companies should redesign outlets as more superior and unique. One of the famous Chinese restaurant chains in Hong Kong, Tao Heung, renovated some of its premises more stylishly after the SARS outbreak and attracted eventually more customers. In addition, the number of outlets should be increased so as to enhance accessibility for consumers.

Marketing implications for the Asian financial crisis and SARS are summarized in Table 12.3.

Table 12.3:   Marketing strategies for Asian financial crisis and SARS

	Asian Financial Crisis	SARS
Product	• Avoid new product launch	• Launch luxury products or premium packages • Use gimmicks/packaging to enhance the perceived values of the product
Promotion	• Kick off 'sales promotion' • Maintain minimal presence of advertising • Deploy public relation activities	• Launch campaigns with special themes
Price	• Implement the 'refund guarantee' or 'pay-the-difference guarantee' • Offer cash incentives and discounts • Use external reference price	• Charge for a higher price for high-quality and value-added products • Drop off the price promotion
Place	• Minimize the stocks • Shift from retail stores to virtual channels (such as the Internet)	• Ensure adequate stocks • Smoothen the logistics • Redesign the channel and renovate the store • Increase the number of outlets

Concluding Remarks

From the life-cycle model analysis, the emergence of a crisis, be it an economic crisis, or a health crisis, will have different impacts on consumption. An economic crisis lowers the expected income and thus the current consumption is lower in order to maintain savings for future consumption. A health crisis lowers life expectancy but the current consumption is raised as savings are cut because smaller future consumption is expected. The Asian financial crisis and SARS are compared to illustrate the different effects on consumption and in turn the impacts on income were also different. From a survey in October 2003 (AC Nielsen, 2003), 86 percent of the Hong Kong consumers said that they would spend on non-essentials. Hong Kong was one of the economies hit by SARS the most seriously. The strong spending incentive supports the higher consumption prediction following a health crisis. Perhaps unsurprisingly, Hong Kong people became more concerned about their health.

The marketing implications for marketers are that a health crisis such as SARS provides totally different consumption patterns compared with the patterns in an economic crisis. The good news is that the predicted strong consumption after a health crisis provides much better business opportunities to firms. However, correct marketing strategies in the face of a health crisis will bring more profits and will gain competitive advantages over its rivals. In contrast to a financial crisis in which the spending on necessities and low-end products become higher, after a health crisis, spending tends to be higher on luxury products and health foods. If a firm prepares well in the face of a crisis, it can get an edge over its rivals.

References

AC Neilsen (2003), 'Consumer confidence in Asia rebounds faster than expected. consumers' major concern switches from the economy to health issues', 26 November 2003, available at <http://asiapacific.acnielsen.com.au/home.asp?newsID=122>.

Aghion, P., P. Bolton and M. Dewatripont (2000) 'Contagious bank failures in a free banking system', *European Economic Review* 44, 713–18.

Ang, S.H., S.M.Leong and P. Kotler (2000) 'The Asian apocalypse: crisis marketing for consumers and businesses', *Long Range Planning* 33, 97–119.

Apple Daily News (2004a) 'Thematic luxury tours as gimmick in the Chinese New Years', 3 January.

Apple Daily News (2004b) 'Hotel rooms with firework view are popular', 14 January.

Apple Daily News (2004c) 'Hong Kong people are getting rich in dining', 24 January.

Asia Times (2003) 'SARS threatening to cripple Hong Kong', online 5 April.

Bernanke, B. and M. Gertler (1989) 'Agency costs, net worth, and business fluctuations', *The American Economic Review* 79(1), 14–31.

Business Day (2004) 'Hong Kong retail sales down', 26 August.

Cole, H.L. and T.J. Kehoe (2000) 'Self-fulfilling debt crises', *Review of Economic Studies* 67(230), 91–116.

Dombey, O. (2003) 'The effects of SARS on the Chinese tourism industry', *Journal of Vacation Marketing* 10(1), 4–10.

Government of the Hong Kong Special Administrative Region (2003) *Half-yearly Economic Report 2003*.

Henderson, J.C. (2003) 'Managing a health-related crisis: SARS in Singapore', *Journal of Vacation Marketing* 10(1), 67–77.

Hong Kong Commercial Daily News (2004) 'Luxury tours are the most popular and 70% luxury tours are full', 3 January.

Hong Kong Economic Times (2004) 'People are Willing to Buy for the Luxuries in Chinese New Year', 14 January.

Hong Kong Standard (1998) 'AMC Information Bank', 5 May.

International Insights (2003) 'Hong Kong market feels effect from SARS', June.

Kang S. and C.C.Hong (2004) 'The psychological impact of SARS: a matter of heart and mind', *Canadian Medical Association* 170(5), 793.

Kiyotaki, N. and J. Moore (1997) 'Credit cycles', *Journal of Political Economy* 105(2), 211–48.

Krugman, P. (1979) 'A model of balance-of-payments crises', *Journal of Money, Credit and Banking* 11(3), 311–25.

Krugman, P. (1999) 'Balance sheets, the transfer problem, and financial crises', *International Tax and Public Finance* 6(4), 459–72.

Ming Pao Daily News (2003a) 'Luxury New Year tour: the fee was increased by 36%', 18 December.

Ming Pao Daily News (2003b) 'Recovery of the dining industry', 23 December.

Ming Pao Daily News (2004) 'Lovers' names printed on roses', 30 January.

Modigliani, F. and R. Brumberg (1954) 'Utility Analysis and the Consumption Function: An Interpretation of Cross-Section Data', in K. Kurihara Kenneth (ed.), *Post-Keynesian Economics* (New Brunswick, NJ: Rutgers University Press), pp. 388–436.

Obstfeld, M. (1986) 'Rational and self-fulfilling balance of payments crises', *American Economic Review* 76, 72–81.

Official Receiver's Office 'Statistics on Compulsory Winding-up and Bankruptcy', April 15, 2005, available at http://www.oro.gov.hk/eng/stat/stat.htm.

Schneider, M. and A. Tornell (2004) 'Balance sheet effects, bailout guarantees and financial crises', *Review of Economic Studies* 71, 883–913.

Shama, A. (1981) 'Coping with staglation: voluntary simplicity', *Journal of Marketing* 45(3), 120–34.

Sing Tao Daily (2003) 'Peninsula's 75th anniversary', 14 December.

The Department of the Treasury (2003) 'The economic impact of severe acute respiratory syndrome (SARS)', *Australian Government*.

Wen Wei Pao (2003) 'Travel tours at Christmas had increased 30%', 12 December.

Wen Wei Pao (2004) 'Higher demand for luxury tours', 3 January.

World Travel & Tourism Council (2003) *The Impact of Travel & Tourism on Jobs and the Economy: China and China Hong Kong SAR,* http://www.wttc.org/.

Index

DATE DUE

DEC 1 7 2009	